U.S. Intervention
Policy for the
Post–Cold War World

CONTRIBUTORS

COIT D. BLACKER, Stanford University

LINTON F. BROOKS, Center for Naval Analyses

KIMBERLY ANN ELLIOTT, Institute for International
Economics

RICHARD L. GARWIN, Thomas J. Watson Research Center

GARY CLYDE HUFBAUER, Institute for International
Economics

ARNOLD KANTER, RAND Corporation

WILLIAM H. LEWIS, George Washington University

GEORGE E. PICKETT JR., Northrop Corporation

JAMES G. ROCHE, Northrop Corporation

TIMOTHY R. SAMPLE, Potomac Institute for Policy Studies

JOHN O.B. SEWALL, Institute for National Strategic Studies

FAREED ZAKARIA, *Foreign Affairs*

THE AMERICAN ASSEMBLY
Columbia University

U.S. Intervention Policy for the Post–Cold War World

NEW CHALLENGES AND NEW RESPONSES

ARNOLD KANTER
and
LINTON F. BROOKS
Editors

W. W. NORTON & COMPANY
New York   London

The text of this book is composed in Baskerville
Composition and manufacturing by the Haddon Craftsmen, Inc.

Library of Congress Cataloging-in-Publication Data

U.S. intervention policy for the post–Cold War world : new challenges and new responses / Arnold Kanter and Linton F. Brooks, editors : the American Assembly, Columbi University.
    p. cm.
  Includes bibliographical references and index.
    1. United States—Foreign relations—1989– . 2. United States—Military policy. 3. Intervention (International law) I. Kanter, Arnold. II. Brooks, Linton F. III. American Assembly. IV. Title: US intervention policy for the post–Cold War world.
   ISBN 0-393-03698-7 (cloth)
   ISBN 0-393-96636-4 (paper)
   E840.U173   1994
   327.73′009′049—dc20   94-27932

W. W. Norton & Company, Inc. 500 Fifth Avenue, New York, N.Y. 10110
W. W. Norton & company Ltd., 10 Coptic Street, London WC1A 1PU

1 2 3 4 5 6 7 8 9 0

Contents

Preface

Intervention by the United States in the affairs of other states has occurred throughout our history, but seldom has it been a more divisive national issue. In an effort to help identify policy guidelines for decision making—especially in the absence of widely agreed organizing principles for our foreign policy following the end of the cold war—The American Assembly commissioned this volume.

Its chapters were first used as background for an Assembly program held at Arden House, Harriman, New York, April 7–10, 1994, where a distinguished group of authorities representing government, academia, business, industry, nonprofit organizations, military, the law, science, technology, and the media convened to make recommendations to U.S. policy makers. Their names and the report of their recommendations are included as an afterword to this volume.

To provide intellectual leadership for the Arden House meeting and to edit this volume, the Assembly commissioned two highly experienced former government and military authorities: Arnold Kanter, former under secretary of state for political affairs, and now senior fellow at the RAND Corporation; and Ambassador

Linton F. Brooks, formerly a captain in the Navy, and head of the U.S. delegation to the START talks, and now a distinguished fellow at the Center for Naval Analyses.

We gratefully acknowledge support for this book and the Arden House Assembly from the Malcolm Hewitt Wiener Foundation, the United States Institute of Peace, and the Rockefeller Family Fund. Additional assistance was provided by the RAND Corporation, which, like The American Assembly and our funders, takes no position on subjects presented herein for public discussion.

It is our belief that this book continues to fulfill the mandate of the Assembly's founder, President Dwight D. Eisenhower, "to illuminate public policy." We hope it will help both citizens and policy makers to understand more fully what is required to develop coherent guidelines for U.S. interventions that will both protect American interests and values, and secure the support of the American public.

Daniel A. Sharp
President

U.S. Intervention Policy for the Post–Cold War World

Introduction

LINTON F. BROOKS
AND ARNOLD KANTER

During the final thirty years of the cold war, perhaps no national security topic was as politically divisive as the question of why, where, when, and how the United States should intervene abroad. From the bitter debates over Vietnam to the equally bitter arguments over Beirut, Americans clashed over the morality, wisdom, and efficacy of becoming involved in the affairs of other nations. By contrast, the first post–cold war intervention, undertaken to reverse the Iraqi invasion of Kuwait, met with almost universal approval. It was easy to conclude from that episode that the long debate was over and that consensus finally existed that intervention was both a proper and a useful tool of U.S. policy.

LINTON F. BROOKS is a distinguished fellow at the Center for Naval Analyses and a consultant on START II ratification to the Clinton administration and the United States Arms Control and Disarmament Agency. During the Bush administration, he served as assistant director for Strategic and Nuclear Affairs, U.S. Arms Control and Disarmament Agency, and as head of the U.S. Delegation on Nuclear and Space Talks and chief strategic arms reductions (START) negotiator. Before becom-

The first year and a half of the Clinton administration provided a quite different perspective. The Clinton foreign policy team entered office in 1993 full of enthusiasm for the United Nations as an instrument of "assertive multilateralism"—in short, of intervention. By the spring of 1994, however, failure of the United Nations' intervention in Somalia, continuing confusion over Bosnia, and American reluctance to send military forces to Haiti had combined to feed growing public and congressional doubts about both the wisdom of U.S. intervention and our ability to intervene successfully. This widespread sentiment made it easy to conclude that intervention had become a discredited relic of a now bygone era.

Both conclusions were and are misleading. Neither the suc-

---

ing head of the U.S. Nuclear and Space Talks Delegation in April 1991, Ambassador Brooks served for two years as deputy head of the delegation, holding the rank of ambassador. He joined the delegation after spending over three years as director of arms control on the staff of the National Security Council. Ambassador Brooks's National Security Council service culminated a thirty-year military career. Prior to his retirement as a Navy captain, Ambassador Brooks served at sea in destroyers, ballistic missile submarines, and attack submarines, commanded the nuclear powered attack submarine USS WHALE, and served in a variety of Washington assignments relating to nuclear policy, military strategy, and arms control.

ARNOLD KANTER is a senior fellow at the RAND Corporation. From October 1991 until January 1993, he served as under secretary of state for political affairs. In this position, he was the State Department's "chief operating officer" with responsibility for the day-to-day conduct of American foreign policy and for crisis management. Prior to assuming his duties at the Department of State, Mr. Kanter served as special assistant to the president for national security affairs and senior director for defense policy and arms control at the National Security Council from 1989–91. Before reentering the U.S. government, Mr. Kanter was at the RAND Corporation from 1985–89 where he was a senior staff member working on issues related to nuclear forces, arms control, and European security. Mr. Kanter served from 1977–85 in the U.S. Department of State, including positions as deputy assistant secretary of state for politico-military affairs, and as deputy to the under secretary of state for political affairs. He has been on the staff of the Brookings Institution and has taught at Ohio State University and the University of Michigan.

cesses of 1991 nor the difficulties of 1993 mean the debate over intervention has been settled. Quite the reverse: the changing nature of the post–cold war world requires a fresh look at the policies, techniques, and consequences of American intervention. To contribute to that reexamination, The American Assembly commissioned this volume.

The Costs and Benefits of Intervention

Intervention, as we define the term, means U.S. involvement in the affairs of another sovereign state. It encompasses the entire spectrum of coercive techniques—diplomatic, economic, military, or new techniques based on new technology—with which we seek to change the character or alter the behavior of another government. We intervene economically when we impose sanctions on Haiti to force a change in government. We intervene militarily when we deploy troops to Somalia or Bosnia to contain violence or to Grenada to overthrow a Marxist regime. Seen this way, intervention is a fact of life; a policy of total nonintervention is neither realistic nor desirable. For this reason, intervention should not be viewed as either intrinsically good or intrinsically sinister. Instead, it must be judged in each case based on its purposes, costs, and prospects.

Because intervention decisions are potentially of great consequence, the United States must weigh their costs as well as their benefits. This cannot be done unless we are clear about objectives. We should resist the temptation to intervene simply in response to an intense but ill-formed desire to "do something." Intervention should have a clear purpose: to defend U.S. interests or to uphold U.S. values. It should also have a reasonable prospect for success, at least in the sense that the probable costs will be outweighed by the probable benefits.

Unfortunately, while it may be easy to agree on these principles, it is not so easy to apply them in the disordered post–cold war world. In the coming years intervention may become both a more frequent and more difficult issue for U.S. policy makers.

There are at least four reasons why the United States may be increasingly tempted to intervene. First, the end of the cold war removed many constraints on U.S. action. No longer must American leaders view possible actions taken anywhere in the world through the prism of our superpower competition with Moscow. Freed of these cold war constraints, the United States may now see fewer risks to intervening, whether militarily, diplomatically, economically, or through new techniques based on new technology.

A second reason why intervention may become a more frequent issue is the increasing predominance of economic considerations in U.S. foreign policy, a predominance demonstrated by President Clinton's stress on the North American Free Trade Agreement, on General Agreement on Tariffs and Trade (GATT) negotiations, and on improving trade relations with Japan. Intervention is one way to advance our economic interests in the global marketplace. Moreover, greater emphasis on economics means a greater premium on the stability of the growing number of nations that—in an increasingly interdependent world—are important to our international trade. Intervention may be seen as a way to foster, or even impose, the stability that is a prerequisite for prosperity.

The renewed American emphasis on democracy and human rights as foreign policy goals provides a third reason for intervention. Increasingly, Americans will be willing to justify intervention to promote American values as well as to defend American interests. Not only are democracy and human rights valued in themselves, but most U.S. policy makers believe they contribute to stability and prosperity abroad and thus to economic opportunity at home.

Finally, U.S. leaders will face intervention decisions simply because the post–cold war world is disorderly and full of dangers. Ethnic, religious, and sectarian conflicts suppressed by the cold war threaten to erupt around the globe. The potential proliferation of weapons of mass destruction, especially nuclear weapons, may replace the threat from the Soviet Union with an equally frightening, though ill-defined, new threat. Terrorism continues to be directed at U.S. citizens, interests, and allies. Internal anarchy and natural disasters have turned some states (the West African nation of Sierra Leone, for example) into little more than bands of ill-disciplined armed men without cohesion or political purpose.

Refugee and migration problems, spawned by external conflict or internal anarchy, spread the results of conflict to otherwise uninvolved states.

Taken together, these factors suggest that, far from being obsolete, widespread intervention will play a growing role in future U.S. policy, becoming both more feasible and more necessary than in the past. But this conclusion, too, is misleading. Increased opportunities for intervention—and even increased ability to intervene—do not necessarily mean that intervention has become either more desirable or more effective. On the contrary, with intervention no longer tied to a global struggle for national survival, the apparent benefits of intervention have also decreased. Such benefits have become harder to see and easier to argue about. This has, in turn, focused increased attention on the costs of intervention.

These costs can be significant. Besides the obvious resource costs, both in lives and in dollars, there are also political costs. Even minor problems during overt intervention, especially military intervention, may have great political impact in the age of global televised news, when vivid images can bring about rapid changes in the national mood. The pictures of the October 1993 desecration of dead Americans in Somalia, for example, led directly to the American decision to withdraw its forces from the United Nations effort in that ravaged nation.

There are also less obvious and less quantifiable costs. Because the mood of the American public is to turn inward, diverting attention from domestic issues automatically imposes costs on political leaders. Intervention may also have costs in terms of American credibility. Threatening to intervene and then backing down is one way to lose credibility. Intervening with halfway measures that prove ineffective is another. Further, resources used to intervene in one situation are unavailable for other situations. In trying to do everything during a time of shrinking resources, we may end up doing nothing well.

The intersection of feasibility, desirability, and costs yields three distinct categories into which a potential intervention might fall. In some cases, the threat to our interests from inaction may be so clear (and thus the benefits of intervention so great) that there is no practical alternative to intervention. In such cases, the only questions are about the most effective means. These might be called cases of "mandatory intervention." Iraq's invasion of Kuwait, which threatened to put Saddam Hussein in control of a significant fraction of the world's oil, might be one example.

In other cases, intervention may serve to promote neither U.S. interests nor U.S. values. In these cases, intervention would be unwarranted even if the costs were low. Put differently, there are cases in which we should not intervene even if we could do so successfully and at minimal cost. Intervention in Sri Lanka, for example, has never been seriously considered because there were no apparent U.S. interests to be served. These might be called cases of "unwarranted intervention."

The most difficult cases for policy makers fall into an intermediate category, in which an intervention decision turns on a careful calculation of costs and benefits. These might be termed cases of "discretionary intervention." Haiti provides an example; if the United States can intervene at an acceptable cost (for example, by using economic sanctions that impose little burden on us) it clearly will. If intervention means invasion, it clearly won't.

Assigning potential interventions to one of these three categories may facilitate analysis but will not necessarily make decisions easier. Real policy issues are seldom clear-cut choices between good and evil. Instead they usually are choices between competing goods or, more commonly, are exercises in picking the lesser of two evils. As a result, we can expect significant arguments over which of the three categories best describes any specific intervention.

Still, this threefold way of looking at a potential intervention decision highlights the importance of the tools available. In cases of "mandatory intervention," we want to intervene at the lowest cost in dollars, lives, and political capital. Better ways of using traditional political, military, and economic instruments can help lower the cost and increase the effectiveness of doing what we have to do in any case. So can new techniques based on new technologies.

In the more numerous cases of "discretionary intervention" where there are more limited benefits, a wider menu of options may allow otherwise infeasible interventions to be undertaken at acceptable cost. But there is a risk: the availability of low-cost, low-risk options borne of new techniques and new technologies may tempt us to make the mistake of intervening in unwarranted cases, intervening because we *can*, rather than because we *should*.

Because of the importance of these issues for future U.S. policy, The American Assembly sought, in April 1994, to examine both the availability and the implications of new tools and techniques for intervention. Such an examination does not imply a thirst for intervention, merely a desire to expand the options available and to understand their consequences.

Looking for new options can mean many things. It can mean more effective ways to use the existing military and economic tools of intervention. It can also mean devising totally new tools and crafting new forms of organization to employ them. Before turning to either new tools or improved use of old tools, however, we must consider the post–cold war environment in which intervention decisions will be taken.

The Nature of the Post–Cold War World

An intervention decision—like any other—is not made in a vacuum. We can only understand the costs and benefits of intervention if we first understand the changed nature of the world following the end of the cold war and the collapse of the Soviet Union. The chapters in this volume by Coit Blacker and William Lewis set the scene by helping to illuminate that world. Their most important conclusion is that both the international system and America's conception of the U.S. role in the world differ in fundamental respects from what policy makers have known for the past four decades.

First, as Blacker demonstrates in his chapter, "A Typology of Post–Cold War Conflicts," the nature of post–cold war conflict is different. During the cold war, the combination of nuclear deterrence and the determination of the two superpowers to maintain order in their respective spheres of influence led to a relatively peaceful—if not necessarily secure—world. Most cold war conflict was within what Blacker refers to as "the periphery," that vast portion of the globe outside of a "center" containing Central Europe, Russia, North America, China, and Japan. Conflicts within the periphery during the cold war were not primarily the result of superpower rivalry; as a result, the end of the cold war does not diminish the potential for such conflict. On the contrary, Blacker concludes that, while deterrence and peace are likely to hold at the center, the periphery will see an increased potential for violence. In part, this is because the post–cold war world will be multipolar in nature, despite frequent characterizations of the United States as the sole superpower. Historically, multipolar, balance of power systems have a propensity for violence.

In surveying the sources of conflict, Blacker suggests that struggles for regional autonomy or independence, civil unrest caused by economic problems, and tensions between indigenous populations and national minorities will all plague the developed world. States in the periphery will likewise face all of these problems, but will have to deal with other conflicts as well. With increasing frequency, these conflicts in the periphery no longer can be viewed as struggles between well-defined, homogeneous states. Instead, they are more often struggles for supremacy within a state or a battle over how a state is to be defined. Frequently there are multiple parties involved, as in Bosnia or Somalia. The boundaries of the groups involved in these struggles may or may not correspond to state boundaries; in some African ethnic conflicts, for example, or in the continued drive of the Kurds for autonomy, they do not.

Blacker concludes that the greatest area of danger in the post–cold war world is where conflicts in the developed and undeveloped worlds intersect, at "fault lines" separating the two worlds. These fault lines have traditionally been viewed as splitting the globe along north-south lines. New fault lines have now emerged following the collapse of the Soviet Union, fault lines running through southeastern Europe and through the Caucasus toward the Russian heartland.

If Blacker's conclusions are correct, they have important implications for how U.S. military forces should be structured, trained, and equipped. In a world in which most conflicts were between or within states in the periphery, the United States would devote less time and fewer resources to preparing for "major regional contingencies" and more time and resources to peacekeeping, "peace enforcement," and other, more limited uses of military power. In such a world, the traditional norms against interfering in the internal affairs of other states also would become harder to observe and, perhaps, less relevant.

A second difference is that the U.S. post–cold war role has changed. The United States is now, at most, the leader of a community of increasingly independent actors, rather than the commander of a military alliance united by a common threat. The United States has become the world's sheriff, rather than the world's police officer. While the police officer acts alone or commands others who must obey, the sheriff must assemble a posse. If the posse won't come, the sheriff can't act. Like the sheriff, the United States must lead but must do so by persuasion, convincing a shifting coalition that intervention is necessary and justified. The early Clinton administration experience seeking to forge a coalition to act in Bosnia demonstrates the difficulty of this new role in a world where the disappearance of a common threat makes cooperation more difficult to secure.

Yet another difference is that Americans' perceptions both of the threat we face and of our national priorities have changed. For example, there is a strong and growing sense in this country that we should shed our international burdens, attend to our problems and concerns at home, and define our interests abroad in terms of narrower—predominantly economic—self interest. This impulse ripples through the political process, affecting not only who gets elected to office, but also which policies they pursue and which political risks they avoid once they get there. It leads to a set of self-imposed constraints on U.S. actions that tend to erode—if not render all but irrelevant—the utility of the U.S. emerging from the cold war as the "sole remaining superpower."

As Lewis discusses in his chapter, "Challenge and Response: Coercive Intervention Issues," in the world that has emerged from the ashes of the cold war, we no longer seek to buttress our side in a global confrontation, but have not yet agreed on what we *do* seek. Indeed, the very characterization of this period as the "post–cold war world" highlights what it is *not*, rather than what it is. There is internal confusion and debate over what should replace the Soviet threat as the organizing principle for U.S. national security policy. Lewis notes several overlapping debates:

- A debate between those fearing that new international burdens will divert resources from domestic needs and those fearing that opportunities for international leadership will slip away if not grasped.
- A debate between those who would continue the cold war national security focus on arming our friends and those who would seek to curb arms proliferation.
- A debate between internationalists who would increase support for collective security organizations such as the United Nations and those who, seeing the United Nations as flawed, would depend on cold war institutions such as NATO or on unilateral U.S. action to protect our interests.
- A debate between those favoring continuation of the cold war emphasis on Europe and those calling for broader emphasis on areas previously neglected.
- A debate between those seeing an increase in the size of the community of democratic nations as a valid American goal and those viewing a U.S. foreign policy of "enlargement" as dangerous romanticism.

In surveying these overlapping debates, Lewis concludes that, on balance, Americans have become increasingly skeptical about U.S. involvement abroad and want the United States to "withdraw from a world leadership role and to concentrate on significant domestic problems."

The complex debate over intervention that Lewis describes is often couched in terms of where our interests lie, although it is, in reality, more a debate over priorities among interests and over the changing threats to those interests. The range of views on what (if anything) should prompt intervention is immense:

- Some neoisolationists argue that there are no present or prospective external threats to our interests great enough to justify intervention.
- Others would limit our actions to steps that directly affect a narrow domestic agenda, for example, by forcing Japan to buy more American goods and services.

- Still others would use intervention to create the kind of stable and prosperous world they believe offers the greatest chance for peace and prosperity at home.
- Finally, some believe that we should intervene to promote American values of democracy and human rights, as well as to relieve suffering and prevent "ethnic cleansing," even if there is no direct security impact on the United States.

The lack of agreement on what threats and objectives should justify intervention is not the only constraint facing policy makers in the post–cold war world. Resource constraints driven by the lack of a perceived military threat combined with the post–cold war emphasis on domestic concerns significantly limit U.S. ability to intervene militarily. At the same time, the growing priority of domestic considerations makes both unilateral U.S. action and U.S. leadership of international coalitions more difficult politically, a self-imposed constraint, but a real one.

Paradoxically, the same publicity—the so-called CNN effect—that is a prod to intervention also imposes limits on military action. Somalia illustrates both sides of this paradox. This limitation is especially severe where American lives may be lost, but loss of life among innocent bystanders may also cause revulsion and erode support for intervention. Finally, the increasingly visible role of the United Nations also constrains U.S. action; unilateral action may be precluded because of the political need for U.N. endorsement, while multilateral action is difficult because of Americans' doubts about U.N. competence.

These constraints do not all move in the same direction, but in the aggregate, they tend to raise the cost—particularly the political cost—of military intervention, often to a point higher than the nation is willing to pay. The diplomatic and economic instruments that are the traditional alternatives to military intervention may not be effective enough to get results. Thus the tools of the past may not be adequate to support U.S. interests—under almost any definition—in the coming years. Even if they are, the growing complexity of the world suggests a benefit to going beyond the traditional instruments. Something better is clearly needed.

New Techniques and New Technologies

The three intervention categories discussed earlier illustrate both the need for and the risks of new intervention capabilities. Because there will inevitably be cases where intervention is all but mandatory, we need to be able to intervene as effectively as possible. Given the new post–cold war constraints described above, this alone would argue that new tools are needed. New tools may also make it easier to act in discretionary cases where we are willing to intervene, but only if the costs are less than the benefits we hope to realize.

As noted earlier, however, such tools may tempt us to intervene in unwarranted cases where we have little or nothing at stake. Avoiding this trap is important. Improved tools for intervention are not a substitute for a clear analysis of where our interests lie. The dilemma of the post–cold war world is that it may be easier to intervene but more difficult to decide where and when such intervention is warranted. This caution must be kept firmly in mind as we evaluate possible improvements in our ability to intervene.

Excluding diplomacy and moral suasion, the traditional tools of intervention are military force and economic leverage. If we are to increase our options, we must adapt our military forces to the changed circumstances of the post–cold war world, augment traditional lethal military force with new, nonlethal tools, improve the effectiveness of economic sanctions, or find entirely new tools of intervention and coercion. Our authors have examined each of these options.

More Effective Use of the Military

The most obvious—and arguably most important—tool of intervention will remain military force. In his chapter on "Adapting Conventional Military Forces to the New Environment," John O.B. Sewall notes the growing importance of "peaceful military intervention," such as preventive deployments in Macedonia or the provision of military observers to the Sinai Peninsula. With intrastate conflict increasingly replacing interstate conflict, the United Nations, NATO, and other international bodies are under increasing pressure to intervene in nations both to engage in peacekeeping or "peace enforcement" and to conduct "nation building," the re-creation of a viable state out of chaos.

Sewall surveys the various types of peaceful military interventions, noting that participation in such operations has implications for civil-military coordination (including coordination with nongovernmental organizations that are playing an increasingly prominent role in humanitarian operations), military doctrine, equipment, training, and education. He argues that American doctrine, devised for high-intensity war, needs changing, while American military organization does not. In his view, the U.S. military should avoid specialized peacekeeping units, but, despite the arguments of some, does need specialized peacekeeping training.

Not all military intervention will be peaceful, of course. Not only might we elect to intervene using force but, as the death of 241 Marines in Beirut in 1983 demonstrates, peaceful intervention can quickly turn into coercive intervention, i.e., into something that looks very much like combat. Coercive intervention requires continued emphasis on intelligence, on precision-guided munitions (so-called smart bombs), and on flexibility and mobility. Sewall suggests it also demands reexamination of service roles and missions and of military command arrangements.

Sewall's analysis raises a number of important policy issues. To what degree should the United States train and equip its forces for intervention? What kind of intervention should we prepare for? Do we, for example, wish to be able to maintain peace and rebuild a nation, as some sought to do in Somalia? Should we plan for long-term or short-term intervention? Most importantly, as it shapes, trains, and equips its future military forces, what balance should the United States strike among traditional high-intensity warfare, coercive intervention, and peaceful intervention. Sewall argues that the United States can do all three, in large part because traditional warfare and coercive intervention require similar forces. He sees the trade-offs primarily in terms of training requirements and response times. Others believe that armor-heavy warfighting forces developed to defend against Warsaw Pact attacks are unsuited for intervention and that resource constraints will make it difficult to preserve all three capabilities. In an era of declining defense budgets, the answers to these questions will be immensely important.

Augmenting Traditional Military Tools with New Nonlethal or Less Lethal Technology

As the world's only remaining superpower, we could, in theory, intervene militarily almost anywhere in the world with a reasonable probability of success *if* we were willing to pay the price. In reality, however, the political constraints discussed by Blacker, Lewis, and Sewall make such intervention difficult, if not infeasible. Put simply, in most cases of discretionary intervention, if the price is dead Americans *or dead civilians in the target country,* America is likely to consider that price too high.

But what if we could intervene successfully without accepting or inflicting significant fatalities? The capability to do so could dramatically reduce the political and human costs of intervention. In addition, with less risk of loss of life, we might be able to muster the will to intervene earlier, when the risks were lower and the chance of success greater. Recent developments in the area of nonlethal weapons—weapons that incapacitate rather than kill personnel, or disable rather than destroy equipment—appear to be a promising source of such a new capability. For their advocates, these new weapons offer a unique opportunity for the United States to seize the moral and political high ground.

Effective nonlethal weapons could reduce the costs of intervention in other ways as well. Intervention that leads to significant deaths could embitter an entire generation against the United States, with inevitable—though difficult to calculate—future costs. Destruction of facilities means that those facilities will need to be replaced, perhaps as part of an international reconstruction effort that we are likely to help pay for. For all of these reasons, many have concluded that augmenting our lethal arsenal with nonlethal weapons should be a U.S. priority.

Richard Garwin explores the potential benefits and limitations of nonlethal weapons in his chapter on "New Applications of Nonlethal and Less Lethal Technology." As he notes, such weapons are neither a new idea nor a new military capability. Tear gas was used by U.S. forces in Vietnam to flush enemy soldiers out of tunnels, and Egyptian radars were electronically jammed by Israeli forces during the Yom Kippur War.

But emerging alternatives to deadly force go far beyond these uses. These new technologies range from caustic substances that destroy weapons sensors to lasers that blind the weapons operators, from microwaves that disrupt electronics to "infrasound" that disrupts human beings' capacity to function, and from lubricants that are so slippery that equipment cannot maintain traction to foam that is so sticky that people cannot move.

Nonlethal techniques such as tear gas and radar jamming traditionally have been employed when they were deemed to be the *militarily* most effective means available. New technologies also might be attractive for the same, predominantly operational, reasons. In particular, some nonlethal weapons might be used to increase the effectiveness of *lethal* weapons. For example, nonlethal weapons might be used to blind or immobilize tanks and other vehicles so that it becomes easier to destroy them with conventional ordnance.

In considering the growing number of post–cold war contingencies in which the United States might contemplate intervention, we are, however, more interested in the potential utility of such weapons as substitutes for, rather than as complements to, lethal capabilities. These contingencies, especially so-called peace operations, are characterized by the absence of an easily identifiable adversary who can be isolated and attacked; by the intermingling of combatants and noncombatants; by limited U.S. stakes that diminish our tolerance for high costs and friendly fatalities; and by a desire to set the stage for "postwar" reconciliation and rebuilding by minimizing the damage, death, and lingering bitterness resulting from "peace enforcement" operations.

Put differently, they are precisely the situations that we are most likely to face in the post–cold war world, but for which our arsenal of state-of-the-art lethal weapons and our doctrine of bringing overwhelming force to bear seem to be particularly ill-suited. The new situations place a premium on the development of new military capabilities that can be used to achieve our objectives while holding fatalities and collateral damage to an absolute minimum, i.e., precisely the promise offered by nonlethal weapons. If we can develop weapons that have the desired military effects, act quickly enough, and last long enough, all without killing people, they could significantly increase our options by reducing the *political* costs of intervention. Nonlethal weapons could make interventions politically more palatable by making them less bloody and costly for all concerned. As such, they would appear to be particularly useful for those discretionary intervention cases in which decisions about whether or not to intervene turn on a close calculation of costs and benefits.

But nonlethal weapons are no panacea. One problem is that "nonlethal" is a relative term. There often is a fine line between what is required to incapacitate an individual and what it takes to cause death. The understandable desire of military commanders to *ensure* their opponents will be unable to fight increases the chances that this line will be crossed frequently, and that weapons intended to be more humane will become indistinguishable from lethal weapons in their results. To complicate matters further, what it takes to incapacitate a healthy adult might well be lethal to the very young, the very old, and the very sick. In some circumstances, using weapons we believe to be nonlethal could well have the opposite of the intended effect, killing the innocent and helpless while leaving able-bodied combatants unharmed.

Developing weapons that disable equipment rather than incapacitate people does not provide a reliable escape from this dilemma. First, it may be more difficult to develop nonlethal weapons that are effective against hardware, in part because it often is easier to design countermeasures to protect equipment than measures to protect people. There are, however, "less lethal" alternatives to nonlethal weapons that have many of their political advantages but also may be militarily more effective against an opponent's capabilities. As Garwin points out, if the objective is to minimize collateral damage and to limit harm to innocent bystanders, many of the advantages we seek from nonlethal weapons can also be realized by utilizing precision-guided conventional munitions such as the smart bombs that were used to such great effect against Iraq during Desert Storm.

Second, many adversaries—particularly those encountered in peace operations—may have relatively primitive weapons and equipment that would not be particularly vulnerable to measures designed to work against modern, sophisticated systems. In such cases, there may be little choice but to target the personnel who operate the weapons and other equipment. Finally, the intermingling of combatants with noncombatants that typically characterizes post–cold war contingencies means that, in many cases, there simply is no alternative to targeting people.

Moreover, employing nonlethal weapons could even work to our disadvantage in certain circumstances. Given our dependence on sophisticated systems, we might well be relatively more vulnerable to such weapons than would be many potential opponents. In addition, some weapons that are technically nonlethal—such as lasers that cause blindness—may be considered so abhorrent that their use would undermine the political objectives that nonlethal weapons are designed to achieve. For reasons such as these, Garwin argues that serious consideration be given to negotiating arms control bans on maiming and blinding weapons.

Finally, the availability of nonlethal weapons could lure us into interventions that soon become transformed into situations in which the costs outweigh the benefits. For example, Garwin notes that an opponent who lacks effective nonlethal weapons (or believes that they would not be the most effective response) could well respond with lethal weapons. We would then face a choice between unilateral restraint in the form of continued reliance on nonlethal technologies, or responding in kind with lethal weapons. The first alternative could put us at a military and political disadvantage. The second alternative, i.e., escalation, would undermine the objectives of minimizing collateral damage and casualties that led to the initial choice of nonlethal weapons. In either case, we could find ourselves bogged down in a now-lethal intervention that threatens rather than serves our interests.

In the end, the development of nonlethal weapons would add an important tool to the kit bag of intervention options by expanding the spectrum of "politically usable" force, but would be unlikely to transform fundamentally U.S. intervention policy, the need for acquisition of lethal systems, or the way in which military force is employed. Such nonlethal weapons appear to have the most promise for those cases:

- In which countermeasures and escalation options are not readily available to the adversary.
- Which resemble domestic law enforcement or riot control situations, especially with respect to a very low tolerance for fatalities (e.g., scenarios such as Haiti or Somalia or rescuing hostages seized by terrorists).
- In which military force is being used to support other coercive measures (e.g., blockades to enforce economic sanctions).

Economic Intervention

One alternative to military intervention is the imposition of economic sanctions. Sanctions have often been used by the United States as a way of demonstrating concern and resolve. Indeed, they have become the U.S. intervention tool of choice in the post–cold war world. But do they work? Kimberly Elliott and Gary Hufbauer have analyzed almost 120 cases of the imposition of sanctions during this century. Drawing upon their extensive research, they conclude in their chapter, " 'New' Approaches to Economic Sanctions," that economic leverage is most likely to work when objectives are modest (so that the cost of complying is low), when the coalition imposing sanctions is broad (so that circumvention by third countries is less likely), and when the sanctions are imposed quickly and decisively.

As the global economic system has become increasingly interdependent, the ability of any nation—including the United States—to impose effective unilateral sanctions has decreased. Sanctions still may serve political and diplomatic purposes by sending signals of disapproval, but only in rare cases can unilateral economic coercion succeed in today's global economy. Many potential target states have large and diversified economies, while the growth in world trade means that most U.S. exports can be replaced at acceptable cost. Exacerbating the problem are the costs that sanctions impose on American allies, on American business, and on the poor and the weak in the target country.

Multilateral sanctions, typically organized through the United Nations, might, in theory, be more effective. But Elliott and Hufbauer's research suggests that sustained, widespread international support for effective sanctions (as was the case for sanctions against Iraq following the invasion of Kuwait) is rare. The greater the number of states involved in imposing sanctions, the longer it will take to impose them, typically weakening their effect. With many participating states, at least some will find the cost to their own economies of continued sanctions erodes their will. As a result, leakage is virtually inevitable.

Faced with these sobering facts, some have advocated increasing the effectiveness of sanctions by targeting them specifically against the target country's leaders and the elites who support them. Elliott and Hufbauer suggest this technique is unlikely to work except in special cases, usually involving financial sanctions and the freezing of overseas assets. In most cases, however, elites can redistribute the burden away from themselves and onto the poor and the innocent. In the end, sanctions are almost always a blunt instrument.

Elliott and Hufbauer identify some steps that would improve the effectiveness of sanctions. They advocate mandating secondary sanctions against states that violate primary sanctions. This stick could be coupled with the carrot of providing assistance to states whose economies bear unusually heavy burdens from enforcing sanctions. Still, they conclude that economic sanctions "should not be viewed as a means of conducting foreign policy on the cheap."

Interventionist economic policy instruments other than sanctions might offset the declining effectiveness of both unilateral and multilateral sanctions. One technique would be to, in essence, buy compliance with our desires by providing positive economic incentives for states to do what we want. A recent example of this approach is Ukraine's decision to give up nuclear weapons despite significant internal opposition, a decision driven heavily by the prospect of gaining both revenue and nuclear fuel from selling the highly enriched uranium scavenged from the weapons. A quite different example might be encouraging a dictator to depart by providing for an economically comfortable exile. While such techniques are likely to be useful only in special cases, where they can be used, they deserve serious consideration.

Finding Something New

In the new security environment that the United States faces, the traditional instruments of intervention may no longer work— or at least no longer work well enough at acceptable cost. Even with nonlethal weapons, military intervention is subject to constraints that can only be overcome when the benefits are clear and substantial. The use of the military still often will mean killing people and having people killed. Economic sanctions avoid the trap of tying down forces and of putting lives directly at risk, but have their own problems. Unilateral sanctions are of diminishing effectiveness; multilateral sanctions are more difficult to enforce and cede at least partial control to others. As a result, it is attractive to look for entirely new techniques.

Timothy Sample has examined possible new approaches in his chapter, "New Techniques of Political and Economic Coercion." Many of these arise from the increasing importance of the emerging global information network, what Sample calls the "infosphere." Coupled with the development of this infosphere are three fundamental changes in the nature of the business world:

- A growing number of international businesses.
- An increasing importance of international business leaders as compared to government leaders.
- The growing dependence of both international and domestic firms on technology, especially information technology.

These changes mean that, whether sought or unsought, the growing ability of businesses to operate on a multinational basis in substantial independence of the policies of their governments makes them an increasingly important source of international prosperity and stability. At the same time, the dependence of businesses on modern information technologies to compete effectively in the global marketplace makes them highly vulnerable to manipulation or disruption. Of particular relevance is the fact that this vulnerability is not limited to advanced nations. Many less developed states are leapfrogging into the information age by creating their own versions of the U.S. information superhighway. Traditional forms of intervention seek to bring external pressure on target governments. Sample suggests that by targeting the business community, the United States can create pressure from within, compelling a government to comply with our desires because of the demands of its business leaders. In today's world, all but the most autocratic states must pay attention to such demands. Among the new techniques Sample discusses are manipulation of design, production, financial, or marketing data. Disruption of any of these data would have a devastating effect on a nation's business elites.

Populations, like businesses, can be directly targeted. Existing technology could allow external seizure of television signals, blocking government broadcasts and substituting our own. Such a technique could allow the United States to bypass a nation's leaders and deal directly with its people. A more focused, longer-term technique would be to provide the population with independent information through computer networks. History suggests that American interests are more likely to be threatened by dictatorships than by democracies. Such dictatorships depend for their power on monopolizing the flow of information to their citizens. Breaking that monopoly could be a powerful tool.

The use of the techniques Sample discusses raises significant policy and ethical questions. In an increasingly interdependent world, disrupting computer or communications networks in one state can have repercussions in many other states. Some techniques might be unknown to the target nation and allow covert intervention using technology as a substitute for agents. For example, we might covertly manipulate a nation's warning system, air control system, or weather broadcasts. Would the traditional American reservations about covert action still apply in such a case?

Many techniques involve a degree of cooperation between the U.S. government and international business that is unprecedented in recent years. The ability to take control of communications signals or disrupt financial networks within a country, for example, may require the cooperation of multinational businesses. What incentives are we prepared to offer business to induce such close cooperation? Finally, not all states are moving into the information age at the same rate. Some may lack the technical sophistication, the business communities, or the social attitudes to make these sophisticated techniques feasible. Are the techniques worth developing if their use is limited?

These questions have no clear answers. Still, as Sample notes, the infosphere of the future is being created today. U.S. ability to manipulate that infosphere to serve our national security interests requires that we study these techniques seriously now and act both to preserve our future options and to devise the necessary policy and technical safeguards. The issues raised above are a reason for more debate, not less.

Combining the New Techniques

Although it is useful for purposes of analysis to consider new techniques and new technologies one by one, the greatest effect will be gained by combining their effects. In particular, there is an obvious synergism between the nonlethal technologies described by Garwin and the information based techniques described by Sample. Suppose, for example, that with U.S. and coalition military forces poised to intervene against a future Saddam Hussein, all electrical power to Baghdad was disrupted—but not destroyed—and military electronic systems throughout the country stopped working. Suppose that, at the same time, commercial businesses discovered they no longer had access to their financial records, while citizens found that their radios and televisions broadcast only messages from the United States and its allies. Finally, suppose that a few critical metal structures—bridges, airplanes, and ships—suddenly had their molecular structure altered so that they became brittle and inoperable. What would be the result?

No one can answer that question, of course, but it is possible that the sense of massive vulnerability engendered by such a sweeping combination of steps would lead to a more accommodating government. At a minimum, such widespread nonlethal intervention should drastically undermine the support of the people for their leaders. Even if neither of these expectations materializes, the use of nonlethal techniques should make military action more decisive, thus reducing loss of life on both sides.

The scenario we have presented is, of course, deliberately fanciful. Only in very special circumstances are we likely to be able to employ new tools in such a coordinated fashion, and even then, the results may not be what we hope. After all, if the real Saddam Hussein of 1990 was not dissuaded by massive destruction, the hypothetical Saddam Hussein of 2010 may not be swayed by massive nonlethal intervention. But if we should not depend too heavily on technological solutions, neither should we ignore their potential, especially if, as their proponents suggest, the development of these new capabilities is relatively straightforward. In the complex post–cold war world, where traditional tools may be losing their value, finding new tools is imperative.

American Intervention Policy for the Twenty-first Century

Neither this book nor the conference for which it was prepared were conceived as abstract intellectual exercises. We survey changes in the world and new intervention techniques and technologies, not out of idle curiosity, but to help devise a sound U.S. intervention policy for the future.

How can we craft that wise policy? Perhaps the first step is to recognize the risks. Intervention is almost always easier to begin than to end. In a messy world it is difficult either to define success or to accept failure. The promise of technology and the new tools we have discussed should not blind Americans to the fact that, ultimately, intervention may require either applying lethal military force and accepting American casualties or an equally unpalatable acceptance of the consequences of defeat. The authors who have contributed to this volume have made many suggestions for improvements in America's intervention capability, but they found no "silver bullets." There may be many reasons to embrace their ideas, but cutting the defense budget or moving to a world of bloodless, painless intervention isn't among them.

Be Selective about Intervention

The costs and risks of intervention make it imperative that we be selective about where and when to intervene. Two of our authors offer suggestions to help the United States in considering this issue. Both argue for intervention only in strictly limited cases. Blacker advocates a narrow definition of U.S. interests. He would limit military intervention to cases involving "critically important" U.S. or allied interests, where clear aggression across an internationally recognized boundary will, if not reversed, result in an unacceptable shift in the regional balance of power. Finally, Blacker would consider intervention only when the local balance of military forces favors the United States and its allies. In his view, only such a cautious policy can be sustained economically and politically.

As Blacker notes, however, the real world is seldom as clear-cut as we would like. Agreeing that intervention is only appropriate in response to clear threats to U.S. interests is not the same as agreeing on what those threats—or even what those interests—are. As we noted earlier, there is and will continue to be significant debate among Americans about exactly what constitutes a sufficient threat to justify intervention.

Taking a somewhat different approach, Fareed Zakaria also calls for a tightly focused approach to any intervention decision. In his chapter, "A Framework for Interventionism in the Post–Cold War Era," Zakaria examines both distant and recent history for clues to guide future intervention decisions. Zakaria recalls the nineteenth century British error in intervening in the far-flung reaches of the empire, while neglecting the true threat represente ' by the rise of Germany. He suggests that the United States faces a similar danger of misunderstanding its interests and cautions against making a similar error.

In contrast to Lewis, Zakaria concludes that since the end of the cold war Americans have reached substantial consensus on the type of world they would like to see and on the preconditions for using military force to gain that world (clear interests, adequate force, unambiguous goals). Policy makers no longer treat claims of sovereignty as an insurmountable barrier to intervention. Further, there is broad agreement that some U.S. involvement (diplomatic, humanitarian aid, or food delivery, for example) may be appropriate in almost any crisis. What remains contentious is whether and when to resort to coercive instruments of intervention, especially the use of military force, a fact made evident by the vast gap in 1993 between rhetoric and action in Haiti, Somalia, and Bosnia.

Zakaria uses the debate over intervention in these three states to illustrate the importance of having a clear sense of priorities. Despite arguments in favor of intervention in each case, he concludes that, ultimately, none of these states is central to American interests. Zakaria argues that intervention in such cases diverts attention from what should be the central U.S. goal: single-minded devotion to its political and economic relations with Europe and with East Asia. Stability in these two crucial regions cannot be taken for granted and depends on continued wise use of American power. Neglecting that fact risks catastrophe.

Zakaria makes an eloquent and powerful argument for clarity and focus in the definition of American interests. Not everyone will agree, however, that placing the greatest emphasis on Europe and East Asia should preclude intervention with military forces elsewhere. If Victorian Britain had dealt with both Germany and the empire, it might still dominate the world. Intervention in secondary areas need not be harmful if it can be done without diverting too many of the resources needed to defend core interests. As we noted earlier, the most difficult decisions for policy makers are in those cases where intervention would bring us net benefits if and only if it can be accomplished at acceptable cost. Zakaria's analysis, like Blacker's, clarifies the debate, but is unlikely to end it.

Look at New Methods of Organization

If America is to continue to contemplate intervention—a course we believe is inevitable—it is important to preserve and expand our options for doing so effectively. One important step is to improve the internal U.S. government organization for dealing with issues related to intervention. Such a step would have three aims: to bring an institutionalized advocate for new techniques to the debate, to improve our ability to develop new tools of intervention, and to improve the integration of various intervention tools when they are used.

In the concluding chapter, "Organizing the Government to Provide the Tools for Intervention," George Pickett and James Roche examine the organization and functioning of the Defense Department with particular emphasis on using lessons from the private sector for organizing to deal with uncertainty and change. Successful businesses, like successful governments, need a strategy. Such a strategy does not come forth full-blown, but evolves over time. Its development can be facilitated by three techniques:

• Emphasizing core competencies. Put simply, there are some things America does well (intelligence, long-range air combat, distant naval operations, long-distance logistics). A successful strategy should play to our strengths.
• Using scenario based planning. Accurately estimating the future is exceptionally difficult. While many believed that the collapse of communism was inevitable, few if any foresaw when that collapse would occur. Scenarios allow developing strategies for alternate futures in an inherently uncertain world.
• Employing time oriented strategies. As the pace of technological change increases, a successful strategy must be able to adapt. Failure to do so will slow the pace of innovation and gradually erode U.S. lead-times in such important military areas as communications, navigation, and intelligence.

To complement these forms of effective strategy development, Pickett and Roche advocate better methods of integration, both within the Defense Department and within the government as a whole. They call for shallow hierarchies—following industry's lead by eliminating layers of management in order to increase responsiveness—and for adaptive organizations, perhaps driven by reexamination of roles and missions of the military services. These structural changes should be augmented by reforms in defense acquisition and in the planning, programing, and budgeting system and by increased use of exercises for training the entire government, including the White House. Ultimately, the authors conclude, the key to successful organization lies with the president and the National Security Council staff.

The ideas Pickett and Roche advance would doubtless improve the organization of the Defense Department in ways reaching far beyond planning for intervention. Even if all their proposals were to be adopted, however, additional issues would remain. Among the other organizational questions: how can the various instruments of intervention (diplomatic, military, economic, financial, technological) be integrated? Are changes in structure (such as merging the National Security Council and National Economic Council) needed? In an age of increasing congressional involvement in foreign and security policy, what changes in executive-legislative relations are required? Is there a need for new mechanisms for oversight, such as a "Select Committee on Intervention"? In this area as in others, the issues are far from resolved.

Wrestle with the Hard Questions, both Intellectually and Organizationally

Our authors have not exhausted the difficult questions facing the United States, much less provided definitive answers. The range of remaining issues is enormous. Perhaps the most difficult is the weight moral and ethical considerations should be given in U.S. intervention decisions. We have said that intervention is only justified to protect American interests or promote American values. There has been a great deal of debate about threats to our interests, but far less about threats to our values. Blacker points out that the need to right an egregious moral wrong may appear so compelling to the American people that intervention will seem necessary regardless of whether or not there is any direct challenge to U.S. interests. Preventing starvation in Somalia or genocide in Bosnia are obvious cases where at least some Americans would intervene, not because it is in our national security interest to do so, but because not to act diminishes our sense of ourselves as a moral people.

On the other hand, intervention, by definition, ignores the sovereignty of another nation. Many Americans believe that a nation committed to the rule of law cannot legitimately impose its will on others absent a clear and compelling threat. For them it is intervention, not inaction, that threatens the American soul.

There are other difficult questions for American policy makers in addition to what, if any, role moral and ethical questions should play in intervention decisions. Among them are the following:

- What about intelligence gathering and analysis? Is a "central" intelligence agency the right approach or is there a need for some form of regionalization of intelligence? If, as Sample suggests, we need the cooperation of international business to make intervention effective, should we pay for that cooperation by sharing commercial intelligence?
- If intervention should defend U.S. interests or uphold U.S. values, what do we do when those goals conflict? If an important state freely elects a xenophobic, anti-American fascist, should we ignore both international law and our commitment to democracy and intervene to change the outcome? How do we decide?
- How should we craft a research and development agenda? Should we, as Garwin suggests, consider joint development of nonlethal weapons by the military and law enforcement? Are new institutional mechanisms needed to ensure a voice for technological innovation in the councils of government?
- If we can't afford to do everything (and we can't), how do we decide what to give up? Currently, the size of the U.S. military is driven by a requirement that we be capable of fighting in two major regional contingencies simultaneously. Should we forgo the ability to intervene in order to keep that capability?
- How should we seek to organize the international community for intervention? Do we depend on the United Nations (and accept U.N. leadership)? On NATO? On ad hoc coalitions?

Some of these issues were dealt with by participants in the 1994 American Assembly. The results of their deliberations are included in this volume as an afterword. Others remain for future debate. All are important.

Closing Thoughts

The decision to intervene in the affairs of another state is one of the most important that the United States can face. Unwise intervention can be costly in terms of lives, of resources, and of U.S. credibility and honor. Unwise restraint likewise can irreparably harm American interests and undermine American values. The authors of the eight chapters that follow offer a variety of perspectives on intervention, suggesting how new techniques and new concepts can contribute to sound decisions. The breadth of their opinions and prescriptions testifies to the complexity of the issue.

Ultimately, however, it is not the experts who must decide. It is the people. In a democracy, wise decisions require informed public debate. Nowhere is such debate more crucial than in contemplating intervention. We prepared this book—and The American Assembly organized its spring 1994 assembly—in order to contribute to that debate.

1

A Typology of
Post–Cold War Conflicts

COIT D. BLACKER

Few issues so dominate the headlines. The electronic media focus on little else, it seems. Images of war that are simultaneously riveting and revolting bombard the senses, leaving us with the impression that the world has become a much more violent place in which to live—or to die, as the case may be. Have the frequency and intensity of conflict increased since the cold war came to an end in 1989–90, or do we simply pay more attention to the phenomenon of organized violence than we used to? If war has become more common, what are the major reasons? Given that some degree of turmoil in the international system is inescapable, where are the most serious challenges to global peace and security likely to arise, and how—by reference to what set of standards, in other words—should the United States respond?

COIT D. BLACKER is deputy director and senior fellow, Institute for International Studies, Stanford University, and, by courtesy, associate professor of political science. Dr. Blacker's areas of interest include international and regional security issues, nuclear arms control, and Soviet and post-Soviet foreign and military policies. He is author or editor of six books and monographs, including *Hostage to Revolution: Gorbachev and Soviet*

The purpose of this chapter is to investigate these and related issues. It begins by comparing and contrasting the nature of conflict *during* and *after* the cold war. It continues with an analysis of the most probable sources of conflict in three increasingly distinct domains: the industrialized North; the developing world of the South; and the impoverished East, specifically, the former Communist states of East Central Europe and Eurasia that are currently experiencing far-reaching political and economic change. The discussion then moves to the problem of regional conflicts from the U.S. perspective. What are the interests that should define and animate U.S. policy? What are the kinds of developments and eventualities that U.S. policy makers will want to prevent? The final section focuses on the ways in which the increasing incidence and complexity of post–cold war conflicts, together with such secular trends as declining defense budgets, will almost certainly constrain the options available to U.S. policy makers, whatever their preferences.

The chapter advances three major propositions. The first is that the global system of relations that is emerging is more likely to be multipolar than unipolar in character, signifying, among other things, that the world will become more, rather than less, violent in years to come. The second is that the collapse of the Soviet empire has shifted the line separating the developed and the developing worlds to the north and west. The third is that the demand for resources to help prevent conflicts, and to manage those that do erupt, will far exceed the supply, making difficult choices for U.S. policy makers inevitable.

Conflict During the Cold War

One of the most remarkable features of the cold war order was its relative peacefulness. Although scores of regional conflicts, many prolonged and some quite violent, perturbed the interna-

Security Policy: 1985–91; Reluctant Warriors: the United States, the Soviet Union, and Arms Control; and, with Gloria Duffy, *International Arms Control: Issues and Agreements.*

tional political landscape between the end of World War II in 1945 and the collapse of the Soviet Union in 1991, none precipitated the kind of global conflict that many had come to expect and that all had learned to fear.

Exactly why the wars that *did* erupt remained limited in scope and intensity is difficult to determine. Among both students and practitioners of international politics, however, there is near consensus that the extraordinary destructive power of nuclear weapons, and the caution that these weapons induced on the part of U.S. and Soviet political leaders in particular, had something to do with it. A number of other explanations have also been advanced, including the stabilizing influence of bipolar international political systems, the status quo orientation of the two great powers, the impact of reciprocal "learning" by political decision makers in Washington and Moscow, and what political scientist John Mueller has termed "the obsolescence of major war."[1] With the exception of the Mueller hypothesis, which explicitly contends that nuclear weapons were irrelevant to the maintenance of peace during the cold war, each of these second-order explanations either derives from or builds upon the logic of nuclear deterrence.

The "long peace," to employ the term first used by John Lewis Gaddis, did not obtain everywhere, of course.[2] If most developed countries, sometimes characterized as the "core" or the "center" of the international system, largely escaped the ravages of war, the same cannot be said for the developing world, or the "periphery," which was the scene of frequent, costly, and often extremely bloody conflicts between the late 1940s and the early 1990s. For purposes of analysis, these conflicts can be grouped into six distinct clusters:

- So-called *wars of national liberation,* e.g., the several dozen wars for political independence that pitted five of Europe's metropolitan powers—Belgium, France, Great Britain, the Netherlands, and Portugal—against many of their colonies, dependencies, and protectorates in Africa and Asia.
- *Wars of conquest or for territorial aggrandizement,* such as North Korea's attempt in June 1950 to defeat the Republic of Korea militarily and forcibly reunify the peninsula.

- *Wars over natural resources,* such as the effort by Katanga province to secede from the newly independent Republic of the Congo (Zaire) in 1960 and Iraq's 1990 invasion of Kuwait.
- *Wars caused or exacerbated by ethnic, racial, and/or religious differences,* such as the recurrent conflicts between India and Pakistan, India and Sri Lanka, and China and Tibet.
- *"Proxy wars,"* e.g., conflicts involving U.S. (or Western) allies, on the one hand, and principally Soviet client states, on the other, in which the armed forces of the two superpowers may or may not have played an active part, but never at the same time.
- *Small- to large-scale military interventions* undertaken by each of the superpowers—from U.S. actions in the Dominican Republic in 1965 (and in Vietnam from the late 1950s to the mid-1970s) to the Soviet invasion of Afghanistan in 1979—in ostensible defense of "vital national interests."

Of these six kinds of conflicts, the first four had little, if anything, to do with the cold war directly; they neither began with the deterioration of U.S.–Soviet relations that followed in the wake of World War II, nor did they end once the superpower competition had run its course. As a result, most are likely to persist—perhaps even to intensify—in decades to come, notwithstanding the remarkable changes in global political relations occasioned by the abrupt disappearance of the Soviet challenge.

A second method for conceptualizing the problem of conflict during the cold war is to correlate the relative frequency of conflict and different pairs of actors. Note, for example, the relatively low incidence of organized violence between developed states (or center versus center conflicts); the higher, though still modest, incidence of conflict between developed and developing states (or conflicts between the center and the periphery); and the relatively high incidence of conflict between developing states (or the periphery versus the periphery). Major conflicts involving the relatively affluent communities of Europe, North America, and parts of East Asia did not disappear entirely between 1945 and 1991, but, as the above schema suggest, war was a particular problem for the governments and peoples of the poorer and more populous societies of the Third World.

Conflict after the Cold War

The relative orderliness of the postwar structure was a function
of both the deterrent effect of nuclear weapons and, throughout
much of the period, the determination of the two superpowers to
maintain order within their respective spheres of influence. Where
neither superpower had much of a political and/or economic
stake, by contrast, conflict was a much more common occurrence.
What, then, does the sudden collapse of the cold war system of
relations portend for regional and international security? Is the
passing of the old order likely to increase or to decrease the frequency and/or the intensity of conflict?

The answer depends in part on whether the global system that is
emerging will be more *unipolar* or more *multipolar* in character.
When a single state dominates world politics, both history and
international relations theory tell us that the level of violence
within the system goes down. Within its own borders, for example,
the Roman Empire was for centuries a relatively peaceful place to
live. When power is more evenly distributed among the states that
constitute the system, peace often becomes the exception rather
than the rule. Balance of power systems, such as the one that
characterized European politics between 1648 and the Napoleonic
Wars, are notoriously violent; because the distribution of power
within such systems can shift suddenly, the fear of abandonment
runs high, and national political leaders must be hyper-vigilant to
any sign of betrayal. The tendency is to ascribe the basest of motives to friend and foe alike. Under such circumstances, both the
strong and the weak can have powerful incentives to go to war:
strong states may decide to resort to force because the prospect of
an easy victory is too attractive to resist, while weak and declining
states may be tempted to strike before they get any weaker.

The sudden demise of the Soviet Union in 1991 prompted publication of a small handful of articles arguing that what Charles
Krauthammer first termed Washington's "unipolar moment" had
arrived.[3] The disintegration of the USSR, it was alleged, had left
the United States the sole surviving superpower. Although less
powerful in relative terms than either the Roman or the British
empires at their height, America, in the aftermath of the Soviet

implosion, had at its disposal material and human resources far in excess of those available to its nearest rival; moreover, so great was the gap separating Washington's power from that of all other states that no credible challenger to the United States was likely to emerge anytime soon.

Others, drawing on the same data, reached the opposite conclusion. In the struggle to maintain its status as the one true superpower, the United States had all but exhausted its industrial and technological potential. So great had the burden on the U.S. economy become that by the time the Soviet Union collapsed, Washington, with chronic budget deficits and the lowest rate of savings and investment in the developed world, was unable to exploit its hard-won victory. At the same time, countries that had managed to limit their exposure to the economic costs of the cold war—Germany in Europe and China and Japan in Asia—were in a much stronger position than the United States to exercise effective political leadership, at least at the regional level. For these reasons, the emerging global system could only be multipolar in character, whatever the precise distribution of power within it. To argue in support of unipolarity, proponents of this school insisted, was not only delusional, but dangerous.

Both interpretations capture elements of the truth. In 1994 U.S. power far outstripped that of any other country. Its economy was more than twice the size of Japan's, the world's second largest, and only the United States maintained military forces capable of fighting two large regional conflicts simultaneously. It was also true, however, that relative to other developed states, the United States was less powerful in 1994 than it had been in the past. To take the most obvious example, since the late 1960s the most successful of these countries have routinely posted annual rates of growth two to three times larger than those attained by the United States. Although such disparities have begun to disappear as the economies of these countries mature, the larger point—that the economic (and political) hegemony once enjoyed by the United States continues to erode and is unlikely to be reestablished—stands.

If, as most international relations theorists contend, multipolar systems are less stable and therefore more susceptible to war than systems dominated by one or, at most, two great powers, does the relative decline in U.S. power presage a more violent world? All else being equal, one would be hard pressed to answer this question in anything but the affirmative. All else is not equal, however. In contrast to previous multipolar systems, the one that is now forming will have among its constituents a sizable number of states armed with nuclear weapons. Countries with an arsenal of deliverable nuclear weapons at their disposal—even more, those with secure second-strike forces—have little reason to fear direct attack from potential enemies; neither are they forced to rely on the goodwill and support of others for their security and well-being. To date, at least, nuclear weapons have probably reinforced general, system-wide stability by enhancing the security of the major powers.

Whether the acquisition of nuclear weapons by countries not now in possession of such forces will have an equally salutary impact is harder to predict. Given State A's ambitions to establish local hegemony and to dominate its regional rivals, and State B's strong incentive to prevent State A from acquiring the military capabilities to make such domination possible, the consequences of further nuclear proliferation could well be disastrous. Such has certainly been the conventional wisdom among scholars and policy makers in the United States, and the non- and counter-proliferation policies of the U.S. government have always been driven by the conviction that membership in the Nuclear Club should be limited to the smallest possible number of states.

Taken together, these two factors—the breakdown of the bipolar order (and rise of multipolarity) and the inevitable spread of nuclear weapons capabilities beyond the seven or eight countries now in possession of such forces—strongly suggest that the international security environment of the 1990s and beyond will be sharply bifurcated.

• At the center of the system, deterrence, and therefore peace, are almost certain to hold; countries with established nuclear weapons capabilities will have essentially no incentive to attack one another; nor are they likely to be victimized by states still in the process of assembling such weapons and their means of delivery, given the manifest ability of the established nuclear weapons states to respond to any provocation.

• In the periphery, however, the potential for conflict, perhaps even nuclear conflict, is likely to be much greater because of the declining ability and willingness of the most powerful actor in the system, the United States, to perform the functions of a global *gendarme*, the growing availability of sophisticated and affordable weaponry of all kinds, the absence of mature deterrent regimes, and the generally volatile state of political and economic conditions throughout much of the developing world.

To complicate matters further, the withdrawal of Soviet power from Eastern Europe, followed by the outright collapse of the Soviet state barely two years later, has for the first time brought the political disorder characteristic of the periphery to within walking distance of the center. This is unprecedented. As recently as 1991, the line separating the developed and the developing worlds ran along a mostly east-west axis that began just south of San Diego, California, continued in an easterly direction across North Africa, and ended somewhere off the East China Sea. By 1994 two new fissures—the first angling off toward southeastern Europe and the second pointing, through the Caucasus, toward the Russian heartland—had appeared along the line's midpoint. Exactly why this happened and what it portends is difficult to know. One early and obvious consequence of the disintegration of the Soviet empire, however, has been to consign millions of people, once considered an integral part of the industrialized world, to its outermost reaches—if not, in fact, to the periphery.

It is along these two fault lines—at the new juncture of the center and the periphery—that the international community can expect to encounter some of the most serious and threatening challenges to the maintenance of regional peace and security. The fighting has already begun, of course, in such places as the former Yugoslavia, Moldova, Georgia, and in and around Nagorno-Karabakh, the predominantly Armenian-populated enclave within Azerbaijan. Although these particular conflicts may burn themselves out in time, there is nothing to suggest that this recent upsurge in organized violence will end anytime soon. On the contrary, the fighting—fueled by a combination of historical grievance, precipitous economic decline, and political chaos—is almost certain to intensify in years to come and to claim many more victims than it has to this point in time.

The Sources of Conflict

The types of conflicts that are likely to preoccupy both local and national political leaders and to tax the resources of regional and international organizations will differ, depending on where they erupt. Their intensity will vary along this and other dimensions, as will the root causes of violence. Some conflicts will be depressingly familiar in form and content, while others, almost certainly, will take the world by surprise.

At a minimum, three types of conflicts will disturb political life in *the developed world*. The first, civil unrest caused by prolonged economic recession, chronic unemployment, profound social alienation, and a general rejection of the social democratic model of development, is hardly a new phenomenon; in Western Europe, where the problem is most acute, governments have learned to cope by maintaining high levels of spending in support of social welfare programs. To this point in time, the mostly urban violence associated with these ills has been sporadic, disorganized, and apolitical in nature.

The second type of conflict is the sometimes violent struggle for greater regional autonomy within, or outright political independence from, existing state structures; it is simultaneously quite ancient and more recent in origin. The campaign of the Basque separatists in Spain is but the most obvious example in this regard, and although similar struggles elsewhere in Europe and in North America—the Lombards and Piedmontese in Italy, the Bretons in France, the Scots in the United Kingdom, and the Quebecois in Canada—have not been particularly bloody, the potential for their becoming so remains quite high, especially if economic conditions remain depressed. Governments challenged in this way have resorted to ceding considerable authority to regional and local decision makers (through a process the British term "devolution" and others call "regionalization"). How much further national political leaders can or should go in accommodating such demands is unclear; there is no evidence to suggest, however, that those issuing the demands intend to suspend their activities anytime soon.

The third, and most troubling, type of conflict in the developed world is the recent explosion in tensions between indigenous populations and national minorities. The problem is most visible in Germany, where Turkish and Vietnamese "guest workers" have been frequent targets of violent attack, and in France, where Algerian nationals and other Muslim residents have been victimized by French citizens disturbed at the influx of tens of thousands of dark-skinned excolonials. Similar episodes have been recorded in most of the industrialized countries of the West, including the United States, where resentment against "illegal aliens" has reached an all-time high. The dramatic upsurge in racially motivated attacks is a clear case of the center striking out as the periphery makes its presence felt in a new and unanticipated way. As the level of violence at the border between the developed and developing worlds increases, the problem will only intensify, particularly in Europe, as thousands of displaced people seek physical safety from and political protection against the ravages of war in their own homelands. The million-plus refugees who have escaped from the fighting in the former Yugoslavia may be only the foretaste of things to come, if, as seems probable, the political chaos that has engulfed much of southeastern Europe spreads to the north and east.

The developing world is host to many of the same ills that have led to an increase in violence in the West, including declining living standards and a pronounced fraying of the social fabric. Governments in the periphery must also contend, however, with a long list of problems that, for the most part, their more affluent counterparts in the developed world have not had to confront. Foremost among these is the persistently high level of civil strife that can be traced either to the unfinished business of the national struggle or to the process of state formation (or reformation), and sometimes to both. The ongoing and so far unsuccessful attempt of the Kurdish people to create a country out of bits and pieces of territory currently controlled by the Turkish, Iraqi, and Iranian governments is an example of this phenomenon, as is the escalating violence between militant Hindus, who demand the establishment of a theocracy in India, and the country's sizable Muslim population, which, for understandable reasons, vehemently opposes such a development. Such conflicts are almost always exacerbated by yawning disparities in wealth between contending groups, which, more often than not, fall out along racial, ethnic, or religious lines. While no society is immune from such tensions, the problem is far worse in developing countries, where the inequities that often accompany early capital accumulation are most pronounced.

Nationalism remains an extremely powerful force. Once thought to have reached its apogee during the nineteenth and the first part of the twentieth centuries, nationalism has gotten its second wind over the course of the last decade, and its force seems far from spent. Although more potent elsewhere (see below), appeals to begin or to finish the task of national construction continue to move people throughout the developing world. At the same time, popular support for the establishment of politically sovereign subnational units, organized by reference to racial and ethnic criteria, is also on the rise. What happens when these two trends collide is unclear, but both cannot be accommodated in the same place at the same time.

In the periphery, conflicts over raw materials seem destined to remain as much a fixture of the new era as they were during the cold war, given the resource needs of most developing countries and the temptation to seize such commodities by force or through invasion, rather than to purchase them with precious hard currency earnings. Wars of conquest or for territorial aggrandizement may well increase in frequency as well, as outside powers, once inclined to intervene to prop up friends and unseat enemies, shy away from such entanglements in all but the most extreme and threatening of circumstances. Conflicts that arise within countries between rival groups not distinguishable by racial, ethnic, religious, or class differences—straightforward struggles for power, in other words—also seem destined to persist in the absence of a fundamental transformation of the human psyche.

The one piece of good news is that Third World conflicts rooted in or made more intense by East-West ideological differences have disappeared and are unlikely to stage a comeback anytime soon. Sadly, however, it is also the case that both nationalism and religion can generate belief systems every bit as messianic—and therefore every bit as destructive—as the ostensibly secular ideologies of Marxism and Western-style liberalism. The politicization of

Islam, which poses a growing threat to a number of governments from Algeria and Egypt to the Philippines, is perhaps the most alarming development in this context, although other examples abound (the radicalization of the Hindus in India comes to mind, as does the quiet campaign of the Orthodox church to reclaim at least some of its former political clout in post-Communist Russia).

It is at *the juncture of the center and periphery,* in southern and eastern Europe and, farther to the east, along Russia's southern reaches, that most of the elements responsible for the violence in the developed and developing worlds come together in a highly unstable mix. This environment is made all the more explosive by the sudden and in many areas virtually complete collapse of state authority that followed in the wake of communism's overthrow and the disintegration of the Soviet Union. An already tragic situation was made many times worse, of course, by the sharp intensification of long-simmering ethnically and religiously based conflicts, many of which spilled over into violence. The most ferocious of these conflicts, the war between and among the Serbs, the Croats, and the Bosnians, has resulted so far in tens of thousands of casualties and the displacement of millions more.

As the fighting escalated, so too did the debate over its causes. Many, particularly in the media, insisted that the violence was a predictable consequence of the break-up of Yugoslavia and the Soviet Union, both multinational states whose leaders had succeeded in maintaining an outward appearance of interracial and interethnic harmony by rewarding some populations while punishing others. As these state structures collapsed, long suppressed ethnic and religious grievances once again came to the fore, and large-scale violence ensued. Others, including many on the scene, fixed the blame on local political elites, who, desperate for a way to maintain their privileged positions in society after the revolutions of 1989–90, cynically manipulated popular fears and resentments based on ethnic and religious differences. Having manufactured the crisis in the first place, they were then able to portray themselves as patriots and saviors, uniquely capable of safeguarding the national honor. Doubtless, both interpretations have merit. The larger point, in any event, is that the scale and savagery of the fighting is without modern precedent in Europe, and that, as of early 1994, all outside diplomatic efforts to bring it to an end have met with failure.

The scale of the human suffering, especially in the Balkans, coupled with the intense media coverage of events, has obscured the unpleasant fact that when countries disintegrate they do so, more often than not, with great violence and considerable loss of life. The process of state deformation, which must precede national renewal and reformation, is typically a bloody affair that can go on for decades. Most developed countries have been spared this experience to date not because they are exempt from it, but because they have demonstrated a superior capacity to coopt by economic and political means those within their borders who might otherwise feel sufficiently aggrieved to take up arms against the state. With precious few assets to redistribute, political leaders in the former Communist countries of Eastern Europe and Eurasia that are currently experiencing high levels of turmoil have essentially nothing to offer their constituents. Civil war has been the result. Absent an extremely large-scale effort to improve the material conditions of the people living in these countries, organized and paid for by the more affluent societies of the West, or outright military occupation—neither of which seems even remotely possible—these conflicts are almost certain to persist until one side or the other prevails, or until the combatants simply exhaust one another.

Regional Conflicts and U.S. Interests

U.S. policy makers must navigate their way through this thicket of issues to determine *which* conflicts in *which* parts of the world constitute genuine threats to the national interest. They must do so with imperfect information and in the context of a political culture that has grown weary of foreign involvements and resents the time its leaders devote to international affairs. To make matters worse, the disintegration of the Soviet Union and the collapse of the Communist challenge have deprived the current generation of U.S. decision makers of the heuristic device to assess the costs and benefits of action upon which their predecessors could and did rely: what are the implications for the relative international positions of the two superpowers if the United States decides to respond militarily to this crisis or conflict? What if Washington chooses not to?

To take an extreme (and contentious) example, every U.S. president from Dwight Eisenhower to Gerald Ford was compelled to ask what would be the consequences were the United States not to stand by its South Vietnamese ally. Would a victory by North Vietnam also signal a victory for the USSR and China? (From the late 1950s to the early 1970s, the answer was yes.) The ability to frame the problem by reference to such an accessible formula enabled political leaders in the United States to simplify the decision-making process; it also ensured that once the decision had been taken, the electorate would be able to follow the logic by which the leadership had arrived at its preferred outcome. The reverse is also true, of course. The lack of such an orienting device complicates decision making and confuses the electorate.

This is roughly the situation that currently confronts U.S. policy makers. If not anti-Sovietism and anti-communism, what is to inform the process by which decisions to intervene or not to intervene must be made? Alas, there is no easy answer to this question, no magic formula to which U.S. leaders can turn for guidance. A reasonable place to start, however, is by posing the one question that should precede any consideration of the possible use of force in defense of U.S. interests: what is it that the United States is proposing to defend? At an even more basic level of analysis, the key question comes in two parts: what is it that we want; and what is it that we would prefer to avoid?

Defining U.S. Interests
in the Post−Cold War Era

Giving positive expression to bedrock U.S. interests in the post−cold war era is a comparatively straightforward task. Whether the strategy be one of "engagement" or of "enlargement," the goals are few in number and easy enough to articulate. Topping the list of U.S. preferences is that the international community be dominated by countries that are more, rather than less, democratic in their political orientation. The goal of policy, therefore, should be to support democratic regimes where they exist, and to proffer assistance of various kinds to those struggling to establish such systems of government. Placing support for democracy at the center of the U.S. policy agenda is based on the conviction that countries with genuinely representative and broadly pluralistic political systems seldom go to war with one another, and are therefore less likely to pose a threat to the United States and to U.S. friends and allies (particularly when the latter are also democratic) than are more authoritarian regimes. This is more an article of faith than it is a law of nature, however, and in this instance the past may be a less than reliable guide to the future.

U.S. interests are also served by the maintenance of an open trading system and a liberal economic order—one in which goods and services produced in one country are free to move across national boundaries with as few constraints and penalties as possible. Ensuring access to foreign markets has been a hallmark of U.S. foreign economic policy since World War II and remains so today, as evidenced by the Clinton administration's extraordinary efforts in 1993 to secure passage of the North American Free Trade Agreement, and to bring to a successful conclusion the most recent round of negotiations in the General Agreement on Tariffs and Trade (GATT). Few goals have been pursued as consistently and aggressively by successive U.S. administrations as reducing barriers to trade, and given the importance of the export economy in the United States, this is not likely to change anytime soon.

This commitment to democracy and, even more, to a liberal trading system predisposes U.S. policy makers to place a very high premium on political stability, both globally and within a number of key regions. Few things are as disruptive to normal commerce as wars, especially when they take place in areas of the world that are economically advanced (and therefore more dependent on exports and imports than most developing regions), rich in resources, or that lie along important trading routes. The relationship between organized violence and democracy is more complex, but there is nothing to suggest, liberation theology notwithstanding, that wars—be they civil or international in character—are a necessary part of the democratization process. Most revolutions that have resulted in more open and representative political systems have been, in fact, relatively bloodless affairs. To the degree that U.S. policy makers welcome political change, their clear preference has always been that it unfold slowly and with as little violence as possible. So it remains today. This is hardly surprising in light of the role played by the United States in the construction of the existing economic and political order and Washington's continuing high stake in its maintenance and preservation.

Recognizing What Is Not in the U.S. Interest

If promoting democracy, encouraging free trade, and safeguarding general systemic stability are positive expressions of U.S. foreign and economic policy interests, what are the kinds of global developments that decision makers in the United States will want to avoid, or, more actively, to prevent?

The most basic of objectives is to deter direct attack against the United States and its closest allies by any would-be aggressor. The United States maintains a full spectrum of military capabilities, up to and including nuclear weapons, for precisely this reason, of course, although such forces also serve other purposes, from strategic reassurance to friendly governments and diplomatic suasion to power projection. The Soviet Union's collapse in 1991 makes the probability of any direct attack against the United States more remote than at any time since the Kremlin's first successful test of a long-range ballistic missile in 1957. It does not eliminate the threat entirely, however. Russia's political future remains highly unpredictable in 1994, and it is not inconceivable that a successor to President Boris Yeltsin, the ultranationalist Vladimir Zhirinovsky, for example, could chart a course in foreign policy that would set Moscow and Washington on a collision course for the second time this century. Three other countries—China, France, and Great Britain—also have nuclear weapons systems of sufficient range to menace the United States directly, although none is currently deemed to constitute a near-term threat to U.S. national security.

If the potential number of global rivals to the United States ranges between zero and one in 1994, the same cannot be said for the population of regional actors with the power to menace U.S. interests and those of its allies. As the war against Iraq demonstrated, even comparatively small states that have advanced to, at most, the midpoint in the developmental process can pose a deadly threat to their neighbors, some of which may have important political and/or economic ties to the United States. Taking large-scale military action in response to all instances of regional aggression would be foolhardy, even if the United States had the will and the resources to do so, which it does not. But there may well be occasions, as in the Gulf in 1990–91, when the costs of doing nothing to reverse the ill-gotten gains of regional aggressors outweigh the anticipated costs of going to war. The challenge that confronts U.S. policy makers is knowing when such decisive action is called for, and when it is not. An essential step in the process must be the development of a template, or a set of standards, by reference to which such decisions can be taken.

Regional actors with hegemonic pretensions are perhaps the most likely candidates to disturb the peace and threaten U.S. interests, but there are others. The most serious of these is the kind of localized political instability that initially centers on one state, but that soon comes to attract the attention of other, neighboring countries. More out of fear than ambition, one or more of these states may decide to intervene, either to impose a settlement or to prevent the spread of the contagion. Suspicions (and jealousies) are aroused throughout the region, and what begins as a local problem comes to engulf a number of countries. The invasion of Cambodia by Vietnam in 1978 may be a case in point.

The results can be calamitous for all concerned. To the extent that U.S. friends and allies are drawn into such conflicts, directly or indirectly, they also become a problem for the United States, which may feel the need to shore up its commitments by dispatching additional aid, including military equipment and, on rare occasions, military personnel. The increase in the level of U.S. support to Thailand in the wake of Vietnam's invasion of Cambodia is one such example. The lesson is not that all instances of regional instability will require that Washington take action; rather, it is that certain kinds of crises, which may not be attributable to the aggressive actions of a single state, may still endanger U.S. interests and call for a response.

Three points, implicit throughout this part of the analysis, should be made explicit. All relate to the potential use of force in defense of U.S. foreign and economic policy interests. The first, and most elemental, is that U.S. and allied power is limited— severely so. According to the International Institute for Strategic Studies between 1990 and 1994, the U.S. defense budget declined by 24 percent, adjusted for inflation.[4] The cumulative reduction between fiscal year 1990 and 1997 is expected to top 40 percent. At 4.5 percent of gross domestic product, the United States spent less in 1994 on defense and defense related tasks than at any time since the conclusion of World War II. Most U.S. allies are curtailing their defense spending at about the same rate. Particularly now, in other words, the demand by others for Western military, material, and financial resources is certain to exceed the supply; competing interests must be weighed, and choices will have to be made.

The second point is an obvious one, or so it would seem: not all wars, conflicts, and crises are equally menacing to the United States. The conflict between Libya and Chad in the mid-1980s was of little direct consequence to the United States. The war between Iran and Iraq, however, was of much greater significance, given U.S. dependence on imported oil and Washington's understandable concern with the regional balance of power. Clearly, part of the U.S. reluctance to take a more active military role in the war in Bosnia-Hercegovina has had to do with the issue of interests: how are U.S. interests materially affected if the Serbs and Croats succeed in their efforts to dismember the Muslim republic? Unless the fighting spreads to other areas beyond the borders of the former Yugoslavia, the answer, at least to this point in time, has been, not very substantially, this despite the fact that no one in the public domain in the United States denies that the war in Bosnia has been and continues to be a human tragedy of significant proportions. No less than in the past, in years to come U.S. policy makers will be forced to shoulder the thankless task of distinguishing between conflicts that are *dangerous* and those that are merely *tragic*.

The third point is derivative of the second. Not all conflicts can be resolved militarily when the coercive instruments that are likely to be employed are circumscribed because of the limited nature of the political objectives. For example, the conflict in Bosnia-Hercegovina in 1992–93 could have been suppressed, at least temporarily, through large-scale military intervention on the part of one or more of the great powers. As a practical political matter, however, policy makers in the United States never seriously contemplated such action, either alone or in concert with their European allies. Military considerations aside, at no point during this crisis did there emerge a durable political consensus in the West favoring substantial intervention. A more limited use of force—air strikes, for example, or the garrisoning of cities—might have generated some degree of domestic support on both sides of the Atlantic, at least initially, but militarily, the value of such operations would have been modest and, almost certainly, not consequential enough to have affected the material fortunes of any of the parties to that bloody conflict. The dilemma for U.S. policy makers willing to use force in defense of American interests, or those of the West more broadly, is apparent.

The Limits of Intervention

When and how U.S. political, economic, and military resources should be brought to bear in the interests of resolving future regional crises and conflicts is treated at length elsewhere in this volume. In concluding the present effort, it is enough, perhaps, to frame the discussion about intervention that will follow by reference to three of the arguments that constitute the analytical core of this chapter.

In considering the conditions under which the armed forces of the United States might be placed in harm's way, U.S. policy makers would do well to remind themselves of the following.

• *Most of the root causes of instability that existed during the cold war are also present in today's world, and several new sources of conflict have been added.* Foremost among these is the political, economic, and social turmoil that has attended the collapse of state structures in East Central Europe and Eurasia; the dramatic increase in racially, ethnically, and religiously motivated violence in many parts of the world, including areas once thought immune to such appeals; and the widening gap in wealth between the relatively affluent countries of the North and the extremely poor societies of the South, especially those of sub-Saharan Africa and South Asia.

• *The end of the ideological competition between the United States and the Soviet Union has left U.S. political leaders without a simple, reliable compass by which to assess who among the universe of possible claimants merits American support, including military assistance, and who does not.* Although the easy availability of such a standard led U.S. policy makers to commit a number of costly blunders during the cold war, it also provided a degree of predictability to U.S. policy, narrowed the range of options to a manageable number, and enabled the American electorate to understand the logic of particular foreign and security policy decisions.

• *In seeking to develop a new template to guide U.S. action in the post−cold war era, those responsible for the formation and conduct of policy should recognize that the most appropriate threshold for U.S. involvement in conflict situations is the degree to which U.S. action, or inaction, will impact this country's political, economic, and military interests, narrowly defined.* To peg policy to any other standard—to the level or intensity of violence, for example—would be to deprive the political leadership of essential flexibility; in addition, such a policy could not be sustained, either economically or politically.

What these propositions suggest is that only across a very narrow band of contingencies should the president of the United States be willing to commit U.S. forces to action. Leaving to one side circumstances in which the danger to U.S. personnel is minimal, such as certain kinds of United Nations sponsored peacekeeping operations, these contingencies would appear to include only those situations in which: a failure to act would place critically important U.S. and allied interests at risk; an aggressive actor has violated internationally recognized borders and is threatening to dismember or absorb a neighboring state that has important political, economic, or military ties to the United States; to allow the aggression to stand would result, from the U.S. perspective, in an unacceptable shift in the regional balance of power; and the local balance of military forces is, or can be made, favorable to the United States and those of its allies that might be engaged in the fighting.

These are, admittedly, extremely demanding conditions that, if respected by U.S. policy makers, could expose them to charges of insensitivity, timidity, and even moral cowardice. Some U.S. allies would object strongly, detecting in the new American profile a thinly disguised blueprint for strategic disengagement; enemies of the United States might well rejoice. Finally, there may be times when the case in support of military intervention—for example, to right an egregious moral wrong—will prove so compelling to the people of the United States and their elected representatives that the costs of such action will become a secondary consideration.

A deliberately cautious policy regarding intervention is not without risk, in other words. It is, however, incumbent upon those who would set out a less restrictive set of guidelines to inform U.S. policy in this area to be prepared to answer two questions. If not the national interest, narrowly defined, what *is* the appropriate threshold for U.S. action, particularly in those circumstances requiring the use of American military forces? And who—or what— is to bear the costs of a more ambitious agenda in the areas of peacekeeping, peacemaking, and peace-building?

Notes

[1] Mueller (1989).
[2] Gaddis (1986).
[3] Krauthammer (1991).
[4] International Institute for Strategic Studies (1993).

2

Challenge and Response: Coercive Intervention Issues

WILLIAM H. LEWIS

Intervention: Challenge and Response

The earthquake that shook the world in 1989 has continued to send seismic shock waves throughout the international community. The demise of communism and the attendant collapse of the Soviet empire have carried in their wake a weakening of international security structures and political-military coalitions. For the United States, in particular, troubling challenges to its national interests have emerged, necessitating fresh assessment of its purposes and goals during the remainder of this decade and well into the twenty-first century. Expectations that the post–cold war world would be characterized by relatively harmonious readjustments and realignments have not been realized. At present, there is vast uncertainty about the volatile forces that have been unleashed in the world at large and the capacity of the "sole" remaining superpower to play a leading role in coping with them.

WILLIAM H. LEWIS is professor of political science and international relations at the Elliott School of International Affairs of George Washington University. He has served as a specialist in political-military and

To comprehend the magnitude of the changes that have occurred on the world stage, we need only look back to when George Bush was elected U.S. president. There still remained a Soviet Union and a Warsaw Treaty Organization capable of wreaking vast havoc on international society, the Communist party and its Moscow headquarters were still the Mecca for lesser ideological groups bound to Marxist-Leninist doctrine, South Africa remained firmly under the control of a white supremacist regime, and Arab-Israeli differences remained despite the 1979 signing of the Camp David Peace Accords bringing an end to armed conflict between Jerusalem and Cairo. We even had established governments, however unrepresentative, in Somalia, Liberia, and Haiti.

In the aftermath of the cold war, the Bush administration and now its successor were expected by friends and allies to provide a road map on how the United States proposes to manage the peace. This would be a daunting task under any circumstance, but the issues and conflicts that abound in the world at large assure that the assignment verges on "mission impossible." In 1994 armed conflicts—some new, some old—continued in Peru, Angola, Burundi, Somalia, Liberia, Western Sahara, Sudan, Uganda, Afghanistan, India, Indonesia, the Philippines, Cambodia, Sri Lanka, Iran, Iraq, Turkey, Northern Ireland, the former Yugoslavia, and the former Soviet republics of Moldova, Azerbaijan, Armenia, Georgia, and Tajikistan. "Ethnic cleansing," or fighting intended to eliminate ethnic communities, was the catalyst for conflicts in Bosnia, Rwanda, Burundi, Sudan, Kenya, and Myanmar (formerly Burma). Hindu-Muslim riots in India, Islamic militant warfare in Algeria, and comparable problems in Egypt threatened the collapse of government authority in these countries. A vast array of peoples is embarked on rewriting boundaries or constitutions, reconstituting political orders, or seceding from existing political and state "systems."

Middle Eastern affairs at the U.S. Department of State and on the policy planning staff of the Department of Defense. He is the author of numerous books and articles on U.S. foreign and national security policy, Middle East and African affairs, and arms transfers.

The disappearance of a unifying, universally understood threat, in part the result of the collapse of the Soviet empire, means that the U.S. policy-making community is required to redefine the nation's security. Gone for the foreseeable future is the requirement for the United States to lead Western democracies in a global effort to protect the Eurasian land mass from Communist domination. In the United States, most Americans are now turning their attention to domestic issues—what strategies to adopt in coping with burgeoning crime? How to provide fresh opportunities for economic advancement for the youth of decaying inner cities? How to accommodate health and medical needs at costs sustainable within limited budgets? What priorities for the nation in education, technology, welfare, and protection of the environment? In the minds of many concerned with public policy, international security should be downgraded in importance to permit addressal of problems at home that impinge on national well-being and cohesion. For them, the Clinton administration's announced international policy—"enlargement of democracy" through development of free markets and support for democratic processes—contains within it the seeds of new, limitless intervention in the affairs of countries with little history or experience of power sharing and representative government. For these people, the United States appears to be tilting in the direction of new burdens, a feckless effort, when the national need is to impose severe limits on our security and political commitments abroad.

At the opposite end of the American spectrum are a substantial number of citizens and foreign policy specialists who feel uneasy that opportunities for U.S. leadership in the international community are fast slipping away. The president's concentration of time and attention on domestic issues and his apparent lack of interest in such complex foreign policy questions as peacekeeping in Africa, spreading violence in the Balkans, and continuing tensions between India and Pakistan suggest that, with the exception of significant issues of commerce and trade—which could impact the domestic fortunes of the United States—the president is inclined to disengage from an international leadership role. For these critics, the rhetoric of enlargement of democracy and support for human rights is a smokescreen behind which a policy of disengagement and neoisolationism is being implemented. In brief, they believe that President Clinton is abdicating the U.S. role as a stabilizing force in the post–cold war world.

Misleading Doctrinal Divisions

Today, we are witness to rising debate in the United States about the relative advantages and disadvantages of various national security strategies to be adopted in the post–cold war world. Changes in the international distribution of power might be expected to shape the terms of the debate. However, the proclivity of most U.S. policy makers is to seek to preserve continuities inherited from the bipolar period. Rather than run the risk of alienating entrenched domestic constituencies that have invested time and treasure in existing policies, policy makers are inclined to be cautious in redirecting policy approaches, preferring instead to fabricate new rationales for existing programs and activities. Thus the Agency for International Development has undergone reorganization and fashioned new supporting rhetoric, but traditional claimants for economic aid such as Israel, Egypt, and Turkey continue to be allocated substantial financing, leaving niggardly sums for dozens of other claimants. Similarly, U.S. Information Agency programs continue to emphasize time-encrusted strategies and themes. Within the Department of Defense its security assistance agency stresses sales of advanced military equipment and technologies to Third World countries, much as in the previous decade, seemingly without great concern for the competitive rivalries such sales generate.

In the foreign policy realm, such continuities in arms sales approach might well fuel competition with West European capitalist democracies. Some academics contend that, with communism discredited, the economic dimension has assumed heightened importance for great power status. The export of military and dual-use technologies assumes significance from an international trade perspective, as well as in terms of the domestic economic health of each contender for great power status. As a result, competitive rivalries with the United States are in prospect, with some West European governments (and Russia) vying to acquire increased market shares in sales to Iran and other Persian Gulf purchasers seeking advanced weaponry. Clinton administration calls for restraint are likely to fall on deaf ears, given the fact that the United States is today the leading marketer of such weaponry.

The fault lines of disengagement concerning the proper U.S. roles in the decade immediately ahead extend to other areas as well. The question of international collective security is perhaps the most bedeviling. Some scholars and foreign affairs specialists urge a leading U.S. role in bolstering United Nations crisis prevention and conflict resolution capabilities. The initiatives they recommend include organization of a U.N. directed standing force of 5,000 to 10,000 volunteers, to be deployed to potential crisis zones at the behest of the Security Council and the secretary-general to "choke off" the crises and to permit mediatory measures to be launched. Similarly, they propose a change in the U.N. Charter to permit humanitarian interventions when sociopolitical upheavals or human rights abuses by tyrannical regimes are fostering large-scale population displacements. They also urge other significant initiatives:

- Resource transfers to the U.N. headquarters to buttress early warning and crisis management capabilities. The resources must include augmented U.S. financial contributions over a fixed period—e.g., five years—to support expanded peacekeeping operations.
- Regeneration of the moribund Military Staff Committee (Article 43 of the Charter) to provide military guidance to the secretary-general.
- Stockpiling of U.S. military equipment for peace operations and dedication of airlift resources under funding arrangements compatible with U.N. financial capabilities.

With respect to other U.S. collective security roles at the global level, members of the so-called internationalist school urge more forceful intervention to enhance the existing Non-Proliferation Treaty (NPT). *Inter alia,* they recommend bolstering the safeguard regime to deal with NPT signatories that import or produce fissile material by strengthening inspections or controls. Violations, they believe, should trigger automatic sanctions. In addition, the International Atomic Energy Agency (IAEA), the international inspection agency, should be adequately funded. The agency, despite expanded responsibilities, has been compelled to function with a zero based budget over the past decade.

A contrary view is presented by a community of specialists that views the U.N. and its ancillary organizations as inherently flawed institutions. They believe that the Security Council, with its "permanent five" veto arrangement, could ultimately paralyze decision making once the national interests of the "five" collide. Recent Soviet actions in Bosnia and Chinese reservations regarding threatened sanctions against a refractory North Korea unwilling to adhere to the NPT are held to portend Security Council dysfunction. Of comparable weight, the U.N. failure to resolve conflicts in Somalia, Haiti, and elsewhere is held to reflect the inherent dangers of U.N. overreach. Finally, critics of a collective security system under U.N. auspices point to the frailties and divisions of the U.N. bureaucracy that defy effective remedial action. To subordinate U.S. national security interests to a poorly guided international conglomeration such as the U.N. is decried as foreign policy myopia.

An alternative organization that might serve as a stabilizing force is the North Atlantic Treaty Organization (NATO). However scholars of a unilateralist or neoisolationist persuasion contend that with the implosion of the Soviet empire NATO's raison d'être has vanished and that European defense issues should become the primary preoccupation of the Europeans. Indeed, the United States should encourage the formation of a European security pillar, one revolving around the Western European Union and the former Common Market. This would permit the withdrawal from Europe of the residual 100,000-plus U.S. military force, and free the Clinton administration to concentrate on strengthening ties with Russia—which continues to dispose of thousands of nuclear warheads. If West European chanceries shoulder the burdens of regional security, the Clinton administration would be free to deal with pressing domestic issues.

The contrary view holds that the United States remains the preeminent stabilizing force in Europe. Despite Secretary of State Warren Christopher's careless 1993 observation that he was more interested in U.S. relations with a vibrant Asia than with a dispirited Europe, the United States must view Western Europe as a valued trading partner and force for stability on the European continent. At last count (late 1993), approximately 40 percent of all U.S. corporate profits earned from abroad derives from that continent, while U.S. firms have an estimated $250 billion—one-half of total foreign investment—concentrated in Europe. It is argued that the United States has a long-term interest in foreign policy engagement with Europe. According to this school of thought, the United States should not become fixated on its relations with a Yeltsin-ruled Russia. The auguries for a democratic Russia are problematic at best. The U.S. strategy instead should be to play a commanding role in NATO—i.e., to enhance NATO as a security organization capable of calming Eastern European fears of Russia. The costs, viewed as quite acceptable, would include an ongoing U.S. military presence and expanded peacekeeping roles in Europe and in the Mediterranean Basin.

The principal policy lines dividing "unilateralists" and "internationalists" regarding U.S. leadership tend to focus on economic desiderata. Many qualified analysts and commentators have a sanguine view of U.S. prospects for economic growth. They argue that the Clinton administration has proved remarkably effective in ordering its economic priorities at home and abroad, pointing to successful passage of the North American Free Trade Agreement (NAFTA) legislation and negotiation of the General Agreement on Tariffs and Trade (GATT) Uruguay Round agreement, both in 1993. The two initiatives underscore U.S. capacities to resolve manifold domestic economic problems while burnishing its role as a forceful leader in the international economic realm. At the opposite end of the spectrum are specialists who contend that the current trade dispute with Japan underscores the need not for international leadership but for unilateralism and forceful competition in matters that can affect adversely the economic health and prosperity of the United States.

Alternative Strategies Considered

Confronted with a wide range of policy issues and challenges, the Clinton administration has directed its energies primarily toward remedial actions to improve the nation's economic performance. At this writing, it is addressing strategies to expand productivity, adapt educational standards to the demands of modern technology, and develop fresh approaches to health care and social welfare problems. On the international level, the Clinton administration has concentrated most of its attention on several issues that it has characterized as primary policy concerns: (1) Russia and its safe passage into a democratic society; (2) Arab-Israeli mutual accommodation under a peace process initiated in October 1991; (3) enlargement of the U.S. trading zone, ultimately to include all of the Western Hemisphere; and (4) comparable efforts, of a less formal character, to include the East Asia and Pacific region. Crosscutting these geographically defined aspirations are several functional goals—notably, enhancing the nuclear Non-Proliferation Treaty and the Missile Technology Control Regime, speeding the dismantling of military nuclear systems in the former Soviet republics, and coping with problems associated with population upheaval, as reflected in the mounting global number of displaced persons and refugees currently estimated at 35–40 million.

Alternative U.S. strategies have been propounded to address these and cognate issues. They are strategies that, throughout modern history, have been available to all major powers: (1) unilateralism; (2) selective coalitions, regionally based, with existing or emerging major powers (e.g., Japan, India, Germany, and so on); (3) a global great power coalition to enforce international peace; and (4) a broad international collective security system under United Nations auspices. Each strategy has its proponents and critics.

The costs and benefits of each strategy vary, particularly in terms of their likely impact on the domestic economy and the desirability of a major U.S. security role abroad. Most Americans are prepared to pay the costs of a downsized military establishment, but they pose two fundamental questions: what national interests are sufficiently important to continue to maintain large numbers of troops in Europe and in Asia? And, under what circumstances should U.S. forces be committed to combat or engage in risky peacekeeping operations? The president has yet to provide a clear response to these questions, but his advisers contend, probably with justification, that he is doing precisely what the overwhelming majority of Americans desire: devoting his energies and political capital to promoting his domestic agenda.

Nevertheless, there is one group of foreign policy specialists—the so-called internationalists—who argue that the president is required to devote equal time and attention to international questions since many will ultimately impinge on the U.S. economy. They urge continued American leadership in the post–cold war world, utilizing a combination of regional coalitions, together with a concert of like-minded states sharing a common global agenda when required. The case for great power intervention is held to be analogous to challenges presented during and immediately following World War I. Failure on the part of a recalcitrant U.S. Congress to approve U.S. membership in the League of Nations relegated that organization to powerlessness when confronting acts of aggression by predatory member states. Even earlier, the decision by the United States and other major players not to intervene in 1917 Russia to suppress the Bolshevik insurrection and to support the democratic Lvov-Kerensky regime also produced unfortunate consequences—notably seven decades of worldwide political and economic conflict. Allied policies of timidity and equivocation in the Balkans and Central Europe are held responsible for power vacuums that, ineluctably, led to World War II. The principal foreign policy requirement confronting the United States today, runs the argument, is to assume a leadership role, in concert with European and Asian major powers, to buttress the existing state system and, thereby, to ensure that order and stability become the hallmarks of the post–cold war world.

At the opposite end of the policy spectrum is a constellation of "unilateralists" who oppose adoption of an "internationalist" strategy, proposing instead selective disengagement from cold war security commitments and concentration of existing resources on amelioration of domestic problems. Neither isolationist nor "free rider" in its approach, this school's brief is based on a return to traditional national interest litmus tests when addressing challenges and fashioning appropriate responses in U.S. foreign policy. According to this view, great peril resides in grounding policies on expectations of major power burden sharing or in effective management of peacekeeping at the behest of the United Nations. Representatives from this school are most vocal in cautioning against messianic policy crusades such as "enlargement of democracy" or protection of "free enterprise systems." Of particular concern to them is President Clinton's assertion that U.S. security requires this country to ensure "a just, enduring and ever more democratic peace in the world."

The more pessimistic within this school contend that pre–World War II history is either irrelevant or, if returning, confronts the United States with choices that can either be deferred or ignored. They underscore the words of French President Charles de Gaulle that we are once again living in a "time of great tempests," a time that reflects the failure of governments to secure the loyalty of national communities. The resulting disorders may burn themselves out or lead to tyrannical regimes. The United States will have to respond selectively since it cannot impose its values and political system on societies lacking the historical and cultural backgrounds essential for democracy building. The consensus emerging within this school is that the unraveling and resulting turmoil in some areas do not threaten U.S. interests, and their irrelevance is a clear indication that the international community has become less than the sum of its parts.

In reality, existing divisions between "internationalists" and "unilateralists" are more apparent than real. Neoisolationism, the *bête noire* of some, represents an abdication of responsibilities that, as already implied, few scholars and pragmatists believe is a realistic course for policy leaders. Many Americans would prefer that the Clinton administration adopt a low profile on most international problems, but recognize that the United States cannot opt out on economic and humanitarian issues. The real divide is the chasm between anticipated crises and U.S. capabilities and national willingness to assume fresh burdens as crises evolve. The seismic changes occurring in the international arena in the wake of the 1989 political earthquakes that hit Europe are manifold and subject to different levels of analysis and interpretation. Within this context, the question frequently arises whether existing alliances and institutions (regional and international), or the United States in concert with others, are in a position to assume widening international promissory obligations. Walter Lippmann, in a much celebrated admonition, pointed to the need to establish a proper balance between national objectives and available resources:

Without the controlling principle that the nation must maintain its objectives and its power in equilibrium, its purpose within its means and its means equal to its purposes, its commitments related to its resources and its resources adequate to its commitments, it is impossible to think at all about foreign affairs.[1]

Decades later, this admonition applies to the United States, its friends and allies, and to existing international and regional organizations.

Contemporary Anomalies

The decline and fall of the Soviet Union has had the ripple effect of unleashing disorders on a global scale that threaten the international system so laboriously fashioned in the aftermath of World War II. Secretary-General Boutros Boutros-Ghali reflected the growing sense of dismay among international leaders when he opined in late 1993 that politically and economically, the international community is now in retreat. President Clinton, in his 1993 address before the twenty-eighth U.N. General Assembly, offered a cautionary admonition: "The United Nations simply cannot become engaged in every one of the world's conflicts. If the American people are to say yes to peacekeeping, the United Nations must know when to say no."

The president was representing the American temper of the time. If anything, in the wake of the Somali debacle of late 1993, public sentiment in the United States swung dramatically against large-scale U.S. military intervention involving peacekeeping operations and nation building. In the existing altered international strategic environment, the majority of Americans perceive few threats abroad that should engage U.S. resources—economic and military. They prefer instead to embrace Lippmann's classic maxim—bringing harmony and balance to national means and ends—which should challenge all notion of "superpowerdom." What American resources remain with the entombment of Communist ideology must be husbanded and offered up parsimoniously if we wish to bolster the existing state system. Where leadership is required, it should occur in defense of clear and present dangers to the national interest, the latter being identified in terms of economic well-being and perpetuation of American institutions and "sacred values."

Pragmatists within the community of U.S. strategic thinkers would support this view, having often declaimed in the past that grand strategy is primarily a question of proceeding from existing resource availabilities to clearly defined national goals. Beyond this, strategy is a matter of getting from where you are to where you want to go. If we are unable to agree on the intended destination of the nation, getting there is likely to become a major problem. A precondition for determining goals and objectives is general agreement on the nature of existing and anticipated challenges to U.S. national interests, and the degree of peril these challenges represent. At the height of the cold war, we confronted a somewhat less complex challenge—a situation of ideological nondifferentiation in the sense that the strategy of containment, with all of its nuances, would be directed against all Eurasian Communist regimes and their surrogates. Rather than defining enemies parsimoniously, the United States enlarged its list of adversaries virtually without restraint.

The challenge today, paradoxically, in the view of some specialists, is to fashion an inverse perspective, that is to identify challenges to the United States at three levels—to the United States directly, to our remaining friends and allies, and to the world community generally. The dynamic interaction among the three is critical if fruitful strategies are to be constructed. These experts argue that the imperative the United States confronts is to avoid entrapment in grandiose missions, i.e., historical determinism of the type that afflicted the authors of a 1949–50 national security memorandum for President Truman who wrote: ". . . in the context of the present polarization of power, a defeat of free institutions anywhere is a defeat everywhere." Such perspectives (which some would call "messianism") produced contradictions and squandered national energies, as well as ultimately eroding confidence in government. The list of U.S. friends and adversaries is in flux. Policy, therefore, should be lodged firmly in long-term strategic objectives.

The starting point to confront the policy challenges outlined above is to determine where the critical interests nexus of the United States and its friends and allies lies. In the case of Western Europe, for example, the U.S. goal throughout much of this century has been to ensure that that region's vast reservoir of human, technological, and economic resources did not fall under the domination of parties or coalitions inimical to basic U.S. interests. As a corollary, the United States has sought through its presence and influence to secure a politically stable Western Europe. Hence, in recent years successive U.S. presidents have supported the creation of common market mechanisms, European institutions for the peaceful resolution of disputes, and organizations capable of serving as pillars for regional security. With the interment of the Soviet Union and the Warsaw Treaty Organization, a number of their erstwhile member states and republics now seek admission to the North Atlantic Treaty Organization and the European Union. Arguments in favor of admission are generally weighted in the United States on the scales of Europe-wide stability. The Clinton administration and the other NATO members have offered an ill-defined "Partnership for Peace" relationship, presumably a halfway house or transition period before full membership is granted. Opponents in the United States contend that Eastern Europe is inherently conflict ridden and not soon likely to become a secure or stable environment. To have NATO embroiled in such a volatile region is to spell that organization's ultimate demise. The area of Eastern Europe does not threaten vital NATO or European Union interests and, therefore, should be treated as a marginal nuisance, nothing more. In addition, to have the United States involved is to squander diminished security resources at a time when the U.S. Department of Defense is struggling to field forces capable of fighting two simultaneous Persian Gulf–sized wars within the Third World. The United States should not be burdened with contingency plans for involvement in self-containable conflicts in Eastern Europe.

Public opinion in the United States harbors comparable reservations concerning the nexus of U.S. interests and needs in the East Asia and Pacific region. While viewing trans-Pacific Asia as an area of rising importance to U.S. economic and commercial growth, most Americans believe that there is a declining need for a substantial U.S. military presence west of Pearl Harbor and Guam. Conflicts arising in East Asia—with the possible exception of the Korean Peninsula—are not likely to prove susceptible to amelioration as a result of the presence of U.S. naval and air units. Moreover, with respect to Japan, public opinion, perhaps erroneously, is shaped by the belief that the United States has assumed a disproportionate share of the financial burden associated with the protection of Japan's "home islands." Considerable savings, in this view, could be realized by redeployment of naval and air units to the United States and their subsequent transfer to reserve status or decommissioning. In brief, the nexus of U.S. interest with friends and allies in both Europe and Asia should shift away from traditional security concerns and toward a congruence of economic interaction.

The Challenge of Strategic Conception

The philosopher Reinhold Niebuhr once observed that it is sometimes necessary to do evil to do good. The doing of evil does not require activist intervention in crisis situations far removed from immediate U.S. national interest. Given the widening number of violent confrontations in the Middle East, Africa, and elsewhere, active intervention everywhere on the part of the United States alone or in collaboration with others would prove counterproductive. Governments offer little instruction to the public at large when they declaim that Bosnia, Somalia, and Haiti have been placed on the "back burner" of foreign policy. Innumerable "back burner" and "front burner" issues will confront the U.S. government in the coming years. Instruction is needed on the litmus tests to be used for critical selection to "front burner" status.

In short, what factors have been weighed to warrant benign neglect or to secure active U.S. involvement? Is policy to be subject to capricious forces and influences outside U.S. capacity to control, such as electronic linkage courtesy of CNN, or has the United States developed a clearly defined strategic endgame? To avoid confusion and contradiction regarding our purposes and ends, a broad foreign policy review with participation by specialists within the foreign policy and academic communities would serve as an excellent point of departure.

Michael Stuermer, director of the Research Institute for International Politics and Security at Ebenhausen, Germany, observed in 1993 that the American spirit of leadership was flagging. In his words:

> In the aftermath of the Cold War, America has grown tired of visions and missions. The "new frontier" no longer fascinates; there is no crusade calling on the country; no "evil empire" mobilizes its powers. At the same time, America feels overburdened by the world economy and its own domestic agenda. It suffers from "imperial overstretch." But this not only intensifies global insecurity, it also deprives Germany of the leading power which was always there for forty years to protect it from the bitter decisions and perils of world politics.[2]

The German scholar's lamentation regarding America's failure to take advantage of its military and economic preponderance was little noticed in official Washington, where the current intention is to return to Wilsonian principles, emphasizing support for emerging democracies and condemnation of governments that engage in gross and consistent violations of human rights. Implicitly, imbedded in this policy posture is support for the inherent right of ethnic minorities and nationalities to self-determination, which appears to go against the grain of internationally mandated respect for the "sovereign rights of independent states." The Clinton administration, recognizing the dangers of broad principle, does insist that borders can only be changed peacefully and by mutual agreement.

The traditional U.S. policy ideal is to serve as the "city on the hill," a narcissistic self-glorification transmuted into a missionary approach to international politics. While shibboleths such as "enlargement" may evoke a positive response within the U.S. body politic, as a guide to policy they are likely to represent posture rather than realism in action. Greeted with cynicism by Europeans, enlargement is viewed as American romanticism even within the chanceries of most Third World nations. Moreover, the strategy of enlargement has not received a warm welcome in the United States. In the decade immediately ahead, geographic realignments will provide critical tests of U.S. policy coherence and patience. Not the least of these realignments will involve emergence of enlarged ethnic units (Greater Serbia–Greater Croatia), regional spheres of influence (e.g., Russian "peacekeeping" in the former Soviet Union republics), and new African states born out of intertribal warfare. Many of these realignments will undoubtedly occur after painful conflict and population displacement. At issue for U.S. policy will be the challenge of accepting such transferrals of boundary and populations as occur through acts of aggression in violation of accepted international norms and human rights standards. These anticipated upheavals will produce special policy pressures for the United States and Western European democracies. The human costs of regime failure and the collapse of economic and social systems as these upheavals occur will carry in their wake immense population transferrals in the form of displaced persons seeking economic and political asylum. The figure is expected to approach 50 million by the end of this century. The absorptive capacity of neighboring countries and the international economic system is approaching overload, and, in the instance of the Western democracies faced with economic recession and rising unemployment, restrictive admission legislation is clearly in prospect.

The Middle East and Active Intervention

One of the fundamental principles of foreign policy, as already noted, is to assume new burdens as parsimoniously as possible. However, given the looming challenges to the cohesion of the international state system, a U.S. retreat from response to the most urgent of these emerging challenges would undoubtedly engender even more far-reaching disorders and instabilities in the international security environment.

The adverse consequences for U.S. interests of an abstemious foreign policy posture are probably best illustrated by the endemic condition of disequilibrium afflicting the Persian Gulf region. The Middle East as a whole, but the Persian Gulf in particular, is a region of persistent enmity between contending local forces. In the Gulf, violent conflict erupted after the withdrawal of British forces in 1971, with Iraq and Iran vying for regional primacy based on expansionist ideologies (messianic Islamic fundamentalism in the case of Iran and secular Baathist socialism in Iraq). The result has been the overthrow of the Pahlavi monarchy in 1978–79 and the Khomeini revolution in Iran, the eight-year Iran-Iraq war (1980–88), and the Gulf War of 1991. We can readily assume that the regional ambitions of Baghdad and Tehran will persist during the remainder of this decade, with a resultant threat to Western access to the region's oil supplies. The continuing threat might be received with studied neglect by the United States were it not for the failure of this country and other Western industrial countries to develop strategies to diminish dependence on the petrochemical resources of that region. All available estimates by energy study groups indicate access to Gulf oil "at reasonable prices" will remain a vital American interest. Given the deeply rooted insecurities and hostilities that abide in the region, the United States will be required to play an interventionist role, balancing off competing forces in a delicate political-military minuet.

The current U.S. strategy of dual containment, involving manifold efforts to deter both Iran and Iraq from acquiring the military and economic means to resurrect their ambitions to become the preponderant power in the Gulf (as well as in the Middle East more broadly), is already in jeopardy. Efforts to establish an effective "weapons of mass destruction" control regime are eroding. The introduction of high- and low-technology armaments, nuclear materials, and missile systems has continued, aided and abetted by Western European exporters, the People's Republic of China, and North Korea. If this trend continues, we are likely to see the first Arab (or Iranian) nuclear weapons placed as warheads on missiles of extended range before the end of this decade. The NPT regime is already under extraordinary stress in the Middle East, South Asia, and East Asia. The safeguards system clearly needs strengthening. At present, there are no effective plans within the U.S. government for countering the ambitions of expansionary states such as Iran and Iraq armed with advanced military technology and weapons of mass destruction. The situation is even more threatening on the Korean Peninsula.

Worldwide arms acquisition has tended to blur the distinction between conventional and unconventional armaments, and has underscored the many infirmities of arms control strategies, particularly the porous nature of existing supply constraint regimes. For the United States, a basic reexamination of these regimes is required, one that addresses the feasibility of global deterrence supported by the United States, Russia, and other declared nuclear weapons governments that covers both weapons of mass destruction and high-technology precision-guided munitions. The precedent for a deterrent approach may exist in U.N. Security Council resolutions that deny Iraq, in the wake of the 1991 Gulf War, "all future right" to acquire weapons of mass destruction or surface-to-surface missiles of extended range.

Intersecting these issues are other opportunities for U.S. policy initiative. Middle Eastern governments, largely ruled by autocratic oligarchies, are beginning to feel the political ground shift under them as populist forces urge redistribution of political power. An ideology of socialist inspiration is giving way to pragmatism. In the aftermath of the Gulf War, Arab states are evincing greater willingness to compromise with Israel. Failure of the Israeli-Arab negotiations would assure a gloomy landscape of widening strife that could threaten the tenure of governments throughout the region. The forces of radicalism, if unleashed, could produce threats of terrorist violence extending to the United States, as the 1993 World Trade Center bombing clearly demonstrated. Taken together with the recent alliance of convenience fashioned by narcotics suppliers and terrorists, the geographic reach of U.S. counterstrategies will require global dimension and involve uninvited intrusion in some areas.

Where the United States is unable to bring together a coalition of major powers dedicated to ensuring orderly change in the international system, it will probably feel compelled to accept unilateral action by others bent upon organizing regional spheres of influence. Russia's attempts to extend its influence in the former Soviet republics is the most troubling policy issue close on the horizon. The Clinton administration has signaled its reservations, but there is little support in the United States for active opposition.

The complex interplay of U.S. interests and divergent forces operating in the international arena will impel the United States, of necessity, toward selective intervention and problem solving. The scale of national priority is becoming apparent—development of additional conflict resolution capabilities on the part of existing regional organizations and strengthening of the NPT, together with consideration of major initiatives to dissuade new membership in the weapons of mass destruction club. Concomitantly, the United States will need to examine when and how to intervene in local conflicts or in situations where governments blatantly abuse the rights of their citizenry. Implicit in such an examination is recognition that when the accepted values and standards of international society are violated, the principle of sovereignty may have to be set aside.

The Way Ahead

The discussion thus far has addressed potential challenges and possible U.S. responses in a community of nation states on the threshold of dysfunctional change. Other major actors confront similar challenges and, in some instances, even more painful policy alternatives. Not to be ignored are so-called secondary actors, notably regional and global organizations such as the United Nations, NATO, and the International Monetary Fund.

The Clinton administration offers clear indication of ambivalence bordering on uncertainty where support for secondary institutions is concerned. This is a far cry from the positive declaratory posture candidate Clinton assumed in 1992 when he called for a U.N. "rapid deployment force . . . standing guard at the borders of countries threatened by aggression, preventing mass violence against civilian populations, and providing relief and combatting terrorism." Perhaps bewitched by such rhetoric, our permanent representative to the United Nations, Ambassador Madeleine Albright, declared support for expanded U.N. peacekeeping functions—U.S. policy was encapsulated in the phrase "assertive multilateralism." (This also became a metaphor for NATO involvement in the Bosnian civil war, as well as for efforts to restore democracy to Haiti.) Reality arrived on October 3–4, 1993, when U.S. forces suffered eighteen killed in Mogadishu, Somalia, against a warlord who purportedly had received advanced military instruction at the National Defense University in Washington, D.C.

The Clinton administration, excoriated by congressional and other critics for its Somalia policy, has since announced general retreat from "assertive multilateralism" in Somalia. Secretary of State Warren Christopher observed on the eve of the U.N. General Assembly late in 1993 that multilateral action is warranted "only when it serves the central purposes of U.S. foreign policy— to protect American interests." Secretary Christopher failed to identify with precision those interests the United States might be inclined to "protect." Subsequently, the Clinton administration has made clear that it intends to be parsimonious in agreeing to future Somali-like ventures under U.N. auspices.

The Clinton administration has found congressional support for a peacekeeping policy that is carefully constrained. The dispatch of U.S. combat forces will be restricted to situations where mandates are clearly specified by the Security Council, when the parties in conflict are prepared to "welcome" U.N. forces, the endgame is clear and the time frame carefully delineated, and where there is broad congressional and public support for military involvement.

President Clinton's reticence on the U.N. is shared by increasing numbers of Americans. A *Times Mirror* Center poll conducted between July and October 1993 reported that only 64 percent of those interviewed thought the United States should cooperate *fully* with the U.N., down from 77 percent shortly after the successful conclusion of the Gulf War. Perhaps most significant, the public overwhelmingly opposed placing American troops under "permanent U.N. command," whereas those identified in the poll as the foreign policy "elite"—foreign and defense policy specialists— were willing to put U.S. troops in a "permanent force" under U.N. command. In the same poll, and after the October 3, 1993, American military debacle in Somalia, the public continued to support the dispatch of U.S. troops to Third World countries to prevent mass starvation. On the other hand, most opposed sending troops to "police foreign nations" where government authority has collapsed.[3]

On other foreign policy issues, the arrows of public opinion pointed in several directions. Fewer than one-half of those polled felt that the United States should promote democracy if the outcome was likely to be a totalitarian, anti–U.S. regime. Fewer than one in three would "promote human rights abroad if such support risked antagonizing friendly nations with different traditions." The obvious thrust of public opinion was to have the Clinton administration withdraw from a world leadership role and to concentrate on significant domestic problems. Neoisolationism, whatever the euphemism of the day, was ascendant, absent a persuasive brief from the president on the need for U.S. leadership in the coming years.

Notes

[1] Lippmann (1943), p. 7.
[2] Stuermer (1993), p. 4.
[3] Toth (1994), pp. 31–35.

3

Adapting Conventional Military Forces to the New Environment

JOHN O.B. SEWALL

The purpose of this chapter is to suggest how U.S. armed forces should adapt to the new environment described in chapter 1. This chapter will examine what new or revitalized roles might be appropriate for peaceful intervention on the one hand, and how coercive intervention might be accomplished more effectively on the other. The focus will be on policy options to ensure that our means—the armed forces—remain suitable instruments for the achievement of our ends—U.S. foreign policy objectives.

JOHN O.B. SEWALL, major general, U.S. Army (retired) is a senior fellow at the Institute for National Strategic Studies, following a thirty-three year career in the U.S. Army. He is a graduate of the U.S. Military Academy at West Point and was a Rhodes Scholar at Oxford University. His military career involved troop command and staff with the 82nd Airborne Division, the 9th Infantry Division in the Republic of Vietnam, and the 3rd Infantry Division (Mechanized) in Germany. Major General Sewall served in the Office of the Secretary of Defense, the Army Staff, SHAPE, and the Joint Staff in the Pentagon. As vice director J-5, his final assignment, he participated in the planning for combat operations in

Implications of the New Environment for Peaceful Intervention

The strategic environment postulated for the remainder of this century and stretching into the next suggests a potential explosion in *intra*state and a diminution in *inter*state conflicts, generated in the main by the unloosing of ethnic, religious, and political differences and instabilities hitherto held in check by the deep freeze of the cold war. The Clinton administration is formulating criteria for U.S. response to recurring instances of civil conflict and humanitarian catastrophe. In the future, not only will the questions of when and how to intervene be weighed against the issue of relevant U.S. national interests, but in the broader context, the legitimacy of intervention will be challenged by the sanctity of national sovereignty or nonintervention in the internal affairs of another state, a concept enshrined in the United Nations Charter.

However this broader policy debate eventually is resolved, several implications for the military are already clear. Future conflicts will, in the main, be more ambiguous in terms of U.S. interests involved, who the "enemy" is, the military objectives associated with political goals, and what constitutes "victory" or success. Desert Storm, in effect, may be a historical anomaly, not the paradigm for the future.

Against a trend of failed or failing states, and the apparent unraveling of a multiethnic state system into monoethnic ministates born under the banner of self-determination, United Nations Secretary-General Boutros Boutros-Ghali has argued for a more muscular United Nations role in resolving conflicts and achieving and maintaining international peace and security. In his *An Agenda for Peace*, published in 1992, Boutros-Ghali suggests an active U.N. multilateral approach to security encompassing a broad spectrum

---

Panama (Just Cause) and in the liberation of Kuwait (Desert Shield/Desert Storm), as well as leading the U.S. delegation to the Joint Military Commission under the U.S.–Soviet Agreement on the Prevention of Dangerous Military Activities.

of peace operations, most of which can be described as peaceful intervention.[1] This spectrum encompasses the following:

- *Preventive deployments:* an instrument of preventive diplomacy aimed at deterring a potential conflict, an example being the U.N. deployment to the former Yugoslav republic of Macedonia.
- *Peacemaking:* diplomatic initiatives of mediation and arbitration to achieve a cease-fire, utilizing the measures enumerated in Chapter VI of the United Nations Charter. The Vance plan and Vance-Owen/Owen-Stoltenberg initiatives in Croatia and Bosnia-Hercegovina respectively are good examples.
- *Peacekeeping:* impartial monitors or observers, deployed with the consent of the parties to the conflict, to assist in maintaining an agreed cease-fire. U.N. observers in the Middle East and peacekeeping forces in Cyprus and on the Golan Heights are good examples.
- *Peace enforcement:* military forces used to restore and maintain a cease-fire, so that the terms of an agreement may be accomplished. Such enforcement measures are authorized under Chapter VII of the United Nations Charter. United Nations Operations in Somalia (UNOSOM) forces and the enforcement of "no fly zones" in Iraq and Bosnia are examples of peace enforcement, as defined by Secretary-General Boutros-Ghali. Boutros-Ghali makes a distinction between this concept of peace enforcement and a U.N. directed Chapter VII response to interstate aggression, where the conditions would include forces being provided under Chapter VII, Article 43 of the Charter and strategic direction being exercised by the Military Staff Committee under Chapter VII, Article 47. These latter conditions have never been met in practice.
- *Peace-building:* the rebuilding of infrastructure and restoration of institutions to create conditions conducive to peace, best exemplified in Cambodia and Somalia.

Again, it is not clear how fervently the United States will embrace peaceful intervention, peacekeeping, and the United Nations as a multilateral instrument to meet U.S. security needs. The Clinton administration's initial enthusiasm for the U.N. as a vehicle for exercising "assertive multilateralism" subsided somewhat as a result of the unhappy events in Somalia in October 1993. Nonetheless, peacekeeping has been adopted by the North Atlantic Treaty Organization (NATO) as a new mission, with promises of NATO forces and resources being made available both to the Conference on Security and Cooperation in Europe (CSCE) and the U.N. More recently, at the January 1994 NATO Summit, NATO launched the Partnership for Peace (PFP) initiative, designed to include former Warsaw Pact adversaries and other non-NATO European states in a number of cooperative military activities, including peacekeeping. In part to provide an organizational underpinning for this PFP initiative, the Combined Joint Task Force (CJTF) concept was also announced, thus facilitating the incorporation of non-NATO partners and NATO forces not part of NATO's integrated military command (France) into peace operations using NATO forces and resources. In addition the CJTF concept provides substance to the idea of a European security and defense identity by providing a command and control mechanism for European forces in those instances where the United States chooses not to become involved.

To conclude on this point, both Boutros-Ghali's *An Agenda for Peace* and the January 1994 NATO Summit envisage a key role for multilateral peace operations in the resolution of post–cold war conflicts. U.S. participation in peace operations can span the gamut from: a vote cast in the Security Council and payment of peacekeeping assessments; to providing certain functional support, whether equipment, strategic lift, communications, or logistics; individual U.N. observers, as we have done in the past for the United Nations Truce Supervision Organization and other U.N. missions; specific combat and support units, as we have done in Somalia; and finally, to assuming command and control of an entire U.N. authorized operation, as we did in Korea and the liberation of Kuwait. Whatever the extent of U.S. participation, limited or major, there will be new roles and revitalized old roles for our armed forces. The implications for U.S. military doctrine, organization, training, and professional military education will be profound.

New or Revitalized Roles
Associated with Peaceful Intervention

By "peaceful intervention," I am choosing those activities from Boutros-Ghali's spectrum of peace operations that are noncombat roles, some of which are traditional and some nontraditional or new, for United States forces. These roles are associated with preventive deployments, traditional peacekeeping, peace-building, and a new term found in the relevant United States Joint Chiefs of Staff (JCS) publication, "aggravated peacekeeping."

Preventive Deployments

U.S. forces have the military capability and strategic lift to do preventive deployments better than anyone else. The objective is to deploy military forces rapidly so that a potential conflict is preempted by deterring the potential aggressor. Military forces may comprise air, maritime, or ground forces, deployed jointly or separately, depending on assessments of what is required to do the job. These are not new military missions or tasks, and although deployed in a noncombat environment, i.e., peaceful intervention, they should be organized and equipped for combat in the event deterrence should fail. The deployment of Nordic and United States forces to the former Yugoslav republic of Macedonia demonstrates a preventive deployment, although in reality they are configured as lightly armed traditional peacekeeping forces, with insufficient military capability to defend against a determined attack. One can conclude that their deterrent effect is primarily political, in the sense of a "tripwire," not military.

Traditional Peacekeeping

This presents a somewhat different picture for United States forces. The role of individual observers—observe and report—is not a new one for the United States. In fact, we have been active participants in the United Nations Truce Supervision Organization (UNTSO) for some time with observers stationed in Egypt, Israel, Syria, and Lebanon. Besides UNTSO, American observers have recently participated in a number of other U.N. missions in the Persian Gulf, Western Sahara, and Cambodia. The Department of the Army is the executive agent for overall supervision and management of all United States U.N. observers, and has built up considerable expertise in terms of personnel management, predeployment training courses, and coordination with the State Department and U.N. headquarters in New York.

Over the years, the U.N. has developed an effective corpus of knowledge and training guidance associated with traditional peacekeeping, supplemented very effectively by a number of national training programs—Canada and the Nordic countries being excellent examples.

United States participation in U.N. directed peace operations with military units, however, has been a fairly recent phenomenon. This is a legacy primarily of cold war sensitivity to superpower involvement in U.N. peacekeeping, but also a United States military reluctance to become involved in what some view as nontraditional, noncombat roles that can only detract from the military's traditional role of fighting the nation's wars. An exception was, first, United States participation in the Multinational Force and Observers (MFO) in the Sinai—not a U.N. but a tripartite effort with Israel and Egypt to ensure successful implementation of the Camp David Accords—and more recently, United States participation with a Quick Reaction Force (QRF) in UNOSOM, the U.N. mission in Somalia. In addition to the QRF, U.S. logistical units were also included under the direct operational control of the United Nations military commander.

Hence United States participation with military units in U.N. directed traditional peacekeeping, or "aggravated peacekeeping," is a relatively new military mission with important implications for military doctrine, equipment, psychological preparation, area-specific training, and professional military education.

Peace-building

United States defense planners have previously defined peacebuilding as nation-building. It is not a new role, but is an area where revitalization is needed if the United States is to become actively involved in the future. In United States military history, nation-building, as in the development of the West and taming of rivers through flood control, has been a traditional albeit noncombat role. United States Army engineers have a proud history of effectively assisting in the development of United States and other national infrastructure. United States military forces were also heavily employed in providing not only the protective shield but also the expertise in infrastructure and rural development projects in the Republic of Vietnam under the Pacification and Civilian Operations and Revolutionary Development Support (CORDS) programs.

U.N. activity in peace-building, however, is new, and recent U.N. efforts in Cambodia and Somalia are receiving mixed reviews. What is also new is the heavy involvement of nongovernmental organizations (NGOs) and private voluntary organizations (PVOs), requiring a degree of civil-military cooperation rarely seen before, and for which the United Nations is not now well structured. A revitalized U.S. focus on special military skills such as psychological operations and civil affairs also requires attention, with implications for military doctrine, force structure, and active and reserve component mix.

Adapting the United States Military to New or Revitalized Peaceful Intervention Roles

While it is recognized that the United States government has not come fully to grips with the role the United Nations should play in meeting United States security concerns, some implications for United States military forces are already clear. These implications are relevant whatever the degree of future U.S. participation in U.N. peace operations.

Doctrine Rationalization

A major effort must be undertaken to rationalize military doctrine relevant to the entire spectrum of peace operations so that the United Nations, NATO, and the United States are all marching to the same drummer. The military doctrine associated with a particular United Nations mandate is the capstone from which organization and structure, equipment, training, exercises, and rules of engagement governing the use of military force are derived. Common doctrine or understanding of how one goes about a particular military mission is essential for any multinational force to effectively move in a coherent, effective fashion toward a common objective. Until the doctrinal underpinning is firmly established, it does not make much sense to rush into large-scale multinational training and exercises for peace operations. Although high visibility, cooperative security activity has considerable political appeal, modest training activities focusing on basic individual and unit skills associated with peace operations are more appropriate.

The problem is that while the United Nations has grown comfortable with traditional peacekeeping doctrine, United States military forces are conditioned by AirLand Battle, a highly synchronized, integrated application of military power designed to overwhelm an opponent. Neither is suited to the conditions found in Somalia, Bosnia-Hercegovina, or numerous other potential conflict situations. United Nations doctrine, stressing consent of the parties to the conflict, impartiality of the intervening force, low force levels, restrictive rules of engagement, use of force only in self-defense, and light armament, is clearly inappropriate to conditions where full consent of the parties is lacking, the perception of U.N. impartiality has been eroded, and overly restrictive rules of engagement put the safety of U.N. forces in jeopardy. These conditions are what define the JCS term "aggravated peacekeeping." Likewise, U.S. military war-fighting doctrine, exemplified by the use of overwhelming force and massive firepower to achieve decisive results, is inappropriate to intrastate conflicts or civil wars where the "enemy" is uncertain and the civilian population is intermingled with military combatants.

The military doctrinal community is hard at work both here and at NATO, but more coherence and centralized control and guidance are needed. One would hope the lead would come from the United Nations Department of Peacekeeping Operations, but the overall U.N. Secretariat is in the process of reorganization and incapable at present of effective output. In the United States, the doctrinal focal points are the Joint Staff and the United States Atlantic Command, but they have yet to fully assert themselves to bring order and rationality across service lines. NATO, as always, is captive of the consensus rule among sixteen nations, perhaps more if the North Atlantic Cooperation Council of thirty-eight nations becomes the focal point for the Partnership for Peace initiative. Both the United Nations and NATO cry out for effective United States leadership to force rationalization across the multinational doctrine development process. As the world organization involved in peace operations, the United Nations should provide the umbrella guidance for regional organizations and participating nations; however, it must be given the resources to accomplish the task.

Organization and Equipment

Some argue that nations, including the United States, should organize and equip units specifically for peace operations, thereby overcoming the ad hoc nature of the United Nations' response to conflict resolution. That argument, though perhaps valid for nations with modest defense establishments and a national security policy oriented on U.N. peacekeeping—e.g., the Nordic neutrals and Canada—does not apply to the United States. Because the United States faces worldwide responsibilities involving treaty commitments and other bilateral and multilateral security agreements, it has since World War II been forced to prioritize these commitments to handle the reality of inadequate conventional forces to meet all commitments simultaneously. This has invariably generated a degree of risk, and has put a premium on multipurpose conventional forces with a high degree of mission flexibility and mobility. The only exception that quickly comes to mind is the Special Operations Forces (SOF) assigned to the United States Special Operations Command (USSOCOM), a reservoir of highly specialized combat forces with special equipment designed for unique combat and counterterrorist missions. For noncombat missions, and specifically for peacekeeping, the military preference has been to use conventional forces tailored to the specific mission.

Military planners have consistently rejected any suggestion for U.S. "designated units" or "standby units" to be placed on call for U.N. peace operations and have opposed any suggestion to contribute to a U.N. "standing force," sometimes referred to as a U.N. "rapid deployment force." In their view, such suggestions only serve to reduce the reservoir of conventional forces available for U.S. worldwide commitments, directly increasing the risk involved by degrading our capability to meet more than one major regional contingency simultaneously.

Nonetheless, there are still organizational and equipment issues that our armed forces need to address, if we are to participate effectively, whatever the degree, in U.N. directed peace operations. Current peace operations require a high degree of integration and coordination among participating civilian organizations (NGOs and PVOs) and military forces, and constant interaction with local governing authorities in both peacekeeping and peacebuilding situations. This places a premium on Civil Affairs and Psychological Operations units, many of which are located in the reserves. This should force the services to readdress their active/reserve mix to avoid recurring reserve call-ups to meet contingencies involving peaceful intervention.

With regard to equipment, the focus should be on that equipment and those weapons that support and are consistent with agreed rules of engagement. Recalling the emphasis on the use of force only in self-defense, and avoidance of civilian casualties in situations where combatants and civilians are frequently intermingled, our armed forces need to emphasize the use of precision weapons and related target acquisition capabilities to minimize collateral damage. This would suggest a higher allocation of trained snipers per ground combat unit, more countermortar and counterartillery direction-finding systems, and a greater effort to develop and field nonlethal munitions—those munitions that incapacitate temporarily rather than kill.

Civil-Military Planning and Coordination

The requirement for Civil Affairs and Psychological Operations capabilities deployed as part of a U.N. peace operation has already been mentioned, but there is also a requirement for a much higher degree of integrated planning at the strategic and operational levels. NGO and PVO representatives must be included with military planners at the earliest planning stages, both at national capitals of contributing nations and at U.N. headquarters in New York, prior to a U.N. deployment. Likewise, if coordinated, integrated field operations are to be achieved at the outset, PVOs/NGOs must be included in all deploying headquarters to the theater. This might seem obvious to the uninitiated; however, bureaucratic sensitivities and inertia have resulted in an uneven track record.

Training and Education

As indicated in a previous section, training and education related to peace operations are derivatives of the basic doctrine and concept of how one goes about such an operation, whether it be traditional peacekeeping, peace enforcement, or peace-building. Although some uniformed military still maintain that no special training is required for peace operations, informed opinion stresses that effective, well-integrated peace operations can be achieved only by proper psychological and special skill preparatory training. Hence it is essential that training and professional military education programs be modified to include the relevant subjects. Although the U.S. Army's Training and Doctrine Command has been working with the Center for Low Intensity Conflict to develop peace operation scenarios for use at the Joint Readiness Training Center (JRTC) at Fort Polk, Louisiana, and similar training has been instituted at the Combat Maneuver Training Center (CMTC) in Germany for U.S. and other forces deploying to U.N. directed peace operations, the overall U.S. response in the training and education area has been somewhat ad hoc. This is understandable, given the lack of guidance emanating from the United Nations headquarters in New York and the lingering lack of consensus on doctrine.

Nonetheless, there are certain basic and special skills associated with peace operations that should be candidates for training blocs in both a unit's annual training program and any special predeployment refresher training. Some of these subjects are already included in the Canadian and Nordic regional training courses for peacekeeping, and others have been distilled from lessons learned from U.N. peace operations in Central America, Cambodia, Somalia, and the former republic of Yugoslavia. A sampling of these subjects would include:

- The role of military force.
- Impartiality of the peacekeepers.
- Coordination of cease-fire agreements.
- Establishment of demilitarized zones.
- Road blocks and checkpoints.
- Mine awareness and demining.
- International legal issues.
- Humanitarian and human rights issues.
- Area-specific training (geography, language, culture, religion).

In like manner, the armed forces need a more structured approach in the professional military education programs at the Command and Staff and War Colleges. Here the focus should appropriately be more at the strategic and operational levels. A sampling of relevant subjects includes:

- The role of the United Nations.
- Peace operations and their relationship to United States national security strategy.
- The spectrum of peace operations.
- Civil-military relations.
- Establishment of military coalitions.
- Multinational operations.
- Command and control.

In summary, just as the success of the U.S. forces in Desert Storm can be directly attributed to the complete integration of AirLand Battle doctrine into professional military education courses, service training programs, and the National Training Center, the future success of U.S. forces in U.N. directed peace operations will depend on how effectively and quickly this subject matter is incorporated into the training and education establishment.

Peace Operations as Part of
United States Security Strategy

Ultimately, how our armed forces adapt to the new strategic environment and participate in peace operations will be driven by how the administration views the United States and United Nations role in the world. This view has yet to be fully incorporated into the *National Security Strategy of the United States,* published by the White House, and the related *National Military Strategy of the United States,* published by the chair of the Joint Chiefs of Staff.

A marker was set by the outgoing Bush administration when it declared: "The United States should do its part to strengthen U.N. conflict prevention, peacekeeping and peacemaking capabilities by: . . . taking an active role in the full spectrum of U.N. peacekeeping, and humanitarian relief planning and support. . . ."[2] Whether this promise of U.S. activism in peace operations is carried through by the Clinton administration will depend on the case made for multilateralism, the role of the United Nations in helping to meet United States security concerns, and the balance between conflict prevention and support for the United Nations on the one hand, and security assistance to allies and conflict management on the other.

Implications of the New Environment
for Coercive Intervention

The discussion thus far has focused on peaceful intervention and related military missions and tasks, basically noncombat in nature, that are associated with peace operations and humanitarian assistance. We have seen that the United States military will be challenged with certain revitalized roles and new roles if it is to adapt sufficiently to the new strategic environment and be an effective instrument in the achievement of U.S. foreign policy objectives.

We turn now to those combat missions such as coercive intervention, peace enforcement, or, as some would describe them, "traditional roles," which constitute the *raison d'être* of armed forces, that is, the ability to successfully fight the nation's wars. Although the new strategic environment might suggest a greater incidence of intrastate conflict fueled by ethnic and religious differences, as opposed to interstate aggression, military planners must prepare for the worst contingency even if the probability of occurrence may have decreased. The American public's memory of failed U.N. directed peace operations, even with U.S. participation, may have a short half life, but the American public will not forget easily American failure when American treasure, sons and daughters, and national interests are all involved. The armed forces may not have to be as eternally vigilant for *"the* big one" as was the case with respect to the Soviet Union during the cold war, but we cannot afford to be ill prepared for "*a* big one" in the sense of a major regional contingency requiring either U.S. unilateral intervention or U.S. participation in a multinational coalition.

The most plausible major regional scenarios are not new: the Middle East/Persian Gulf and Northeast Asia. Whether a Korean Peninsula or Iraq/Iran scenario, the United States has security obligations involving either a treaty, bilateral or multilateral security agreements, or vital interests. The fact that these regions have also been the recipients of high levels of military technology and military equipment, as well as the delivery systems associated with weapons of mass destruction (biological, chemical, and nuclear), presents the United States with a challenging and dangerous threat environment.

The implications for our armed forces with regard to coercive intervention and peace enforcement are different in nature from those associated with peaceful intervention. Doctrine, equipment, training, and education are basically sound for U.N. authorized peace enforcement operations in the nature of Korea and Desert Storm—that is, a military response to outright interstate aggression. They are less so for peace enforcement operations as in Somalia and Bosnia—less than all-out warfare in conditions of anarchy or civil war.

The problems associated with a major regional contingency are more related to declining resources and competing noncombat priorities. While defense resource trends continue to plummet, mirrored almost without exception by our NATO allies, U.S.

commitments and deployments remain at a high level. Military spending is down to 3.6 percent of gross domestic product, the smallest since before World War II, and our armed forces are heading toward 1.4 million men and women under arms and some 900,000 reservists, again the smallest since before World War II.

The continuing loss of forward basing, either through choice or foreign pressure, has meant that forward presence must be maintained more by periodic forward deployments of air, maritime, and ground forces than by forces permanently stationed overseas. Expected savings from base closures abroad will become invisible as they become increasingly consumed by higher operating expenses associated with forward presence and greater investment in strategic airlift and sealift to provide the capability to move U.S. based forces to contingency areas. The dilemma is that these hoped-for savings can only be realized by either consciously reducing commitments or consciously accepting a higher degree of risk through reduced forward presence that can translate into reduced U.S. regional influence and regional stability. Again, there is no free lunch.

Making Coercive Intervention More Effective

To meet this new strategic environment characterized by a number of regional actors with high threat potential, in the face of a declining resource base, the U.S. armed forces are already moving toward a new military strategy. Building on previous Chair of the Joint Chiefs Colin Powell's Base Force, and the components of the Bush administration's defense strategy (*strategic deterrence and defense, forward presence, crisis response,* and *reconstitution*),[3] the United States is adopting a strategic concept better described as power projection. Although U.S. strategy during the cold war clearly contained elements of power projection, the emphasis was more on reinforcement of forward stationed U.S. forces located in the vicinity of regional hot spots than on a military response projected from the United States itself.

As previously intimated, this strategic refinement has been necessitated by the dismantling of forward bases and the overflight and transit rights associated with the post–World War II containment strategy aimed at the Soviet Union. The collapse of the Soviet Union and concomitant U.S. reductions in defense budgets and force levels left no real alternative.

In early 1993, Secretary of Defense Les Aspin announced how crisis response would be maintained in the face of significant reductions and what programs would be emphasized to be able to execute two nearly simultaneous major regional contingencies, the force sizing criterion used in the "bottom up review." In brief, the acquisition strategy contained four pillars: improved and additional sealift and airlift to enhance power projection; an increase in pre-positioning ashore and afloat to reduce deployment times to potential trouble spots; an acceleration in the development and acquisition of greater numbers of precision-guided munitions with improved accuracy and lethality, thus using technology and more effective firepower to compensate for personnel reductions; and an improvement in battlefield surveillance to speed up the process of detecting, analyzing, and destroying targets.[4] The compass has been set, and the argument is now focused on first, whether planned reductions are too great, given the chaotic world situation; and second, whether the planned force levels are adequately resourced to avoid a return to the "hollow" forces of the 1970s.

In any event, to ensure that coercive intervention is more effective in the new environment, the U.S. armed forces need to continue their emphasis on:

- Better intelligence acquisition to improve early warning for crisis prevention and crisis response.
- Maintaining the technological edge to achieve better precision strike weapon systems and munition lethality.
- Leveraging force flexibility and mobility for more rapid crisis response.

As mentioned before, improving coercive intervention associated with regional contingencies is more an issue of adequate resourcing than a major overhaul of doctrine, training, and education. Peace enforcement in conditions of anarchy or civil war, however, is the exception where our forces do face important doctrinal and training issues. Nonetheless, there are three key areas where progress must be made if we are to achieve overall improved defense output from declining defense budgets.

Defense Acquisition System. Rationalization and improvement of the entire defense acquisition system are needed to ensure expeditious fielding of new equipment and weapon systems, capturing the best technology at an acceptable cost. This is not a new idea, to be sure, and there is every expectation that the leadership at the Pentagon is well equipped and motivated to take it head on.

Service "Roles and Missions." "Roles and missions," or more appropriately, service functions and tasks, need an intensive and rigorous analysis, going far beyond General Powell's initial efforts in the training, maintenance, and administration areas. This will be a difficult task because it touches the very soul and ethos of the individual services. Functions and tasks drive force structure, weapon system acquisition, personnel acquisition, training and education programs, overall budget requests, and not unimportantly, flag officer billets. "Roles and missions" carry historical and cultural baggage, hence, a lot of potential bureaucratic bloodletting is involved. The answers will not come easily, because what some view as redundant and unnecessary will be viewed by others as complementary, synergistic applications of combat power. Furthermore, not all redundancy is bad, in the sense of hedging against neutralization of a particular capability by a sophisticated enemy. But if ever the time has come to take this one head on, it is now. Unnecessary duplication in an era of fiscal austerity is irresponsible management of our nation's resources, and will directly impede the fielding of appropriate capabilities for both peaceful and coercive intervention from shrinking budgets.

Unified Command Plan. United States command organization, or the Unified Command Plan, likewise needs a rigorous review. This should be a natural by-product of a "roles and mission" review, but it has historically been considered the protected preserve of the military. Not surprisingly, large headquarters with large numbers of flag officer command and staff positions have a tendency to perpetuate themselves long after their usefulness and relevance may have passed.

The second and third areas will be highly sensitive, and there will be an inevitable tendency for the civilian side of the Defense Department and the U.S. Congress to encroach into what the chair of the Joint Chiefs views as his rightful and legally constituted domain, quite apart from the roles and missions independent commission called for in the 1994 defense bill. The chair's constituents—the service chiefs and unified commanders—will want to keep things just as they are, and this will put enormous pressure on the chair to stonewall or aim for marginal improvement. How the chair proceeds, in the sense of fulfilling the role envisioned by the Goldwater-Nichols Act as "principal advisor to the Secretary of Defense and the President," and whether he is able to lead and build support among his four-star constituents, will define the playing field and determine whether he is able to preempt, or at least shape, the competing efforts of independent panels, the Department of Defense, and Congress.

Trade-offs

As a final thought, as one examines the noncombat roles associated with peaceful intervention and the combat roles associated with coercive intervention and peace enforcement, one inevitably has to ask: can U.S. forces do them both, and what are the trade-offs?

The recent explosion in the fielding of United Nations peace operations with the promise of continuing requirements in the peacemaking, peacekeeping, humanitarian assistance, and peacebuilding areas puts the issue squarely to U.S. policy makers wrestling with intervention criteria—whether to become involved, and if so, how, when, and under what conditions. As already indicated, some in the military view these noncombat roles as "nontraditional," with participation causing a direct degradation of traditional combat tasks, functions, and skills. In their view, personnel, technology, doctrine, and training trade-offs are unacceptable. Coercive intervention, or traditional "war-fighting," with its emphasis on highly orchestrated, technology-intensive AirLand Battle doctrine demands full-time preparation and training. Participation in peaceful intervention operations, the argument continues, with the focus on personnel-intensive, lightly armed forces and decentralized operations under restrictive rules of engagement dulls the fighting edge and presents an unacceptable diversion of time and resources into predeployment, deployment, and postdeployment activities.

What is the answer? The answer, in my judgment, is that our armed forces must be able to do both. They have done it in the past, and ultimately will execute whatever the national command authorities and American public view as legitimate missions. The priority, however, *must* remain on traditional combat tasks—the fundamental purpose of our armed forces. Again, a failed humanitarian mission does not carry the same weight as a failure of American arms in defense of U.S., as opposed to global, interests. But that does not mean that our military settles into an "all or nothing" posture. Desert Storm clearly exorcised the ghosts of Vietnam, civilian micromanagement, and the incremental use of force, but it would be wrong to draw the lesson that the discrete use of limited military force for discrete missions is inappropriate. The president and the American public must have options for the use of military power other than a rerun of Desert Storm or cases with a guarantee of no risk and no casualties.

I have argued that our armed forces must be able to do both missions—that is, noncombat or peaceful interventions associated with preventive deployments, peacekeeping, aggravated peacekeeping, and peace-building, as well as combat or coercive interventions associated with peace enforcement, interstate conflicts, and the nation's wars. There clearly are trade-offs, and the trade-offs center primarily on the preparatory time needed to get ready for a peaceful intervention, the execution time of the mission itself, and the recovery time necessary to rehone combat or war-fighting skills. There are accompanying doctrinal implications, requirements for integrated planning with civilian components, organizational tailoring, special equipment training, and the training and education related to coalition formation and multinational operations, which all drive the preparatory time. In addition to these primarily military subjects, predeployment training must include the very important area-specific aspects of culture, language, religion, and whatever other environmental knowledge is required to operate effectively once introduced into the mission area. Experience gained from Canadian peace operations and our own rotations with the Multinational Force and Observers in the Sinai suggests a predeployment training period of three to six months, and a recovery period of six months or more.

While a unit is involved in a peaceful intervention, it cannot be available for a concurrent coercive intervention contingency, the trade-off being a direct loss of combat capability for the latter. This loss, however, is larger than the actual unit deployed, for normal planning suggests that three times the force to be deployed will be affected in order to ensure personnel and equipment fill at 100 percent or greater for the deploying unit and an efficient rotation schedule. In other words, a snapshot in time would show a unit deployed, a second unit undergoing preparatory training to replace the deployed unit, and a third unit providing personnel and equipment fill for the unit in the rotation queue. Hence, the larger the requirement for a peaceful intervention, the greater the impact on U.S. ability to respond to nearly simultaneous major regional contingencies. Finally, the profound doctrinal differences between traditional peacekeeping and peace enforcement, to use an example, mean that units involved in peaceful and coercive interventions are not easily interchangeable. They need recovery and re-training time before they are ready for redeployment to a different mission. The loss of combat capability is not recovered simply by adding the flying or streaming time between contingency areas. The trade-off in time is far greater.

What does this mean for U.S. policy makers? Clearly there is no ironclad set of criteria for a peaceful intervention. Each potential intervention must be assessed on a case-by-case basis with such factors as the anticipated length of the commitment, the likelihood of a concurrent major regional contingency, and the relevance to U.S. interests weighing most heavily.

There is one set of conditions, however, that suggests most careful assessment and extreme caution—coercive intervention or peace enforcement in conditions of civil war or near anarchy. As we have seen in Bosnia and Somalia, peace enforcement in these conditions involves a combat mission less than total war that is inconsistent with the objectives and doctrine associated with traditional peacekeeping. When the consent of the parties to the conflict for an intervening U.N. force is not total, and the perception of the impartiality of that force has been eroded, inevitably the

U.N. force will be perceived by at least one party as a belligerent. Casualties will ensue, and the choice facing policy makers will become a painful one. One either withdraws, as we did in Somalia, or escalates the use of force and commitment of personnel to a level where a solution can be imposed by the coercive use of force. The political implications of either choice are enormous, with the probability of being drawn into a "quagmire" and ultimate failure being extremely high, especially in the case of escalation. Although the secretary-general of the United Nations himself may have initiated this concept of "peace enforcement" in *An Agenda For Peace,* such a mission under the conditions described should be undertaken only with the most careful assessment of all the trade-offs involved. All the implications must be placed in full view on the table. Good intentions alone are not a sufficient rationale for action, and military action without a political framework is counterproductive.

As a final thought, the principal trade-off in macro terms is, again, between investment in conflict prevention and related support to United Nations peace operations on the one hand and investment in security assistance to allies and conflict management and war-fighting on the other. The argument should be made that successful peace operations are a good, cost-effective bargain when compared to the long-term costs of a destructive conflict that timely action might have prevented. Where the balance lies between combat and noncombat roles and their related resource investment in doctrine, training, education, and equipment will ultimately depend on what role the United States sees the United Nations playing in meeting U.S. security needs. This vision will only be formulated with the highest skills in political judgment and military advice. The stakes and need for United States leadership are both high.

Notes

[1] Boutros-Ghali (1992), pp. 11–12, 20–34.

[2] *National Security Strategy of the United States* (1993), p. 7.

[3] *National Security Strategy of the United States* (1993), pp. 14–15.

[4] Secretary of Defense Les Aspin's remarks at the National Defense University Graduation, Ft. McNair, 1993.

4

New Applications of Nonlethal and Less Lethal Technology

RICHARD L. GARWIN

Introduction

The changing environment for intervention has been accompanied by changes in the world structure and in the views of electorates, policy leaders, and those who might be involved in military intervention. Any logical and responsible approach to the creation and exercise of military capability must welcome the consideration of novel tools of military and strategic intelligence, assessment, weapons, logistics, or any other potential contributor to getting the job done at lower cost for a given effectiveness, or more effectively at the same cost. Planning for military capability in general, and for intervention in particular, differs from industry or commerce primarily in the definition of benefits and costs, and in the magnitude of the resources available for planning, development, acquisition, and evaluation.

RICHARD L. GARWIN is vice chair of the Federation of American Scientists and chair of the FAS Fund. He is also IBM fellow emeritus at the Thomas J. Watson Research Center, adjunct professor of physics at Columbia University, and has been professor of public policy at Harvard

This chapter on nonlethal and less lethal technology must therefore consider the nature of the benefits and costs affected by this set of technological options, their reality and readiness, and the degree to which special mechanisms might be needed to create and utilize their capabilities. Potential benefits include the possibility that nonlethal weapons will achieve military goals better than will lethal weapons, that the avoidance of enemy casualties would result in the avoidance of U.S. casualties, or that deaths or injury to bystanders (or even to the opponent) are politically or morally unacceptable and that a nonlethal weapon is, therefore, preferable or necessary even if less effective or much more costly than a lethal weapon for achieving the same military goals.

I conclude that there is substantial overlap between the applicability of nonlethal weapons (NLW) and of improved conventional lethal munitions, that NLW that would be effective per se would, in general, also increase the effectiveness of lethal munitions, and that exploration and development of NLW should be conducted by normal Defense Department procedures rather than in a special new Pentagon office. It is important to note that the utility of NLW in many cases is limited by the possibility of countermeasures and by their use against ourselves and our allies, with implications for caution and perhaps secrecy in deciding to develop and use such weapons, as is the case with some lethal weapons.

A View on Intervention

The reader should be aware of my views on intervention, which are cautious and to some extent principled. I believe we should be

University, a member of the president's Science Advisory Committee, a member of the Defense Science Board, and a consultant to the Defense Department and other agencies of the U.S. government, including the Los Alamos National Laboratory. Dr. Garwin's contributions to the development, analysis, and choice of weapon systems extend from 1950 to the present and include many technologies, including those of communications, surveillance, navigation, and population. He has published many papers, both classified and unclassified, on defense technology and arms control, energy, transportation, and environment, and has testified to many congressional committees in both closed and open session.

ready to intervene as part of a U.N. response, to support our commitments to NATO or other collective security organizations, or to follow through on a security guarantee. I do not believe our military actions in Grenada or Panama were justified by the long-runway airfield construction or the capture of General Noriega; I believe we should have been involved much earlier in Bosnia, given the magnitude of the destruction of material and societal values and the bad example set for other nations by our nonintervention. Our experience in Somalia inspires both caution and the wish to have better tools for such activities. Some NLW were indeed used in these activities—loud music outside Noriega's headquarters—and an analysis of proposed specific NLW programs should include an evaluation of their potential contribution in these specific instances, whether the given intervention was proper or not.

My personal experience includes chairing or being a member of various panels of the president's Science Advisory Committee, including panels on Vietnam, military aircraft, naval warfare, strategic military, conventional weapons, and the like, as well as similar activity of the Defense Science Board and visits to the theaters of conflict during the wars in Korea and Vietnam. In recent years I have helped with some development needs and opportunities of the U.S. Special Operations Command as well as some national law enforcement activities. More than four decades of experience with what has worked and has not worked in the military and commercial world have instilled some caution, but have not totally destroyed my optimism about improved mechanisms and capabilities. I am wary, however, of new technologies that only work if new mechanisms are used for their selection and development, and for their employment outside the military activities to which they are intended to contribute.

The Concept of Nonlethal Weapons

For the last few years a few visionaries have advocated the acquisition of nonlethal weapons. Prominent among these advocates are Janet E. Morris and Chris Morris of the United States Global Strategy Council and John H. Alexander of the Los Alamos National Laboratory. They argue that the United States needs and must develop and plan to use nonlethal weapons in order to be able to minimize U.S. casualties, casualties among bystanders and neutrals, and even among the adversary of the occasion. They tend to emphasize measures that disable or degrade military or civil equipment, while not ruling out some technologies intended to temporarily incapacitate individuals.

The range of NLW concepts includes the following, roughly categorized, in which brief descriptions in quotations are taken from either the U.S. Army Training and Doctrine Command (TRADOC)'s "Operations Concept for Disabling Measures (Draft)" of September 1992 or from a 1990 paper by Janet Morris and Christopher Morris entitled "Nonlethality: A Global Strategy." There are many more potentially effective NLW concepts, but these are among the most commonly cited.

Physical Degradation of Equipment

Supercaustics—"Supercaustics can be millions of times more caustic than hydrofluoric acid. A round that delivers jellied superacids could destroy the optics of heavily armored vehicles, penetrate vision blocks or glass, or be employed to silently destroy key weapons systems or components."

The Grime from Hell—A layer of paint weighing less than a gram per square meter can totally block light through a windshield, viewing window, or sensor lens. Alternatively, encountering very fine dust at the speed of a fast aircraft can micro-crater (sand blast) a windshield or exposed sensor window. In either case, a tiny surface layer destroys the utility of a weapon unless or until the surface can be cleaned or restored.

Nonnuclear Electromagnetic Pulse—Electromagnetic pulses can destroy or disable power systems, electronic circuitry, communications, and computer systems. These concepts almost always use high explosive as an energy storage means.

High-Power Microwave—Again using energy stored in high explosive or in high-power pulses from conventional sources, high-power microwaves can destroy or damage electronics, explode ammunition, or disable vehicles with electronic ignition or controls.

Short-Circuiting Power Distribution or Switching Systems—It is widely reported that certain of the other hit-to-kill weapons (the Tomahawk sea-launched cruise missile and comparable air-launched cruise missiles) used against Iraq in Desert Storm instead carried carbon fiber nonlethal weapons, the purpose of which was to float through the air onto high-tension wires and to short out the electrical grid in a nondestructive but disabling fashion.

Mobility Inhibitors

Antitraction Technology (or "Slickum")—"Using airborne delivery systems or human agents, we can spread or spray Teflon-type, environmentally neutral lubricants on railroad tracks, grades, ramps, runways, even stairs and equipment, potentially denying their use for a substantial period, because such lubricants are costly and time-consuming to remove."

Roach Motels (or "Stickum")—"Polymer adhesives, delivered by air or selectively on the ground, can 'glue' equipment in place and keep it from operating."

Jacks—Simple tubes welded into the form of the "jacks" of our childhood, a few inches in size, provide a nonlethal weapon that has been used since the Second World War to puncture tires and to deny roadways or runways for a time to vehicles.

Foam, Sticky or Hard—to immobilize people or to render them less effective. Imagine trying to conduct your normal business in a world covered with raspberry jam.

Combustion Alteration—"Internal combustion engines can be disrupted through special chemical compounds. These chemical compounds would temporarily contaminate fuel or change its viscosity to degrade engine function." The military has long sought a gas or dust or fog that when ingested by internal combustion engines would terminate the combustion reaction (stop the flame propagation in the cylinder or burner).

Temporary Incapacitation of Personnel

Laser Weapons—"Resembling conventional rifles, low-energy laser rifles with power packs can flash-blind people and disable optical and infrared systems used for target acquisition, tracking, night vision, and range finding."

Flash-Bang Grenades or Mines—Widely used in hostage rescue, these devices distract and dismay people in close proximity (particularly when used inside buildings or at night), allowing the stunned individuals to be overcome or killed.

Irritants—"Tear gas" such as CS-2 smoke used in riot control repels or temporarily disables people. Tiny darts loaded with irritant can be fired at individuals with similar effect.

Anesthetics—"Gas" could be used to put people to sleep, or tiny darts loaded with an appropriate anesthetic (fentanyl, for instance) could do this more selectively and with a wide safety margin.

Infrasound—"Very low frequency sound generators could be tuned to incapacitate humans, causing disorientation, nausea, vomiting, or bowel spasms. The effect ceases as soon as the generator is turned off, with no lingering physical or environmental damage."

Imposing Costs on the Population

Window Breaking via Sonic Boom—Not totally an NLW for people on the streets below high-rise buildings, this could be accomplished by low-altitude supersonic flight.

Information Warfare

Computer Virus Technology—"This technology focuses on computer systems that control fire support systems, data transmission, fire control systems, avionics, etc. It involves the covert intrusion of a computer virus, logic bomb, or worm that may remain hidden until the system is used or meets specific parameters."

Jamming—communications; or disabling or disrupting communications and other equipment by the use of electromagnetic pulse effects.

Nonlethal "Lethal" Weapons

Land Mines—Are they "nonlethal weapons"? An effective minefield prevents passage, and it can be argued that land mines put the initiative of injury on the other side. According to the long-held rules of war, such minefields should be marked, and they should be mapped to aid in their sanitization when they are no longer needed. Land mines can thus be classed with other effective weapons, lethal or nonlethal, the effects of which are readily countered at a substantial reduction in one's effectiveness or at substantial increase in one's vulnerability.

Discussion

While not exhaustive, the preceding list includes most of the concepts commonly advocated. Stickum or slickum might be very thin layers of material suitable for applying to very large areas, while a similar mass of disabling foam could cover only a much smaller area either to entangle individuals or to block motion. These are not simply theoretical concepts; foam, slickum, and some additional means are in use in the "safe secure transport" vans used by the Department of Energy to carry nuclear weapons within the U.S.

Wish or Reality?

Some of these "weapons" would require unusual cooperation on the part of the adversary: fuel systems are not normally accessible to chemicals sprayed on their exterior; electromagnetic pulse generators against electronics work much better if actually connected to the wires of a computer network or power system. In some cases, additional design effort of the delivery system can compensate for the absence of cooperation, but this effort must be included in the design and evaluation of the system. For instance, if an agent that converts fuel into jelly requires a delivery system that punches holes in fuel storage tanks, injects the agent, and then plugs the hole, it needs to be compared in effectiveness with a simpler system that explodes or ignites the fuel either immediately or with some desired delay.

The Question of Relative Effectiveness

For use in military operations, nonlethal weapons pose a peculiar conceptual problem, but perhaps the real conceptual problem is relating military activities to limited political goals. One imagines that NLW are to be used to convey a military advantage; in fact, it would be ideal if the United States and its allies of the moment could use nonlethal weapons to terminate or win a conflict with no casualties on our side and preferably with no casualties on the other side (or, more importantly, among the bystanders). But if the other side is not hurting, why should it concede? Why should it not just wait out the period of incapacitation and resume its activities whenever the pressure is off? One possibility is that NLW themselves cause serious pain or penalty, as in the case of the sonic boom or as would accompany switching off the public power or telephone system. Alternatively, they might be used in order to impose on the other side respect and fear for what may follow.

In the latter case, leverage would arise not from the NLW themselves, but from the improved effectiveness of the military operations that could follow—perhaps because of the additional time made available for mobilizing our forces or the inflicting of damage or destruction during the time that the other side is held transfixed. But a nonlethal capability to transfix the adversaries so that they can be killed more readily may not merit the term "nonlethal weapon." "Prelethal weapon" has been suggested to describe this use.

What does one want to achieve from the use or threat of use of NLW against a sovereign state: release of hostages; cessation of support for insurrection; the shortening of a planned runway; the extradition of a political leader; election of a leader with views more acceptable to the U.S.; improvement in human rights; restoration or establishment of civic order; the nonuse of lethal weapons against U.S. forces intervening on the territory of the state? Each of the above seems to have been the goal of an actual or planned intervention by the United States, but the link between coercion and result is not always evident. Taking a less absolutist view, the result of an election in a quasi-democratic state would be influenced by our use of NLW, but would the change be favorable to our cause?

Interventions differ. In some cases one is fighting a dedicated force equipped with tanks, heavy artillery, mortars, and the like. If these weapons are immobilized only imperfectly by NLW, their fire power will be reduced but not eliminated, and we will take casualties while our NLW inflict no casualties on our opponent. If U.S. freedom of action is constrained by a reluctance to cause casualties among bystanders, but even more constrained by per-ceived public and congressional reluctance to accept casualties among our volunteer military force, our use of NLW might be no more than a more acceptable means of escalating to lethal conflict. If so, the CNN pictures of dead innocents will hardly be compen-sated by the reminder that the other side could have conceded but didn't when we were besieging them with NLW; after all, they could have conceded to the initial demands without any use of weapons at all.

A Lot of Experience with One NLW. If NLW are militarily more effective than lethal weapons, then they should be developed and used without special consideration. In this there is historical expe-rience.

For the last forty years, U.S. air forces have faced the need to overcome enemy air defenses, either within the former Soviet Union or largely supplied by the Soviet Union. In many cases, the approach of choice was not to destroy the air defenses (although this may have been feasible), but to use deception and jamming in order to penetrate the defended air space. Techniques included simple jamming to provide "snow" on the radar displays or com-puter detection systems, deception to prevent accurate tracking of the aircraft by the enemy radars, and fuze jammers or deception systems to detonate the fuzes on air defense missiles prematurely or to prevent them from detonating as they passed within lethal range of our aircraft.

This was a pretty sporty activity, which needed to be carried out successfully every time our aircraft passed within range of opposing air defenses. Such an approach might have been necessary if we were protecting surveillance or reconnaissance vehicles operating in peacetime over denied territory, but it was also used by allied air forces operating against air defenses during a hot war, such as Israeli activities in the war between Egypt and Israel. The Israeli cause might have been better served by actual destruction of Egyptian radar by means of laser-guided bombs, or bombs guided by remote radio command, or by so-called antiradiation missiles that would strike the radars either by homing on the radar transmission or by the use of the radar transmission to get a location within a few meters, against which the bomb or guided missile could be directed by accurate navigation. Instead, the NLW approach of jamming and deception was taken, probably to the detriment of the effectiveness of the Israeli Air Force.

The point in this case is not whether the nonlethal approach was in fact less or more effective than the lethal approach; it is simply to show that there has been no prejudice against NLW when it was *considered* more effective militarily. On the other side of the argument, however, is the dismay often expressed by commanders who are offered a means for disabling rather than destroying enemy targets—for "mission kill" rather than destruction. Skeptics argue that if there are no unambiguous external signals, then the same opposing tank might be marked for destruction again and again, even though its capability for accurate gunfire may have been destroyed.

Some of these problems are no longer so important in the modern era, in which it is finally accepted that one might have a "digital battlefield" in which information could be stored and keyed geographically. When a tank (or something that might be a tank) is seen at a particular location, the corresponding precise location is brought up from the digital battlefield database and shown to contain a destroyed tank. Immobilized and nullified weapons might even be incorporated onto battlefield displays using an appropriate symbol. Because commanders can be sure they know the status of the battlefield, they may more readily accept a disabling weapon (if it is cheaper or more effective than an old fashioned destructive weapon).

Effectiveness, Countermeasures, and the Decision to Develop

Of course, the ideal for the United States would be to have effective NLW that could not be countered, and to which we ourselves were somehow inherently invulnerable. Logically, such circumstances might arise in the intervention context when they would not in full-scale war with a major power, if the weapon were so large or of such technology or so costly that it could not be afforded by the other side. Because we assume the impossibility of countermeasures, such weapons would need to be used in a region where there are no U.S. or friendly or neutral forces, or civilians. An example might be the very fast electromagnetic pulse created by a nuclear explosion at an altitude of 100 kilometers or more, which is harmless to people but may damage unshielded electrical power distribution systems.

Next best might be a weapon to which countermeasures exist, but which countermeasures we would attempt to keep to ourselves and our allies. In general, countermeasures need to be more widespread than the NLW themselves and ordinarily require more training as well; this makes it much more difficult to keep secret the existence and nature of an NLW that is readily countered. For instance, it is a lot more complicated to manage protective garb against chemical weapons (or even against tear gas) than to fire the shell or drop the bomb that delivers such agents. Of course, if we can arrange things so that our personnel and our equipment are not subject to our own NLW, we don't need countermeasures; but if we do need to provide them to our troops, we also will need to train with them and with the actual or simulated NLW, in order to provide those who will be involved confidence that they can operate under those circumstances.

Finally, if we identify an NLW we choose not to develop or to deploy, what do we do about countermeasures if it is used against us? A simple example is a laser blinding weapon: we may choose to develop one at one wavelength and provide ourselves simple shielding glasses or filters to protect ourselves against our weapon, without significant reduction in visibility. But an adversary or a freelance weapons manufacturer might choose a different wavelength, one almost as effective or even more effective. Obviously if we needed to provide countermeasures against the opponent's use of our own weapon, we also would need to provide it against their version; and we would need those countermeasures whether or not we deployed any such weapon. Evidently, intelligence on what is actually being manufactured and bought in the rest of the world is important for our own protection. Naturally, in considering NLW and intervention, as is true more generally, one should distinguish between what *might* be done and what is actually being provided.

The use of "stickum" provides an interesting example of countermeasures. If some such contact adhesive were sprayed on the pavement, it could very well inhibit foot traffic or even passage by certain vehicles. Bare feet would soon be bloody because of the removal of a layer of skin with each step. However, sand spread on the stickum-coated pavement would presumably stick (what else?) and provide a "sandpaper" surface on which one could walk or drive. Before sand could be spread, attaching a pad of newspaper to the sole of each shoe would allow one step per page—enough to cross a small region of stickum-covered pavement at high speed. This is an example of an easily countered NLW, but one that might be effective under specific circumstances, given surprise.

Similarly, there is an enormous spread in vulnerability to electromagnetic pulse (EMP) or electrical interference between a system that is designed with no thought to such interference and one that is carefully shielded. The shielding may cost very little if included in the design process or if specified at the beginning of development. Such shielding may increase the energy requirement for the EMP generator by a millionfold, making such NLW ineffective. Other design techniques also work. For instance, if computer networks use readily available optical fiber for interconnection, the network becomes no more vulnerable than the individual computers used in it. Even normal surge suppressors can do a good deal to mitigate the effects of EMP weapons.

Temporarily disabling open-wire electrical power distribution systems (and switch yards) by the use of munitions that dispense carbon fiber is much discussed, but no air defense system that is designed to have any capability against lethal attack (and that is what they are designed for) will do without independent power to each of the radars, missile launchers, direction centers, and the like. The same is true of all combat elements. Loss of grid power, however, would cut production and retard transport, and probably inhibit the activities of much of government and the rest of society. The point is simply not to overstate the specific utility of this tool.

Steam locomotives came equipped with a "cow catcher"—the grilled plow-like device in front, and that prevented a number of derailments caused by cows or other large debris, although it still left the problem of smaller impediments like pigs. The cow catcher is a countermeasure to the cow, with its own counter-countermeasure—the pig. Similarly, if one has a surefire material that plugs the air inlet to an internal combustion engine (like sand in a sandstorm), typically only a small modification to the filter system will impede this NLW and allow it to be ignored.

It is important to note that it is not only the opponent in warfare who needs to develop these countermeasures. They will be available commercially from freelance suppliers the world over, just as are Teflon-coated bullets for piercing body armor. If the weapon is kept secret, countermeasures may be avoided for some months after first use (and forever, in some regions), but secrecy imposes difficulty on training and dissemination of the technique.

It is often much easier to conceive of nonlethal weapons that would be effective against our own capabilities than against the typically simpler equipment that might be encountered in intervention. Anyone with spectacles entering a building in cold weather envies those who manage without glasses, and mechanically fired weapons are immune from electromagnetic pulse weapons in a way in which electrically operated ones are not. The high performance required of airborne equipment like helicopters imposes large penalties from additional filters, shields against infrared emission, and the like, so that U.S. helicopters in the Iran hostage rescue operation were disabled by a sandstorm that a camel would have walked through.

In similar fashion, the United States worried for years that Soviet aircraft with vacuum tube airborne electronics—"avionics"—would be immune to electromagnetic pulse from space nuclear

explosions, while our aircraft with solid-state avionics would succumb. In the present context of NLW used in intervention, if
material and not people are the sole targets, an adversary with
only people and almost no material may well be immune to most
of the NLW.

Unique Characteristics for Intervention?

In discussing NLW for "intervention" we may ask whether such
technologies need to be developed specifically for that purpose.
This is an important question. If NLW are effective and economical, they could be used in large-scale war either independently of
lethal force or to enhance the use of lethal force, putting their
development into the mainstream of defense needs, rather than
have it dependent on the perhaps lesser justification of support of
intervention.

For instance, if trucks and tanks can be reliably disabled in large
numbers by an EMP weapon, which will effectively flood large
areas, why bother to hunt them out and to kill them one by one?
Furthermore, if they can be disabled in this way for a time, it
would be extremely useful in preparation for finding and destroying the vehicles in the normal lethal manner. For instance, tear
"gas"—in Vietnam used by the United States as the volatile pow-
der CS-2—was used as an adjunct to lethal force to prevent combatants from hiding in bunkers or caves; if they came out shooting,
they were shot or burned in return, and if they came out not
shooting, that was often the result in any case.

The point is that NLW would have a lot of use in plain old
conventional warfare. If so, the relative paucity of NLW at present
might be the result of the lack of effective NLW technology. Alternatively, it might result from bureaucratic deficiencies.

It might be that even if NLW are too costly either in themselves
or in the required delivery capability to pay their way in conventional warfare, they might still be extremely valuable in intervention, where the "CNN effect" puts a great premium on minimizing or eliminating casualties, particularly among noncombatants.
Where else would minimizing casualties, especially among bystanders, be useful? At least as great a premium is placed upon law

enforcement operations, in which the culprits or suspects are often to be found among a much larger number of innocent people in an urban environment; this makes it unpopular to use large-scale lethal force against the suspects, as empirically demonstrated in the operation against the MOVE group in Philadelphia. Furthermore, the ratio of good bystanders to bad guys is usually far more in our favor in law enforcement, as exemplified by Waco, than in an intervention; so there is every interest in achieving the benefits for law enforcement claimed for NLW in warfare. Aside from flash-bang grenades, NLW for law enforcement are conspicuous by their absence. Perhaps this is due to a lack of national technical support for law enforcement, even for the FBI, or to bureaucratic incompetence.

To take a specific example, it would be useful to: (a) be able to monitor the walkie-talkie used by a group of miscreants, (b) at a certain time, locally jam, reliably, their radio communication, and (c) at the same time provide a very high level of acoustic noise so that they could not communicate with one another verbally (except by shouting in the ear). Countermeasures are obvious, including ear plugs, alternate frequencies, and the like. If such a group prepares itself for conflict by acquiring appropriate weapons and concealment, it also could readily stock earplugs if they made a difference, and *if* it were common knowledge that acoustic NLW were an important U.S. asset.

Police in a highway chase should prefer to be able to disable the ignition system of the fleeing vehicle by means of a directed microwave burst, or to glue it to the road. Because of a favorable ratio of good guys to bad guys, the police would have much more opportunity to use such a weapon (if it were practical) than would be available in a typical intervention. There is, of course, a problem of aggregating the market. Each local police force does not develop its own NLW, but one would imagine that the equipment suppliers would have this in mind, and in any case there is a substantial FBI or DEA activity that could be a central resource for such things. They would be valuable, just as similar capabilities in the case of intervention. Indeed, "flash-bang" NLW, widely used in hostage rescue operations, could be supplemented by instantaneously deployed obscurant smokes, lights, and screens.

In the wake of Waco, the attorney general requested both the CIA and the Defense Department to assist with an NLW capability. I judge this an important means to provide new tools for law enforcement, and at the same time to validate and improve NLW for intervention or for use in warfare.

Discussion

Recently, I have talked a good deal with Russian and Chinese scientists and technologists. As a result, I believe that U.S. programs to investigate or develop a given military technology have a profound impact on the decisions of our potential adversaries. Mimicry is a much more powerful force than logic, and what we do affects what others do. So I reject the view that if we do not develop something, others will if they think it is in their interest to do so. Sometimes they will, but often they will not.

On the other hand, we have often had our heads in the sand. For decades we fielded military helicopters and aircraft with no countermeasures against attack by hand-held homing infrared-guided missiles such as our own Red-eye or the Soviet SA-7. The fact that there was no conflict and we therefore did not need such protection is hardly compelling; absent a conflict, we did not need the aircraft either.

Looking ahead to an era in which we will have possessed NLW for a long time, together with requisite countermeasures, we need to be cognizant of the fact that as new generations of more effective or convenient NLW come into the inventory the old ones will become surplus. They will trickle down to allies and even to the world munitions market. Although some seem to believe that because we have 1980s nuclear weapons, we should not much care whether others have 1960s-era nuclear weapons, that is clearly not so, and the decision to field an NLW on our part must not commit "the fallacy of the last move" to which Herbert F. York, former director of the Lawrence Livermore Nuclear Weapons Laboratory, ascribed much of the responsibility for the U.S.–USSR nuclear arms race. He cautions that one must not calculate the benefit of acquiring a capability on the basis that the United States has it, and no one else does. The benefit of exclusive possession is often positive, but the balance swings negative when both sides (or the world) have the new weapon.

Maiming Weapons

Perhaps the simplest kind of nonlethal weapon is a pulsed laser that will cause blindness to the unaided eye. Full protection against such lasers can of course be obtained simply by not opening the eye, and substantial protection by opening the eyes only very occasionally or with a limited field of view. Provisions to counter simple countermeasures would add complication, but even the simpler laser blinding weapons would be effective against those who did not adopt the countermeasures.

Some advocate the use of maiming weapons even in preference to lethal weapons with arguments like "killing a person removes a single individual from the battle; blinding a person removes at least two—the casualty and the person who has to tend for him or her." The argument is doubly defective: if an otherwise functional person is sidelined, that person will be eventually transported to a noncombat area, and then fed, educated to take care of himself or herself, and the like. It will not take one attendant per blinded person. But since the person is of no use as a combatant, why not leave him or her to be cared for by the United States? In that case, if it really did take one person to care for this blind person, for each such casualty we inflicted on the other side we would sideline one of our own people.

The United States would suffer from the political consequences of TV coverage of the maimed adversary, from our own casualties inflicted by laser blinding weapons, and (in the case of close conflict as is typical of intervention) by the burden of caring for the wounded of the other side. We can do something about this prospect.

Policy Questions

Dual-Use Weapons

By dual use in this context I mean weapons that are used in riot control and against criminals on the domestic scene, and thus might be perfected and practiced domestically and thus be available for use in warfare. In general, there are many nonweapon technologies that are used this way, ranging from clothing to vehicles to information technology, and there is no reason not to use in warfare those items that are used in this way domestically.

The statement has implications for the development of weapons, since there is a dual benefit to be obtained, both for law enforcement and for military use. Thus there should be coordination and, in many cases, dual funding, so that each of the sponsoring organizations (and this includes not only the federal government, but states for law enforcement) would feel that it has a stake in the technology. In the category of dual-use weapons would be acoustic weapons, anesthetic darts, less lethal bullets, and tear gas, among others. If the technology is such that the effect does not depend on surprise, and thus that the technology is not seriously compromised by use, development and employment in law enforcement are highly desirable. Such development would provide the opportunity for incremental improvement that has brought such an evolution in consumer goods.

Nonlethal weapons need not be perfectly effective to be valuable. An epidemic can be quenched or prevented without curing or vaccinating each and every individual, it is only necessary that the product of the probability of encounter and the probability of transfer of the agent be reduced to be less than unity for an epidemic to be impossible to start, or to die out once it has started. Similarly in human behavior, a curfew cannot reasonably be expected to keep everyone off the streets at night, but it may sufficiently reduce the numbers so that social interactions that might lead to riot no longer do so. Inhibiting mobility by a nonlethal agent may mimic a curfew in this regard.

Improved Less Lethal Military Weapons

By this I do not necessarily mean weapons that are not lethal at all, but those that have greatly suppressed collateral damage potential. This could involve not only increased accuracy and the corresponding lower explosive yield, but also provisions to dispose of the weapon without exploding it. One could incorporate a "good-guidance" signal, so that the weapon would not explode or probably even continue to strike its target unless it receives continued assurance that it has been properly guided.

Among the nonlethal or less lethal weapons that are closest to field use are darts the size of common steel phonograph needles, equipped with tiny tail fins and bearing a load of systemic anesthetic such as fentanyl, which has a particularly large ratio between lethal dose and effective dose.

Arms Control to Support National Security

Laser blinding weapons are relatively low technology, and will proliferate by manufacture and sale by industry the world over if they are regarded as effective. This was apparent by the time the laser was demonstrated in 1960, and the Military Aircraft Panel of the president's Science Advisory Committee soon thereafter raised the policy question of an arms control initiative, proposing that the United States government take the lead in calling for an international convention to ban the use of battlefield lasers that would blind participants. Unfortunately, this proposal was not adopted, and it is reported that the United States government stood aside from international effort to this end.

There is certainly a policy question that should be addressed as soon as possible, preferably in the Clinton administration, as to the trade-off between the loss of international and domestic support for the armed forces, on the one hand, and an increase in effectiveness that would result from U.S. use of battlefield blinding or other maiming weapons. It is unrealistic to believe that a ban on laser blinding weapons would actually eliminate them worldwide, but if banned, blinding lasers would be made in much smaller numbers by outcast operations. It would, therefore, be much easier to keep track of them by normal intelligence means than if they were legitimate articles of commerce.

I believe that we are extremely vulnerable to such weapons and that it would be highly undesirable for the United States to legitimize them by their possession by our military or by our use of laser blinding weapons. We have a lot to gain by an initiative to ban them, coupled with a unilateral declaration that we will not use them first. In early 1994 the International Committee for the Red Cross announced an initiative to ban laser blinding weapons. Such a move would serve the security interests of the United States; we ought to consider arms control in conjunction with other weapons as well.

Secrecy

The defense against some weapons (lethal or nonlethal) is so simple that their effectiveness would be lost if they were once used, or if information about them leaked to begin with—for instance, as a result of the training of U.S. troops with countermeasures to these weapons. This fragile effectiveness is not an absolute argument against the acquisition of such weapons, but rather a caution that their value is limited largely to the utility of their first use. Two conclusions follow—first, that secrecy may be relatively more important for some NLW programs than for more conventional weapons, and second, that weapons that are more robust may be preferable, even if they are somewhat less effective.

Recommendations for Development

One problem in adapting technologies to the military purpose is the very long time scale of military planning, in which (ideally!) the evolution of doctrine is supposed to call forth technology, organization, and tactics, all carefully worked out in experimental units, which then result in a major development and procurement program and the outfitting of the entire force. This "arsenal" approach has been demonstrated empirically on the commercial scene in the United States and the world over to be inadequate in the 1990s. Central direction cannot compete with the freedom to fail and the rewards of success in an open technical and changing marketplace. Although military confrontation is not so cruel and definite an arbiter as is commercial competition—since a 10 percent or 20 percent increase in overall cost compared with benefit is scarcely discernible on the military stage—there is a lesson here, and not just for nonlethal weapons applied to intervention.

What is responsible for the demise of the once-proud system of military arsenals and development?

The information technologies have been evolving more rapidly on the commercial side than in the military, particularly in those areas driven by individual choice and experience—for instance, in personal computers and cellular communications. As a result, the technical leadership of the Department of Defense now properly emphasizes commercial, off the shelf (COTS) technology, in the expectation of better value and function in any year than would be available in specially developed military items. Of course, there are strictly military innovations—prominent among which are Stealth technology, some aspects of camouflage, and certain implementations of information and microcircuitry in hit-to-kill weapons—for which we can't depend on the consumer market.

The combination of Stealth, intimate knowledge about the air defense system and the resulting defense suppression made possible by that knowledge, and the laser-guided bomb (LGB) made an enormous impact in the war against Saddam Hussein. The combination was not developed as a system. For instance, the LGB was taken from the weapon used in Vietnam; in fact, some 40,000 LGBs were used in that conflict, beginning in 1969, while only about 10,000 were used in the Gulf War. Of course, substantial improvement had been made in the interim, and the LGBs used in Iraq were almost invariably targeted against a spot designated by laser from the same aircraft at high altitude. This precision delivery capability for various payloads, including lethal high-explosive, is both a competitor and a potential basis for nonlethal weapons; such precision is now available by appropriate use of the Global Positioning System (GPS) navigation satellite system, with accuracy of a meter or less against fixed targets, and without the necessity of target designation during the strike.

Hit-to-kill weapons themselves may be regarded in a certain sense as nonlethal or less-than-lethal weapons, in that a single weapon may replace hundreds of weapons of similar explosive yield, achieving both greater effectiveness and enormous reduction in collateral damage. Indeed, in the discussion of nonlethal weaponry, too little attention is paid to a competing concept: improving the effectiveness and reducing the unwanted damage from lethal weapons, which would enable them to be used in an essentially nonlethal fashion. One example is the suggestion that a cruise missile or other precision delivery vehicle carry an electromagnetic pulse generator to within a few feet of a commercial TV or radio broadcast antenna, to disable the transmitter by the impulse powered by explosive in the missile. It has even been suggested that damage caused by the explosive itself would be a "bonus." But it would be much easier and more reliable to destroy the antenna itself with a small explosive charge, or with a cable or bar carried by the weapon, without depending on the intermediary of the pulse generator.

As in any development activity, one needs to choose among potential candidates for development and deployment of nonlethal weapons. This should be done, as always, by analysis. There needs to be some incentive for individuals to propose systems and to analyze their potential, and then for the customer (or the venture capitalist) to choose the most effective or the most profitable. Too often, in every field ranging from nuclear power to propulsion to conventional weapons to laser weapons, a kind of Gresham's Law operates, so that systems for which exaggerated claims are made are likely to be supported to the exclusion of those that have real but modest merit.

The process is imperfect in the commercial world, in part because of the difficulty in capturing the benefit of innovation and the related lack of adequate effort devoted to analysis and choice. As regards the U.S. military, the scale of overall procurement and operation is large enough to support the creation and use of a system of analysis, but massive political and bureaucratic influence impede the process. It is often stated that secrecy, in itself, prevents effective and objective choice, but in my experience the matter is more nuanced; some of the best programs I have seen have been highly secret, but large enough and with sufficient internal integrity that they were able to do the job of providing options and making choices without some of the impediments of our open system.

Some have proposed that a nonlethal weapon directorate in the Pentagon is essential to the development and acquisition of nonlethal weapons, but I don't believe that such an office would be appropriate or useful. If one believes that the Department of Defense can make useful choices among lethal weapons, then it should also be able to make useful choices among NLW. If it cannot do the first, then that problem should be fixed, because it is more important than an NLW initiative.

In fact, exploratory development and demonstration of the key elements of a technology are typically not very costly—below $1 million in many cases. There are fundamental limits that can be taken into account in interactive analysis between a would-be supplier and an informed potential customer. For instance, if one contemplates the use of the magnetic field of an electromagnetic wave to erase all computer floppy disks within an area of interest, this could be done readily only against those floppies that were not enclosed in even simple metal cases or storage boxes. It is easy enough to figure the amount of energy that would need to be radiated in a pulse to erase floppies in a region, say, one kilometer across and one kilometer deep.[1]

It is also simple enough to determine the size of the antenna that would need to be coupled to the explosive generator and pulse conditioner to radiate the signal, and all of this can be done before there is any expenditure on hardware or experiment. At the same time, the effectiveness and cost of countermeasures could be explored (without any necessity to have an experimental prototype NLW of this nature). This exploration could be done in a few days in a small lab.

Only when an NLW passes the early screening test should any significant expenditure (substantially more than $1 million) be committed to it. One could thus afford to do the exploratory development on hundreds of technologies if one had a responsive development system that could continuously evaluate and choose among ongoing programs, rather than be fitted to the Procrustean bed of the annual budget and preparations therefore. My point is not to set a firm limit of $1 million below which any exploratory NLW can be conducted, but simply to indicate the scale of expenditure that can typically result in dropping a concept or preparing a substantiated proposal for a full development program.

When a lot of people in organizations make their living by development rather than by the sale of hardware, "fly before buy" may protect against large purchases of things that do not work, but it does not necessarily do much to obtain things that *do* work in a timely and responsive manner. As a result of the astounding evolution of the information technologies ubiquitous in the personal computer and high-performance (computer) workstation, the GPS navigation system, fiber-optic and radio communication at high data rate, and the elements of "virtual reality," it is now not only possible but widely accepted in the Department of Defense to use simulation and modeling in the exploration, evaluation, and refinement of new weapon options. Such an approach contributed greatly to the evolution and perfection of the military capability used by the United States to such good effect in the Gulf War, and simulation and modeling in turn received a big stimulus as a result.

Too often in the past, effort and time were expended on development and demonstration of technical achievement of a novel technology without asking in a disciplined fashion about the utility and value the technology would have to the consumer even if it worked as claimed. In many cases it was apparent that even if the development succeeded technically, the approach was "dominated" in the economic sense by an existing capability or by an alternative—meaning that another approach was cheaper or did the set of jobs better. Adding to the difficulty of analysis is the fact that different approaches are applicable to somewhat different sets of circumstances or scenarios, and proponents of one approach are likely to choose that one circumstance in which their horse has unique or superior performance, to the exclusion of other more likely or more important circumstances.

With the advent of useful simulation and modeling of some actual force engagements has come the recognition of the greater value of those approaches that lend themselves to modeling. The change is somewhat subtle—for decades the utility of training has been recognized, but the nature of combat was such that training and evaluation were difficult and unrealistic. Rather than optimize hoped-for combat effectiveness without the ability to train for combat or to document its effectiveness, it is worthwhile to settle for combat organizations and methods that can be analyzed and for which one can train realistically. Rather than "train the way you fight" (which may be difficult and dangerous), "fight the way you train" offers more assured performance and puts a premium on those approaches that do lend themselves to simulation and training in a realistic and economical fashion. Hence the emphasis on "video game" war. This emphasis on analysis, modeling, and training more readily accommodates new ways of achieving old effects—destroyed tanks, silenced radars, and so on—than it does new effects themselves. How and in what direction new effects (as from nonlethal weapons) influence military and political goals is an important question; I regret not having addressed it in this discussion.

As for effective and timely development mechanisms, the contrast with the past is striking. A task force on advanced tactical fighter aircraft that I chaired for the Defense Department in 1968 recommended a modular approach with competition (and flight test) of mix-and-match airframes, engines, and avionics. This was to satisfy both Air Force and Navy needs for new fighters, while providing at every step the virtues of competition and the assurance of multiple potential sources of supply; it was the right solution a quarter century ago. In the 1990s incremental development and choice of subsystems already proven in commercial activity can largely replace such special purpose programs. In short, COTS is replacing "fly before buy." This new system of incremental development, on the one hand, and system configuration from available elements by reliance on simulation and modeling should be used to evaluate, choose, and train for the combined use of nonlethal and more conventional weapons.

Conclusion

We have discussed a number of concepts for nonlethal weapons, ranging from those aimed like a rifle against specific antagonists (darts, stickum) to those that affect a whole region or society. The first type has less hazard to bystanders and, in most cases, less permanent damage. Such weapons are, therefore, expected to be more politically acceptable to the United States and world populace. Those weapons with broader effects have much in common with a blockade or other sanctions, typically affecting the populace as a whole.

The potential for use of nonlethal weapons does not resolve the question of legitimacy of interference in the activities of another state, but it reduces its poignancy. Of course, legitimacy is conferred by the exercise of a security guarantee, by action within a coalition, or in support of U.N. activities. But legitimacy is hardly questioned in law enforcement activities, and that should be expected to be a fruitful application and proving ground for assessing those nonlethal weapons that might be used in conflict.

There is much merit in *robust* nonlethal weapons that may be incrementally improved by use in riot control or law enforcement or interventions, without losing effectiveness. Indeed, a truly robust NLW would gain in effectiveness because of its deterrent value.

Like lethal weapons, NLW can have both tactical and strategic effects. On the tactical plane they can reduce or eliminate effective opposition to a U.S. deployment, while on the strategic plane they can influence the decision or the ability of a society, a community, or its leaders to conduct terrorism, to mount an invasion, or to pay its bills. The strategic use has much in common with sanctions or blockade, and effectiveness of an NLW needs to be measured on both of these scales.

Highly effective NLW can be a problem for the rest of the world as well as for the United States; carbon fiber weapons launched by mortars or other means can repeatedly short out power systems, and this can be not just a strategic response by those under attack at the moment but a terrorist or even nihilist tool. If NLW are used by the United States or the forces of "good" in the world, they inevitably will be perfected and sold by arms merchants worldwide. If effective, they will ultimately cause a problem for the United States in interventions, unless we have appropriate countermeasures.

So perhaps even more than in the case of lethal weapons, there will be a measure, countermeasure, counter-countermeasure race.

Strictly nonlethal compulsion might be delivered from afar— something the United States or its allies might be willing to do, even in cases where they are not willing to use lethal force. In this case, response on the ground against U.S. forces is precluded if there are no forces present. Response against hostage communities is possible, however, as is strategic response, with lethal or nonlethal terrorism. Perhaps such use of NLW primarily serves to add a conveniently accessible rung on the lethal escalation ladder.

The same caution applies to the use of NLW on the ground. If the conflict is worth the candle, the other side will respond with lethal weapons and we will not long remain only with NLW.

I recommend that developments of nonlethal weapons be done in the same way as with lethal weapons, navigation systems, and other military technological research and development and procurement. There is a similar necessity for secrecy in many cases, but public discussion can focus on some specific or surrogate technologies—slickum, stickum, irritant, or anesthetic darts.

Finally, like some lethal weapons, some nonlethal weapons appear not to be in the net U.S. interest. For these we ought to consider the possibility of arms control. In particular, I believe that it would aid U.S. security to push for a binding international treaty banning laser blinding weapons.

Notes

[1] Actually, about 3,000 megajoules. High explosive liberates about four megajoules per kilogram, of which it would be unreasonable to imagine more than about 25 percent becoming available in useful form—so about one megajoule per kg into the magnetic field. So 3,000 megajoules would require at least three tons of high explosive.

5

"New" Approaches to Economic Sanctions

KIMBERLY ANN ELLIOTT
AND GARY CLYDE HUFBAUER

Economic sanctions have been imposed on more than 120 occasions thus far in the twentieth century. They have been used in pursuit of a variety of goals, from the weakening of military opponents in the two world wars to settlement of compensation claims between the United States and Ceylon (now Sri Lanka) in the 1960s. They have also taken many forms, encompassing all

KIMBERLY ANN ELLIOTT is a research associate at the Institute for International Economics. She is a coauthor of *Measuring the Costs of Protection in the United States* (1994), *Economic Sanctions Reconsidered* (1990), and *Auction Quotas and United States Trade Policy* (1987), as well as the author (numerous articles on U.S. trade policy and economic sanctions.

GARY CLYDE HUFBAUER is the Reginald Jones Senior Fellow at the Institute for International Economics. Formerly he was the Marcus Wallenberg Professor of International Financial Diplomacy at Georgetown University. From 1977 to 1980 he served as deputy assistant secretary in the U.S. Treasury where he was responsible for trade and investment policy during the Tokyo Round. Previously he was director of the International Tax Staff at the U.S. Treasury. He has published books and articles on international trade, finance, and tax policy, including *NAFTA:*

trade and financial relations in some cases—such as the U.N. embargo of Iraq—and targeting a single product in others—for example, the Australian decision to end uranium sales to France over its nuclear testing policy in the South Pacific. Economic sanctions have been used by large powers and small, as well as by the League of Nations before World War II and the United Nations since. In short, this tool of statecraft has been frequently deployed, and the literature is correspondingly vast.

So, is there anything new to say about economic sanctions? In a 1990 study, *Economic Sanctions Reconsidered,* we documented 116 of these cases, from World War I through 1990.[1] Of those cases, seventy-eight were initiated by the United States, most often alone or with only minor cooperation from its allies. The United Nations, by contrast, was able to garner the needed Security Council support for mandatory sanctions only twice before 1990—comprehensive, but widely violated, trade and financial sanctions against Rhodesia (now Zimbabwe) following the unilateral declaration of independence by the majority white regime in 1965, and an arms embargo against South Africa in 1977.

What may be new is that this pattern has been largely reversed since the end of the cold war. From 1990 through the end of 1993, the United States imposed new unilateral sanctions in only three cases: against Russia and India, and then against China and Pakistan, over missile technology transfers; and against Thailand following the military coup in early 1991. Over the same period, the U.N. has imposed comprehensive trade and financial sanctions against Iraq and the former Yugoslavia, an air traffic and arms embargo against Libya, oil and arms embargoes against Haiti and the UNITA rebels in Angola, and arms embargoes against Liberia and Somalia.

The emergence of the U.N. as a major initiator of economic sanctions reflects the decline of the U.S.–Soviet rivalry, which blocked most Security Council resolutions in the past. The United

An Assessment (1993), *U.S. Taxation of International Income* (1992), *Economics Sanctions Reconsidered* (second edition, 1990), and *Europe 1992: An American Perspective* (1990).

States energetically sponsored most of the U.N. initiatives, so the recent pattern also reflects substitution between unilateral U.S. sanctions and multilateral measures. This chapter explores the extent to which the shifting locus of sanctions activity is likely to continue. It analyzes the circumstances under which unilateral U.S. sanctions might still be useful, and concludes with suggestions as to how the U.N. process for imposing and enforcing multilateral sanctions might be strengthened.

Economic Sanctions as a Foreign Policy Tool

We define economic sanctions as the deliberate, government inspired withdrawal, or threat of withdrawal, of customary trade or financial relations. "Customary" does not mean "contractual"; it simply means levels of trade and financial activity that would likely have occurred in the absence of sanctions. Although the use of economic carrots is probably more prevalent than the use of sticks, for reasons of time and space we generally excluded from our analysis cases in which positive economic incentives (e.g., new aid or credits) have been used to achieve foreign policy goals. For example, this analysis does not treat cases like the negotiations with Ukraine on increasing financial aid in exchange for the surrender of nuclear weapons inherited when the Soviet Union collapsed.

We define foreign policy goals to encompass changes expressly and purportedly sought by the sanctioning state in the political behavior of the target state. We exclude from foreign policy goals the normal realm of economic objectives sought in banking, commercial, and tax negotiations between sovereign states. In other words, possible U.S. sanctions against Japan in retaliation for alleged barriers to U.S. exports would not be covered by this analysis.

Sanctions serve important domestic political purposes in addition to sometimes changing the behavior of foreign states. As David Lloyd George, then a leader of the British political opposition, remarked of the celebrated League of Nations sanctions against Italy in 1935, "They came too late to save Abyssinia [from subjugation by Italy], but they are just in the nick of time to save the [British] Government."[2] The same is true today. What president has not been obsessed with the need to demonstrate leadership, to take initiatives to shape world affairs, or at least to react forcefully to adverse developments? And what president is eager to go to war to make his point? The desire to be seen acting forcefully, but not to precipitate bloodshed, can easily overshadow specific foreign policy goals.

Motivations Behind Sanctions

The United States has deployed sanctions frequently in this century to assert its leadership in world affairs. Figure 1 shows the sharp increase in American use of economic sanctions after World

FIGURE 1.
Trends in the Use of Economic Sanctions

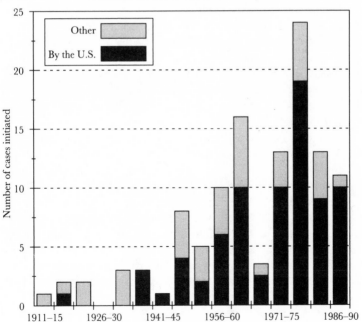

War II, particularly in the 1970s. In addition to seeking to coerce changes in policy, the United States has used sanctions to deter and to punish, and, of course, to "demonstrate resolve."

U.S. presidents seemingly feel compelled to dramatize their opposition to foreign misdeeds, even when the likelihood of changing the target country's behavior seems remote. In these cases sanctions often are imposed because the cost of inaction—in terms of lost confidence (both at home and abroad) in the ability or willingness of the United States to act—is seen as greater than the cost of the sanctions. Indeed, the international community often expects such action from the United States, to demonstrate moral outrage and to reassure the alliance that the United States will stand by its international commitments. The impact of such moral and psychological factors on the decision to impose sanctions should not be underestimated, even if it is hard to document.

Deterrence—the notion that a country can use sanctions to discourage future objectionable policies by increasing the associated costs—is another frequently cited reason for sanctions. In most cases, such as the U.S. sanctions against the Soviet Union over Afghanistan in 1980–81, it is difficult, if not impossible, to determine whether sanctions were an effective deterrent against future misdeeds.

Finally, sanctions are sometimes used as a surrogate for other measures. A diplomatic slap on the wrist may not hit where it hurts, but more extreme measures, such as covert action or military measures, may be excessive or unpopular. Sanctions provide a popular middle road, adding teeth to international diplomacy even when the bark is worse than the bite. But the civil war in Bosnia-Herzegovina is a depressing reminder of how sanctions may also become a symbol of indecision and impotence.

The parallels between the motives for sanctions and the three basic purposes of criminal law—to punish, to deter, and to rehabilitate—are unmistakable. Countries that impose sanctions, like states that incarcerate criminals, may find their hopes of rehabilitation unrealized, but they may nevertheless be satisfied with whatever punishment and deterrence are accomplished, even if the deterrent effect is difficult to establish.

Though these motives are undoubtedly important in explaining the use of sanctions in many cases, the discussion that follows focuses on the utility of this tool of statecraft in changing the policies, capabilities, or government of the target country. In this endeavor, we found it useful in *Economic Sanctions Reconsidered* to classify the case histories into five categories, according to the primary foreign policy objective sought by the country imposing sanctions:

- Change target country policies in a *relatively* modest way (modest in the scale of national goals, but often of burning importance to participants in the episode); this type of goal is illustrated by the human rights, terrorism, and nuclear nonproliferation cases.
- Destabilize the target government (including, as an ancillary goal, changing the target country's policies); this category is illustrated by the U.S. campaigns against Fidel Castro and Panama's strongman, Manuel Noriega, and the Soviet campaign against Marshal Tito in early postwar Yugoslavia.
- Disrupt a *relatively* minor military adventure, as illustrated by the United Kingdom's sanctions against Argentina over the Falkland Islands.
- Impair the military potential of the target country, as illustrated by the sanctions imposed during World Wars I and II, and the Coordinating Committee for Multilateral Export Control (COCOM) sanctions against the Soviet Union and its allies.
- Change target country policies in a major way (including the surrender of territory), as illustrated by the U.N. campaign against South Africa over apartheid, and the Indian sanctions designed to reverse Nepal's pro-China line in 1989–90.

It is apparent from these examples that assigning cases to one or another of the five categories for comparative purposes is inherently subjective. It requires balancing the relative weights that each party places on the policy change being sought, which may be quite different. The policy change also is judged in terms of its importance to the *nations* involved, not just the individuals in power at the time. So, for example, though the Falklands War was quite important to the military junta in Argentina, which fell following Argentina's military defeat, and to the Thatcher government in Britain, it was not critical to the national security or future well-being of either country. In spite of the difficulty of assigning cases to categories, we found this an essential step in analyzing the efficacy of sanctions.

A Brief History of Modern Sanctions

Historically, and through the first half of this century, economic sanctions usually foreshadowed or accompanied warfare. Of the eleven cases identified in our book between 1914 and 1940, all but two were linked to military action, with sanctions usually imposed to disrupt military adventures or to complement a broader war effort. For example, the League of Nations imposed sanctions on Paraguay and Bolivia in the years 1932–35 in a fruitless effort to halt the Chaco war. In July 1940 President Roosevelt restricted U.S. exports to Japan of arms, aluminum, magnesium, airplane parts, optical instruments, and machinery in an effort to slow Japanese military threats against Indonesia. In September the embargo was extended to all grades of iron and steel scrap. In July 1941, following Japan's occupation of Cam Ranh Bay, Roosevelt froze Japanese assets and halted petroleum shipments. The oil embargo was a factor in the Imperial Conference's decision in September 1941 to prepare for war.

Although other foreign policy motives became increasingly common in the period following World War II, sanctions were still deployed on occasion to try to force a target country to withdraw its troops from border skirmishes, to abandon plans of territorial acquisition, or to desist from other relatively minor military adventures. In most of these instances, the United States played the role of international police officer.

Aside from the 1956 Suez incident, however, when the United States pressed the French and the British into withdrawing their troops from Egypt, major powers have never been able to reverse the military adventures of other major powers simply through the use of economic sanctions. In that case, the United States had unusual leverage arising from the scarcity of dollar reserves in Europe, which prevented Great Britain and France from importing oil from the Western Hemisphere to alleviate shortages resulting from blockage of the Suez Canal. But even much smaller countries rarely succumbed to economic pressures intended to disrupt minor military adventures. For example, U.S. sanctions contributed to decisions by Egypt's Gamal Abdel Nasser to withdraw troops from Yemen and cease supporting rebels in the Congo, but failed to deter Indonesia's Sukarno from meddling in Malaysia in 1963 and had little effect on Turkey's intervention in Cyprus in 1974.

Closely related to these military adventure cases are those episodes in which sanctions are imposed to impair the economic capability of the target country, thereby limiting its potential for military activity or foreign adventurism. Cases in this category include the Arab League boycott of Israel, the U.S. embargoes of North Korea and Vietnam, and, most importantly, the broad based multilateral controls on strategic trade that the United States instituted against the Soviet Union and China in the late 1940s. Although COCOM largely succeeded in denying Western arms and key technologies to the Soviet Union and its allies, it is doubtful whether it yielded significant positive foreign policy results, not least because it is difficult to hamper the military capabilities of a major power with marginal degrees of economic deprivation. In other cases, there were opposing major powers, which offset the economic and military impact of the sanctions with their own financial assistance and concessional arms sales. Even when sanctions have significant economic impact, they may have unintended consequences: some historians have suggested that U.S. sanctions against Japan in 1940–41 backfired, inasmuch as they were used by prowar forces as an argument for striking Pearl Harbor.

Increasingly, as the cold war era progressed, the United States used sanctions in pursuit of a number of foreign policy goals not directly related to warfare and national security. Especially noteworthy is the frequent resort to sanctions in an effort to destabilize foreign governments, usually in the context of a foreign policy dispute involving other issues. As documented in our book, the United States engaged in destabilization efforts fourteen times between World War II and 1990, often against other countries in the Western Hemisphere such as Cuba, the Dominican Republic, Nicaragua, Brazil, Chile, and Panama. Many of these episodes involved civil wars or the overthrow of unpopular or weak civilian governments by military elites. Sanctions increased the unpopularity of governments by exacerbating already poor economic performances, and signaled U.S. support for opponents of the regime. Economic sanctions in these cases also frequently were accompanied by supplementary measures, such as covert or quasimilitary support for internal political opponents of the targeted government.

Sanctions contributed at least modestly to the overthrow of Rafael Trujillo in 1961, of Brazilian dictator João Goulart in 1964, and of Chilean President Salvador Allende in 1973; sanctions played a minor role in the electoral defeat of the Sandinistas in Nicaragua in 1990. On the other hand, Cuba under Fidel Castro has not succumbed, despite three decades of U.S. economic pressure, in large measure because Castro (until recently) received compensating aid from the Soviet Union. Likewise, despite costly U.S. economic sanctions, Noriega was able to retain power in Panama; it finally took U.S. military intervention to dislodge him. The Soviet Union also picked on its neighbors, though less successfully. Each time the Soviets used sanctions in an effort to topple a rebellious government within the socialist bloc—Yugoslavia in 1948, China in 1960, Albania in 1961—the effort failed.

Since the early 1960s sanctions have been deployed in support of numerous other foreign policy goals, most of them relatively modest compared to the pursuit of war, peace, and political destabilization. Confrontations with developing countries over their foreign policies and attitudes toward foreign direct investment propelled the use of sanctions in the 1960s. Five of fourteen cases initiated by the United States in this period involved responses to the expropriation of American property. In the 1970s efforts to protect human rights and to halt nuclear proliferation dominated the sanctions agenda. In recent years, that effort has expanded to include controls on technologies potentially contributing to the proliferation of chemical and biological weapons and the means to deliver them, especially ballistic missiles.

Empirical Evidence on the
Effectiveness of Economic Sanctions

The Hufbauer, Schott, and Elliott study had two objectives: first, to provide empirical evidence regarding the utility of sanctions in achieving foreign policy goals; and second, to identify the circumstances in which sanctions are most likely to be effective. Our judgments about success in each case had two parts: the extent to which stated foreign policy goals were achieved, *and* the contribution made to that outcome by sanctions. We then selected for close examination several political and economic variables that we thought would be important in determining the effectiveness of sanctions.

For economic sanctions to succeed, the economic and political costs to the target of the sanctions (and any accompanying policies) must be greater than the costs it expects to incur from complying. A key problem in evaluating the prospects for success, however, is that while the economic costs of defiance can be measured with some degree of confidence, the political costs of compliance cannot be measured in any precise way. In other words, there are concrete trade and financial flows that can be measured and used as a basis for assessing the likely economic impact on the target of sanctions. But the political and strategic implications for the target country of changing its policy to comply with its sanctioner's demands are much harder to measure and assess. A second problem is that the same economic cost, measured as a percentage of gross national product (GNP), may be valued differently by different types of regimes. For example, an authoritarian government may be less responsive to the pain inflicted by economic sanctions than a democratic government whose survival depends on the support of its citizens.

Overall, we found that economic sanctions had contributed to at least partially successful outcomes in 34 percent of the cases studied up to 1990. However, the success rate varied significantly depending on the type of objective sought. Episodes involving destabilization succeeded in half the cases, usually against target countries that were small and shaky. Cases involving modest goals, as defined above, and attempts to disrupt minor military adven-

tures were successful about a third of the time. Efforts to impair a
foreign adversary's military potential, or otherwise to change its
policies in a major way—for example, ending apartheid in South
Africa—succeeded less frequently (23 percent of the time).

Overall, the empirical evidence suggests that sanctions are most
likely to be effective when:

(1) The goal is relatively modest, thus lessening the importance of
    multilateral cooperation, which often is difficult to obtain, and
    reducing the chances that a rival power will bother to step in
    with offsetting assistance.

(2) The target is much smaller than the country imposing sanc-
    tions, and economically weak and politically unstable.

(3) The sanctioner and its target were friendly toward one an-
    other, in a diplomatic sense, prior to the sanctions and con-
    ducted substantial trade with each other (the sanctioner ac-
    counted for 28 percent of the average target's trade in all
    success cases but only 19 percent in failures; in cases involving
    "major" goals, the ratios were 36 percent and 16 percent, re-
    spectively).

(4) The sanctions are imposed quickly and decisively to maximize
    impact (the average cost to the target as a percentage of GNP
    in all success cases was 2.4 percent and 1 percent in failures; in
    cases involving "major" goals, the figures were 4.5 percent and
    0.5 percent, respectively).

(5) The sanctioner avoids high costs to itself.

There is an important caveat to those lessons. If one splits the
case sample roughly in half, into those initiated before 1973 and
those begun between 1973 and 1990, a striking difference emerges.
Almost half the sanctions episodes in the pre-1973 period succeeded, whereas the success rate among the cases begun after 1973
was just under a quarter. The results for cases in which the United
States took a leading role are similar. In the earlier period, just
over 50 percent of U.S. sanctions efforts produced positive results;
between 1973 and 1990 U.S. sanctions have succeeded even partially only 17 percent of the time.

The Declining Utility of U.S. Sanctions

Reflecting its roles as economic hegemon and political and military superpower, the United States in the decades following World War II attempted to impose its will on a wider variety of targets and sought a broader array of objectives than did any other country, including the Soviet Union, which generally confined its use of sanctions to trying to keep rebellious allies in line. Although U.S. goals in sanctions episodes became relatively more modest in the 1970s, and the typical target even smaller and weaker, the United States found that it actually had less leverage than before.

In the early years after World War II, the U.S. economy was the reservoir for rebuilding war-devastated countries. It was also the major if not the sole supplier of a variety of goods and services. Well into the 1960s the United States remained the primary source of economic assistance for developing countries. Since the 1960s, however, trade and financial patterns have grown far more diversified, new technology has spread quickly, and the U.S. foreign aid budget has virtually dried up for all but a few countries. Recovery in Europe and the emergence of Japan have created competitive economic superpowers, while successful development in the Third World has reduced the pool of potentially vulnerable targets. These trends are starkly illustrated by the declining average trade linkage between the United States and its targets (from 24 percent of the target's total trade prior to 1973 to only 17 percent since), and the lower costs imposed on targets (from 1.7 percent of the target's GNP to just 0.9 percent).

Although the relative decline of the U.S. position in the world economy is the most obvious and important explanation of the sharp decline in the effectiveness of U.S. sanctions, the evidence from the cases suggests three other contributing causes. First, there was a sharp increase in the number of sanctions imposed in pursuit of relatively modest objectives, which may have increased the chance of conflict between these efforts and other, higher priority objectives. Although detente allowed the number of cases involving modest goals to multiply, concerns about Soviet influence or strategic position still claimed first priority in the strategic planning of the U.S. government and frequently undermined the pursuit of less central goals. For example, the United States was reluctant to enforce sanctions vigorously against El Salvador, Guatemala, and others for fear of weakening the regimes in power and allowing leftist rebel victories, which would benefit the Soviet Union. It also backed off on sanctions against Pakistan's nuclear program following the Soviet invasion of Afghanistan.

A second and related trend is the growing assertiveness of Congress in foreign policy matters in the past twenty years. The Hickenlooper amendment to the Foreign Assistance Act of 1962 (originally sponsored by Senator Bourke B. Hickenlooper [R-IA]), which prompted executive branch action in many of the expropriation disputes of the 1960s, was a rare example of congressionally mandated economic sanctions in the early postwar period. In the 1970s, however, Congress increasingly forced the president's hand and constrained his discretion in various foreign policy situations by passing legislation requiring the use of economic sanctions. The confused signals sent by administrations that were forced to implement legislatively mandated sanctions may have led target countries to believe, often correctly, that the sanctions would not be sustained.

Third, whereas financial measures—namely, cutting off aid, or slowing International Monetary Fund (IMF) or World Bank loans, or discouraging private lending—were part of the sanctions package in more than 90 percent of episodes prior to 1973, they were present in only two-thirds of the cases after that. In the antiterrorism and nuclear nonproliferation cases in the 1970s and 1980s, denial of key hardware was typically as important as inducing a change in policy, and so selective export controls were the tool of choice. Because alternative suppliers of the sanctioned goods were usually available, both goals proved elusive. For example, U.S. sanctions on uranium sales and nuclear technology exports under the Nuclear Non-Proliferation Act of 1978 largely failed either to slow the development of nuclear programs in Brazil, Argentina, India, Pakistan, or South Africa, or to induce them to sign the Non-Proliferation Treaty or accept full-scope safeguards.

The preferred type of financial sanction also changed in the 1970s. Economic aid was the dominant choice in the earlier period, whereas military assistance was prominent in the later period, especially in the human rights cases, where military governments were often the target. Again, in some cases alternative sources of arms and financial assistance were available. Even more important, the target governments perceived internal dissent to be a greater threat to their longevity than U.S. enmity and sanctions.

Economic Sanctions after the Cold War

The inevitable decline of U.S. hegemony has substantially reduced the utility of unilateral U.S. economic sanctions. Two questions may thus be asked about the future of sanctions. Can anything be done to restore the utility of unilateral U.S. sanctions? Does the U.N. embargo of Iraq presage a new approach to international diplomacy, with multilateral sanctions playing a more important role?

Can Unilateral U.S. Leverage Be Restored?

The collapse of the Soviet Union partially offsets declining American leverage. A significant factor in a number of cases where U.S. sanctions failed was the willingness of the Soviet Union to provide assistance to countries sanctioned by the United States. Soviet support undermined the impact of U.S. sanctions against China, North Korea, Vietnam, and Cuba. For the foreseeable future, however, Russia will not have the resources to play the "black knight" for those countries that seek assistance to offset the impact of U.S. sanctions. Although Libya has sometimes played a black knight role, as has South Africa for Rhodesia and Saudi Arabia for Pakistan, the resources and commitment of potential new black knights are certain to pale beside those of the Soviet Union at the height of the cold war.

Even if black knights go the way of dragons in the 1990s, the scope for unilateral U.S. action will continue to diminish. Changes in the international economy in recent decades have reduced the number of targets likely to succumb to unilateral economic coercion. Many potential targets have developed strong and diversified economies that will never again be as vulnerable as they once were. Even relatively weak economies are less vulnerable today as a result of the growth in world trade and the rapid dispersion of technology, which mean that most U.S. exports can be replaced at little additional cost, and alternative outlets to the large U.S. import market can often be found.

Thus greater economic interdependence would appear to increase the importance of international cooperation in sanctions efforts. Simultaneously, increased competitive pressure from around the world also has diminished the enthusiasm of U.S. policy makers for unilateral economic sanctions. Thus the trends observed in the first four years of this decade—fewer unilateral sanctions and more multilateral sanctions—are likely to continue. But how likely is it that multilateral measures can reverse the decline in the effectiveness of economic sanctions observed over the past twenty years?

U.N. Sanctions: Lessons from Iraq and the former Yugoslavia

Sanctioning countries often seek cooperation when the goal is ambitious. Since major changes in policy are more difficult to achieve than relatively modest objectives, cooperation in most cases will be a necessary but not sufficient condition for success. Multilateral cooperation has often been prized by those who plan economic sanctions. But—as the sanctions against Libya, Serbia, and Haiti show—the end of the cold war guarantees neither that cooperation will be forthcoming, nor that cooperative sanctions will succeed.

For many, the response to Iraq's invasion of Kuwait provided a vision of a post–cold war world in which the United Nations, freed of superpower rivalries, would finally play the peacekeeping role originally intended. The end of the cold war opened the door for an unprecedented degree of international cooperation against Iraq, but the real source of virtual unanimity was the threat to global prosperity and political stability posed by Saddam's aggression. Had the invasion of Kuwait not placed him in control of a large portion of global oil reserves, with an army of 500,000 troops poised on the Saudi Arabian border, it is unlikely that the world would have been so united.

Even with the stakes so high, China was a reluctant participant in many of the U.N. actions against Iraq. China might have blocked those actions, using its veto in the U.N. Security Council, were it not for Beijing's desire to rehabilitate its own international image and see the sanctions imposed after the Tiananmen Square massacre lifted. More recently, China announced in February 1994 that it would not go along with possible U.N. sanctions against North Korea. (Such sanctions were being contemplated if the Kim Il-Sung regime refused to comply with international inspections of its nuclear facilities.) Even if China does not exercise its Security Council veto, an abstention and failure to cooperate would severely undermine any sanctions against North Korea.

The Russian government, which also holds a veto in the Security Council, has come under increasing domestic criticism for going along with the continuation of sanctions against Iraq since the end of the war and for acquiescing in the isolation of Serbia in the Balkan crisis. In both cases, right wing nationalist factions have argued that the government was trying to appease Western powers rather than pursuing Russia's own foreign policy interests. In the future, therefore, Russia may not be as cooperative in supporting U.N. operations as it has been to date.[3]

Though the formal U.N. sanctions against Serbia are quite similar to those imposed against Iraq, the embargo of Iraq remains unique among sanctions efforts in this century. The sanctions were imposed quickly, comprehensively, and with an unprecedented degree of support. The economic embargo was agreed by the U.N. Security Council less than a week after the invasion of Kuwait. Within a month the Council approved the use of naval forces to enforce the sanctions. Within two months, the Security Council had added an air embargo and authorized secondary boycotts of countries violating the resolutions.

By contrast, it was two to three weeks after the outbreak of civil war in Croatia before the European Community (EC) and United States embargoed arms, and several months passed before they suspended aid flows and trade preferences for Serbia. It was three months before the U.N. called on its members to embargo arms shipments, and almost a year after the fighting had begun before comprehensive U.N. sanctions were mandated by the Security

Council. Even then, because the former Yugoslavia serves as a land route for Turkey to Eastern and Central Europe, and because the Danube River enables Eastern and Central Europe to reach open water, the sanctions contained a pragmatic but devastating loophole: the transshipment of goods, including petroleum and products, was permitted through Serbia. By siphoning off transshipments, Serbia was able to maintain vital stocks of fuel and other supplies. Finally, in November 1992, more than a year after the crisis erupted and five months after the sanctions had been mandated, the Security Council approved naval interdiction on the Adriatic to enforce the sanctions, called on Serbia's neighbors to crack down on abuse of the transshipment allowance, and placed U.N. provided customs officers on the ground in neighboring countries to monitor enforcement. Even so, Serbia still draws important supplies from waylaid transshipments.

There were other physical and structural differences that made enforcement of the sanctions against Serbia and Montenegro more difficult than in the Iraq case. Iraq's economy, geographically isolated and skewed toward oil, was far more vulnerable to economic coercion than most countries. Because 90 percent of Iraq's export revenues come from oil, which can be readily monitored and interdicted, sanctions-busting on the export side was largely contained. Moreover, in terms of imports vital to Iraq's economy, smugglers have had less incentive to evade the sanctions as Iraqis exhaust their reserves of cash and tradeable goods.

There is another reason why even the tightest sanctions usually weaken over time: the sender countries may inflict high costs on their own economies, thereby eroding domestic support for the coercive measures. To counter this tendency during the Middle East crisis, the United States and its allies went to extraordinary lengths to ameliorate the costs of oil shortages, especially for the hardest hit members of the sanctions coalition. Saudi Arabia and other oil exporters boosted oil production to offset losses from Iraqi and Kuwaiti production. In addition, the United States took the lead in organizing an "economic action plan" to recycle the short-term windfall profits gained by the Saudis and other oil producers, and to encourage Japan, Germany, and others to provide grants and low-cost loans to developing countries hurt by higher oil prices, and lost trade and workers' remittances. The International Monetary Fund and World Bank provided concessional loans to developing countries suffering balance of payments stresses because of the sudden jump in oil prices.

There is no provision in the Serbian case for secondary sanctions and no compensation scheme for countries severely injured by enforcing the sanctions. In early 1994 Hungarian diplomats reportedly "complained bitterly" in meetings in Geneva about the high cost of the sanctions for their own economy, which they estimated at $1.3 billion. The lack of financial assistance for severely affected frontline states such as Hungary threatened to unravel the sanctions coalition.[4] Both the carrot and the stick would have been helpful early in the crisis to limit abuse of the transshipment allowance on the Danube and to reinforce the sanctions spirit in neighboring countries.

Despite their economic effectiveness, President George Bush concluded that economic sanctions alone would not be sufficient to force an Iraqi withdrawal from Kuwait within an acceptable period of time. Whether Bush's conclusion that military force was needed was correct can never be definitively known. But the embargo of Iraq, buttressed by military threats in some instances, largely succeeded in achieving the U.N.'s postwar goals of dismantling Saddam Hussein's weapons of mass destruction and forcing him to accept, however grudgingly, international monitoring to ensure those capabilities are not rebuilt.

The much leakier sanctions against Serbia and Montenegro did little to influence the course of the civil war in Bosnia. Besides the greater enforcement challenge, the U.N. had a more difficult task than in Iraq because the sanctions were expected to work indirectly—by squeezing Slobodan Milosevic who, in turn, would pressure the Serbs in Bosnia. By the time the sanctions began to impose real pain, Bosnian Serb forces were already in control of a large part of Bosnia and were less dependent on assistance from Serbia to press their remaining territorial claims. In early 1994 Milosevic reportedly was desperate to get the sanctions lifted, but by then, the options available to the Bosnian Muslims and would-be peacemakers in the West were severely circumscribed.

Comparing the chronologies of these two cases reveals much

about the difficulties in organizing and maintaining international cooperation. Comparing the results as of early 1994 supports the conclusion from the earlier history that economic sanctions are most likely to achieve foreign policy goals when they are imposed quickly, comprehensively, and decisively. At the same time, these cases and others have raised concerns about the effects of sanctions on the poor and powerless, and have stimulated questions as to whether more targeted sanctions could achieve positive results at a lower human cost.

Can Sanctions Be Effectively "Targeted"?

The impact of the U.N. sanctions on the impoverished nation of Haiti, in addition to reports of increased death and disease from sanctions-induced shortages of food and medicines in Iraq, have led many observers to ask whether more finely tuned sanctions could be both more effective in changing target country behavior and less devastating to innocent civilians. In this context, two issues must be analyzed. First, can a sanctions package be fashioned so as to hit political, military, and economic elites, but not innocent civilians? Second, can more narrowly targeted measures improve the utility of economic sanctions in achieving foreign policy goals?

The U.S. General Accounting Office (GAO) in a 1992 study concluded that the "ability to use sanctions as a precision instrument to pressure certain population groups in the target nation while exempting others is very limited." The GAO noted:

Sanctions are a blunt instrument and have many collateral adverse effects. Sanctions imposed on one sector of an integrated economy will spill over into other sectors. Furthermore, the target government can take measures to help redirect the costs of sanctions from groups that support it to groups that oppose it or are politically weak.[5]

The wisdom in the GAO's analysis is underscored by the Iraq case. It would have been possible to target just Iraq's oil exports and not impose any sanctions on Iraq's imports. But because of Iraq's extreme dependence on that one commodity, a boycott of Iraqi oil exports alone would inevitably have exerted a severe impact throughout the economy as industrial firms and households were denied the foreign exchange to purchase vital imports.

Similar observations can be made about oil sanctions against oil importing countries. Take North Korea, for example. Because of its ideological emphasis on autarkic economic development, North Korea imports only products that are essential to keep the economy running. It has no oil reserves of its own and must import whatever is needed to meet energy demands that cannot be met with domestic coal. An oil embargo might have sufficient impact on the Kim Il-Sung regime to convince it to allow inspections of its nuclear facilities. This sanction would also have a severe impact on the people of North Korea, however, perhaps even resulting in the collapse of an economy that is already tottering.

Given the dependence of today's modern industrial economy on petroleum and its products, sanctions affecting oil might be expected to be fairly effective in foreign policy terms. This was the thinking behind oil embargoes that were proposed or implemented against Italy (1936), Japan (1940–41), Rhodesia (1966), South Africa (1973), the United States and the Netherlands (1973), and Haiti (1993). Whatever their effectiveness in foreign policy terms, however, oil embargoes are unlikely to leave the broad populace unaffected, as can be seen in Haiti. The adverse impact on the populace at large reflects not only the fact that oil is an essential input to wide swaths of a modern economy; it also reflects the fact that political elites can usually redistribute the burden of sanctions on imported or exported commodities so that innocent civilians bear most of the cost.

Other than arms embargoes and export controls on technology that might be used in the development of missiles or nuclear, chemical, or biological weapons, it is difficult to think of targeted trade controls that primarily affect political and military elites. Selective trade sanctions are also harder to enforce than sanctions covering all trade. Goods get mislabeled; close substitutes are found for items on the embargo list; and dual-use items, such as heavy trucks, find their way into military hands as troop carriers. In the case of dual-use items, it is often difficult to get agreement on where to draw the line between technologies representing significant potential threats that should be controlled and those that should not. Another problem is that political and military elites usually can manage to live without the newest arms or best technology if necessary.

Certain financial sanctions, on the other hand, may be more likely to hit the pet projects or personal pockets of government officials and economic elites who could influence policy. When financial sanctions are put in place, alternative financing may be hard to find and is likely to carry a much higher price (i.e., sharply higher interest rates) and require far greater credit security because of the uncertainties. In addition, financial sanctions, especially those involving trade finance, may interrupt a wide range of trade flows even without the imposition of explicit trade sanctions. On the sanctioning country's side of the equation, an interruption of official aid or export credits is unlikely to create the same political backlash from business firms as a direct interruption of private trade.

Historically, the most common type of financial sanction is the interruption of official development assistance. Although Export-Import Bank financing, multilateral development bank loans, and other forms of official and private credit have been linked to political goals from time to time, the majority of cases involve the manipulation of bilateral economic and military assistance to developing countries. Development assistance usually is intended to improve the lot of the average citizen, but in the short run it benefits primarily the government officials who gain prestige and popularity from dispensing it. If a government is corrupt, which is often the case when sanctions are contemplated, key officials also suffer direct financial losses when aid flows are interrupted. These observations must be set against the fact that the U.S. foreign assistance budget has been trimmed to the bone for all but a few countries. In most areas of the world, there is no remaining leverage from cutting U.S. bilateral assistance.

In recent years there has been a greater willingness on the part of the international financial institutions (IFIs), including the World Bank, the International Monetary Fund, and others, to condition loans on political factors, especially when corruption erodes the effectiveness of IFI funding. While the IFIs are prohibited by their charters from manipulating funds for political purposes, in fact, through such means as consideration of project loans, slowed disbursement, and structural lending, political factors do find their way into the process. However, this potential source of leverage is usually used in a muted fashion in deference to sensitivities within the governing councils of the IFIs.

Sanctions on other financial flows, such as private international lending or assets freezes, may buttress trade sanctions. For example, asset freezes and other financial sanctions that restricted Iraq's access to international capital markets, coupled with an oil boycott, would have been nearly equivalent to the comprehensive trade sanctions imposed on Iraq by the U.N. Security Council. The resulting shortage of foreign exchange would eventually have prevented Iraq from buying goods in international markets even without an explicit U.N. ban on Iraqi imports. But this degree of effectiveness requires that the target country export a limited range of commodities that can be relatively easily controlled, so that it cannot offset financial sanctions with foreign exchange from increased merchandise exports. Comprehensive financial sanctions also often require the cooperation of numerous private banks located in such havens as Switzerland, Luxembourg, Cayman Islands, Hong Kong, and elsewhere. Securing their cooperation is not always easy.

Moreover, in the Iraq case and others, targeted financial sanctions do not necessarily exempt innocent civilians from their effects. Returning to the North Korean example, since North Korea's exports are insufficient to pay for its imports, other sources of foreign exchange—aid, foreign investment, and remittances from North Koreans living in Japan—are critical to its ability to supplement domestic sources of energy and food. Financial sanctions targeting those flows would just as likely inflict severe economic distress as trade sanctions.

A counterexample is the Haitian case, where carefully crafted financial sanctions, swiftly applied, might have captured the attention of the economic elite, without whose support the military would not be able to rule. The Haitian elite keeps little of its wealth in Haiti and enjoys spending time and money in the United States and Europe. A global assets freeze, coupled with a travel ban, would have hit primarily that class. Moreover, because the distribution of income is so skewed in Haiti, very little of the wealth concentrated at the top trickles down, and it would be difficult for the economic elite to shift the burden of targeted financial sanctions to other Haitians, who already are barely subsisting.

Unfortunately, the gradual, partial, and on-again off-again nature of the sanctions did not provide a fair test of the finely tuned approach. Initially, only members of the Organization of American States imposed sanctions—allowing Haiti to continue trading with Europe, Asia, and Africa—but those sanctions were not enforced with any vigor. Moreover, these limited sanctions were further weakened a few months into the crisis when President Bush, under pressure from American firms with investments in Haiti, exempted duty-free imports from Haitian assembly operations. The U.N. oil and arms embargoes were imposed, then lifted, then imposed again when the Haitian military did not implement the Governor's Island agreement for stepping down as promised. Throughout, substantial smuggling reportedly occurred across Haiti's border with the Dominican Republic.

Despite the flawed execution of Haitian sanctions, we entertain some hope that, where the income distribution is very skewed and the economic elite very narrow, targeted financial sanctions, accompanied by restrictions on travel, might influence governmental behavior with limited impact on the populace at large. It is difficult, however, to identify other circumstances where targeted sanctions could have sufficient impact to influence policy without also affecting innocent civilians. Furthermore, it must be considered whether targeted sanctions are so limited that they undermine the political credibility of the sanctioning coalition.

Finally, the empirical evidence suggests that targeted sanctions are typically less likely to achieve the sanctioner's objectives. We find that limited sanctions that only affect tenths of a percent of GDP are usually ineffective. We also find that a progressive expansion of targeted sanctions—a gradual "turning the screws" strategy—gives the targeted country time to adjust—to find alternative markets or suppliers if the sanctions are not multilateral, to stockpile key commodities, or to move liquid financial assets to safe havens. A gradual approach is also likely to lengthen the amount of time required for a response since the target will wait to see if the screws are tightened as promised. If the threatened escalation does not occur—because of intra-alliance differences or domestic political opposition—the sanctions not only drag on longer, they may be fatally undermined. In fact, a "hit 'em hard, hit 'em fast" strategy that maximizes both the short-run economic impact on the target country and the political credibility of the sanctioning country can be the most humane course if it accelerates resolution of the situation. For exactly these reasons, Randall Robinson in 1994 recommended not a relaxation, but a tightening of the sanctions against Haiti.[6]

Conclusions and Recommendations

The evidence from nearly 100 years of experience with sanctions indicates that economic leverage is most likely to contribute to the achievement of foreign policy goals when the objective is relatively modest. The more ambitious the goal, the greater the economic pain that is likely to be necessary to induce the desired response. This, in turn, increases the importance of international cooperation so that all or most of the target country's trade and financial flows will be covered by sanctions. Also, the broader the coalition imposing sanctions, the less likely that a third country will offer offsetting assistance to the target. Finally, both economic impact and political credibility are enhanced when sanctions are imposed quickly and decisively. This may shorten the time that sanctions have to be in place, which considerably eases enforcement problems, not least by minimizing the costs to the countries imposing the sanctions.

Increasing economic interdependence around the world spells the decline of unilateral economic sanctions as an effective tool of U.S. foreign policy. The United States no longer possesses sufficient leverage to coerce any but the smallest or most dependent countries, and even then the Haiti and Panama cases suggest that only modest objectives may be within reach. The debate in the spring of 1994 over whether to renew China's most-favored-nation (MFN) status illustrates many of the dilemmas the United States faces in using economic leverage. History offers few examples of large countries that succumbed to economic pressure in foreign policy disputes. Withdrawing China's MFN would also entail large costs for the U.S. economy, not just for American consumers, who would have to pay more for clothing and other items previously supplied by China, but also for U.S. exporters, because China would almost certainly retaliate. Moreover, these costs would grow over time as Airbus replaced Boeing and Komatsu replaced Caterpillar, because America's allies have indicated no support for U.S. sanctions in this case.

Nevertheless, unilateral economic sanctions will continue to serve the political and diplomatic purposes of demonstrating resolve and seeking to deter and punish objectionable behavior. Both to provide some discipline on such sanctions so that their effectiveness is not eroded by overuse, and for reasons of equity, Congress should consider mandating compensation for the domestic firms that shoulder the burden of unilateral sanctions. When sanctions are imposed multilaterally and comprehensively, the international competitive effects are evened out and the domestic burden is more fairly distributed; under these circumstances, compensation might be authorized but not mandated, depending on the severity of the injury.

Recognizing, however, that U.S. leverage is declining, and that unilateral sanctions undermine American competitiveness, U.S. policy makers have turned increasingly to the United Nations for support. Simply securing a Security Council resolution is not sufficient, however. Details in implementing and enforcing economic sanctions make all the difference. There are two additional supplementary measures for evening out the international burden that play a role in enhancing the effectiveness of multilateral sanctions. First, any U.N. sanctions resolution passed should also mandate "secondary sanctions" against members violating the "primary sanctions." An independent monitoring capability should also be established to identify sanctions busters. Currently, the U.N. must rely on member governments to report or to confirm sanctions violations. Second, as in the domestic case, there are practical and equity reasons for providing compensation to countries that are particularly hard hit economically from enforcing sanctions. The U.N. should systematically incorporate such potential needs into the budget process. It might also try to improve coordination with the International Monetary Fund and other international financial institutions that could help with financial assistance for developing countries.

Finally, rather than searching for the rainbow of targeted sanctions that leave innocent civilians unharmed, it might be more effective to ensure that humanitarian assistance is forthcoming in situations where basic needs are not being met. Nongovernmental organizations may be helpful in undertaking the actual delivery of key supplies, but may be financially strapped or may need help in transporting available food and medical supplies. In any case, the U.N. should take responsibility for trying to meet humanitarian needs. This alternative does not automatically resolve the dilemma of sanctioning a government while trying to protect innocent citizens. An authoritarian government may refuse to accept humanitarian shipments for political reasons, or may accept shipments but then seize the goods and distribute them to its own supporters.

In sum, economic sanctions should not be viewed as a means of conducting foreign policy on the cheap. The costs of sanctions are largely off-budget for governments, but they are nonetheless real. Sanctions impose potentially large costs, not just on the poor and powerless in target countries, but also on less prosperous allies that cooperate with multilateral sanctions, and on private firms in the sanctioning countries.

In most cases, if the sanctioning country or coalition is not prepared to bear the political and economic costs necessary to make sanctions effective, then the economic losses and human suffering caused by sanctions are wasted, and the sanctioner should reconsider the use of economic leverage as a foreign policy tool. The sanctioning countries may wish to use limited, targeted sanctions as a symbolic gesture, and as an answer to their own domestic constituencies who demand that "something be done." But those who sit in the highest councils of government should not delude themselves that half-hearted sanctions will change the policies of a target country.

Notes

[1] Unless otherwise noted, the empirical evidence about sanctions is based on the case studies that are detailed in Hufbauer, Schott, and Elliott (1990).

[2] Rowland (1975), p. 723.

[3] See Konovalov, Oznobistchev, and Evstafiev (1993) for a discussion of Russian views of recent U.N. sanctions; see also Jonathan Eyal, "From Ceasefire to Quagmire: In the Deceptive Bosnian Truce, the Seeds of an East-West Proxy War," *Washington Post*, February 27, 1994, p. C2.

[4] The Hungarian Foreign Ministry denied a *Washington Post* report that it was considering lifting its sanctions because of the high cost. The week following the report, however, Hungary's Prime Minister Peter Boross announced Hungary would not allow NATO surveillance aircraft in its airspace if they were associated with airstrikes against Serb forces in Bosnia. State Department spokesperson Michael McCurry commented that Hungary appeared to have "plans to increase communication" with Serbia in a number of nontrade areas and said the United States viewed "with great concern any action that might ease Serbia's isolation" (*Washington Post*, February 6, 1994, p. A26; February 15, 1994, p. A14; February 25, 1994, p. A20).

[5] U.S. General Accounting Office (1992), p. 19.

[6] *Washington Post*, February 14, 1994, p. A15.

6

New Techniques of Political and Economic Coercion

TIMOTHY R. SAMPLE

I n January 1994, in his first State of the Union address, President Clinton stated: "We gather tonight in a world of changes
so profound and rapid that all nations are tested." His statement
both summarizes the challenges regarding economic stability and
growth, domestic policy, and international status facing the
United States—and most other developed countries—and points
to the difficulty that the United States will have in controlling and
projecting its influence in the 1990s and beyond.

TIMOTHY R. SAMPLE is executive director of the Potomac Institute
for Policy Studies. Previously he was department manager for multimedia
and education resources for military and intelligence support with GTE
Government Systems. He also has managed a project designed specifically to assess the potential impacts of evolving telecommunications technology and development on various agencies and departments within the
U.S. government. Prior to GTE, Mr. Sample served over sixteen years in
the federal government, holding positions within the intelligence and
policy communities that included deputy negotiator to the Strategic Arms
Reduction Talks at the signing of the START Treaty and executive
director of the Director of Central Intelligence Nonproliferation Center.

The end of the cold war finds the developed, industrialized countries scrambling to capture the illusive but much touted "peace dividend"—a dividend their populations believe should logically flow from the end of the bilateral confrontation and the arms race it fueled—while simultaneously watching themselves become players in an increasingly complex game of multipolar dodge ball. As a result, what appear to be diametrically opposed quests for increased influence and reduced defense expenditures are shaping the debate on the role that the United States should play as lone superpower in this new era.

Policy analysts and national security experts are now busy explaining the trends and challenges of growing instability in a multipolar world, pointing out the pitfalls of isolationism, and questioning the ability (and the desire) of the United States to develop and maintain a sole-leadership status. As a result, the public is left somewhat perplexed. On the one hand, we should now be able to take advantage of a hard-fought peace and focus nearly exclusively on a domestic agenda; on the other hand, there are distinctly fewer ways to project our influence abroad at a time when we should be reaping the international benefits of our cold war victory. (After all, we did win that war, didn't we?)

The purpose of this chapter, then, is to explore the changes of this post–cold war period in terms of opportunities for new and expanded techniques of international influence, especially coercive techniques, that could increase our ability to gain our goals and objectives throughout the world, while also addressing the need to mind our economic and political pocketbooks. Consequently, there are two ideas developed in this chapter. The first is that one of the results of the end of the cold war is that most nations are shifting their focus from military to economic security and that this shift offers a new arena for coercion techniques. The second proposition is that advances in technology provide techniques for coercion that are either new or have become more affordable and thus more feasible.

This chapter begins with a discussion of some of the features that are important to the availability and success of today's and tomorrow's coercion techniques. Next will come a look at two distinct trends—growth in technology and international business—that have a direct impact on developing new techniques and their possibilities for success. These trends lead to a discussion of some specific techniques and their effects. Finally, the chapter concludes with a brief assessment of the ability of the United States to engage in post–cold war intervention using these new techniques.

A Word on Coercion

Prior to launching into an analysis of the new environment, a clarification of the term *coercion* is in order. First, coercion is only one of four basic actions available to achieve our international objectives, the others being influence, intervention, and covert action. All four are enhanced by the emergence of new technology and the growth of international business; examples are found later in this chapter. None of these actions is a panacea for replacing the control and structure of cold war bipolarity. Indeed, all four types were used during that period, though perhaps with more restraint in many cases. Nor should one consider their use as progressive or evolutionary. They are not steps up a ladder. Instead, each can be considered an arrow from the foreign policy quiver that has varying degrees of effectiveness and, sometimes, must be used together depending on the target. To help delineate the differences:

- Influence is a rather benign effort to affect a target government or people. In many respects, the success of influence relies on the target's search for help, more than having "help" thrust upon it.
- Intervention connotes more direct involvement in a country's affairs. The most familiar form is direct military intervention, but intervention can also include public support for one political candidate over another in the form of public diplomacy or financial backing.
- Coercion is an action designed to significantly affect the behavior of a government, thereby inflicting the type of pain that forces a government to submit to our wishes.
- Covert actions are those activities that are accomplished in such a way that the target government is unaware of who is behind an action and may not be aware that the action has taken place.

Some Features of the
Post–Cold War Environment

One can, of course, discuss several aspects of the post–cold war period in terms of significant changes in attitudes that affect our foreign policy and outlook. The reluctance of the United States and its European allies to intervene in 1992–94 in a historically important region such as the Balkans, and the increased U.S. emphasis on international coalition forces, usually under the auspices of the United Nations, are two examples of changes in attitudes toward the use of military power to solve international problems. Although trade was always an important foreign policy objective, the increased priority on economic security holds a particular key to the attitudes and directions of most post–cold war nations. The passage of the North American Free Trade Agreement, the successful conclusion of the Uruguay Round of the negotiations on the General Agreement on Tariffs and Trade (GATT), and the early 1994 decision to lift the economic embargo of Vietnam are all examples of the Clinton administration's conviction that the key to our domestic policy is a foreign policy based on international economic development.

The growing emphasis on economic security may bring about new opportunities for coercion. A primary focus on military security emphasizes government decision making and involvement, while concentrating on economic security brings additional factors into play, especially the business sector of each country. Consequently, the United States can aim future coercion policy in two directions. First, it can take actions that have a direct impact on the targeted government. Alternatively, it can take actions that have a direct impact on business and thus an indirect—but significant—impact on the targeted government. In this chapter, these actions are referred to as external and internal measures, respectively.

External measures directly target the government, usually from outside the country. Examples include most of the traditional actions that countries have used throughout history: diplomatic recognition (both granting it and withdrawing it), economic sanctions, public diplomacy, and military intervention. While advances in technology will have some effect on these types of actions—principally in terms of increased efficiency in implementation—their use will largely be similar to past practices.

Internal measures indirectly target the government by directly targeting sources of influence within the country—the population and the economic sectors being key. Prior to the post–cold war period, such actions were principally limited to public diplomacy and covert action. In this new era, however, the trends in technology and business suggest that specific coercive techniques will also be effective. Two features of such coercion are of particular interest. First, indirect coercive actions are primarily nonlethal, thereby appealing to those repulsed by high casualty rates. Second, because of the relatively low cost of technology, these internal forms of influence or coercion are far cheaper than deployment of military forces, making their use more attractive and realistic.

Regardless of the specific measures used, the goal of internal measures is basically the same—to target and operate on a country's politically important constituencies. Therefore, the targets are the military, business, or the population at large. In the post–cold war era, these targets appear more vulnerable than before. For example, today, popular ideas and opinions matter more in more countries, thus making political targets generally more important. Likewise, the dramatic growth of international business and the technology it relies on make targeting such resources both more feasible and more productive. It is difficult to determine which of these targets are, generally, more important, as each situation will likely involve a unique set of circumstances and interrelationships between these factors.

As previously mentioned, the intersection of two major trends in the post–cold war period has created both these new areas for coercion and the new coercion techniques themselves. These trends are in technology and in the growth of international business. It is true that international business interests and access to foreign markets are priorities that are practically as old as civilization itself. It is also clear, however, that the access to the outside world that high technology provides is seen by many countries, for example the developing countries in Africa and Eastern Europe, as a means to participate in the overall growth of the international marketplace. Regardless of the validity of this argument, the effects of both trends developing coincidentally with the transition to a multipolar world bolster the United States' capabilities for coercion as a foreign policy tool.

The Information Age

There is a race within the telecommunications and computer industries to develop a worldwide communications grid accessible at affordable rates by any individual or institution possessing the necessary (and also affordable) equipment. With this grid comes a massive amount of data—an infosphere—that will also be accessible to all and will become a key tool in government and business operations. These capabilities will allow individuals, businesses, and countries to operate faster and with a broader view than ever before. Information that, heretofore, has been inaccessible due to volume and location will suddenly be available with the dialing of a telephone or the stroke of a key.

Advances in telecommunications will soon supply this access. The refinement of satellite technology, increasing use of fiber-optic cable, and the developments in the areas of switching technology and network management are expanding the potential to send massive amounts of data over tremendous distances in the blink of an eye, regardless of where the sender or the recipient may be. No longer will a business, or even an individual, be required to have special or separate services to physically tap into the infosphere—a simple telephone jack or small satellite dish will be all that is needed.

As with the telecommunications industry, the computer/information processing industry is also a part of this communications explosion. With the boom in computer based technology in developed countries and the continual relaxation of commercial export controls, availability of computer hardware and software is no longer a major issue. The development of even the simplest computer based telecommunications resources, such as incorporating a modem or fax capability into a computer, creates affordable tools that supply the worldwide access that businesses and governments demand, at rates even the poorest country can afford. An unintended result of this increasing dependence on technology is an increasing vulnerability to manipulation of the information being transmitted by that technology. This vulnerability, as will be seen below, offers significant new opportunities for coercion.

The demand for these developments in information processing is based not on military requirements, but on the requirements of growing international and multinational business. Multinational businesses often incorporate computer technology in their offices throughout the world, no matter how remote. Part of the overall demand for computer and communications technology stems from the fact that the new global market focus is no longer limited to larger corporations. More and more, small businesses and individuals interact with counterparts in other, sometimes remote, parts of the world.

These advances are not limited to developed or industrialized nations. The technological breakthroughs are at least as important for developing countries. With increasing frequency, Third World nations are preparing to leapfrog traditional technological evolution and jump immediately into the information age, both as a means to compete in an international forum with whatever products they may have and as a vehicle for promoting their country as a site for foreign business investment. This advancement into the information age can happen surprisingly quickly. Given the advances in satellite communications and access, a telecommunications infrastructure can be obtained by countries that lack a transportation infrastructure.

In addition to the basic telecommunications and business computer capabilities, high-technology applications in multimedia and computer graphics, and in data access and encryption devices, provide other tools necessary to exploit this new age environment. Such technology offers new ways to manipulate public opinion. For example, recent developments in computer graphics provide the capability to take two pictures, digitize them, and combine them in such a way that they look like one original, at a quality that can fool even the most experienced photographer. Alternatively, this technology can take a single photograph and, through the same process, rearrange images within the photograph to create an entirely different scene. As, or perhaps more, importantly, these techniques can also be used with videotape, optical disc, or almost any storage medium.

With the increased use of digitized products in broadcasting and print media publications, such tools could effectively be used in an intervention or coercion scenario by creating false images of leaders or situations. Imagine the worldwide reaction, especially in Tehran or Moscow, if, for example, fabricated (but believable) images of Ukrainian leaders meeting with Iraqi officials to sell nuclear weapons were produced and aired on television or published in newspapers. Such "evidence" would likely draw swift action by the international community on both countries—perhaps before much investigation was done.

Another aspect of the evolving information age is the advance in information security. Stringent information controls were formerly the sole concern of governments. Now similar and possibly more stringent controls are being applied to various areas of industry, such as banking and medicine. These systems, however, are extremely expensive. Consequently, as information infrastructures develop in the 1990s, it is possible that many countries, especially developing countries, will maintain an infrastructure without adequate security devices. Even with advanced security in place, those who are determined and armed with the latest technology can potentially access information. Either way, the United States will probably be capable of access if it chooses to try.

Multinational Business Growth

Today's business arena is clearly global. It is not only the biggest corporations that are "going international." Companies of all shapes and sizes are dealing in a multinational setting. The promise of expanding markets and availability of new resources combined with an intense desire by developing countries to have a place in the international marketplace results in a business focus transcending national borders or diplomatic, religious, or ethnic relationships. These developments also result in an increasingly competitive marketplace that not only sharpens the skills of companies, but also places increased importance on governments' trade policies and trade equities—leading directly to new possibilities for both conflict and coercion.

The influence of business in this revised world setting is illustrated by the attempts at assistance in the development of the former command-driven economies of the Eastern European states. With their economies in shambles and basic necessities wanting, Eastern European countries are desperately looking to Western business to invest in the personnel and resources that those countries have to offer. In fact, the need to access and capture Western business interests has been rapidly overshadowing diplomatic priorities since the end of the cold war. In Eastern Europe, a CEO of a Western company may well command more attention than a diplomatic representative, regardless of rank, unless that representative can directly assist in obtaining business investment.

While the end of the cold war competition had an impact on various aspects of business development, the explosion of technology promises to propel these developments at a much faster pace and with a much broader scope than many would have thought possible. Such advances allow a country to participate more readily in the international community and make possible the multinational business expansion previously mentioned.

Applying These Trends to Coercion

The changes in attitudes and actions of many countries in the post–cold war era challenge the effectiveness of more traditional, external measures. With some countries and for some purposes, traditional coercive techniques will still be successful. For a growing number of countries and objectives, however, these pressures may not bring about the desired outcome. Casting an eye toward internal measures is necessary in order to obtain the results that will both sustain and advance our position in the so-called new world order.

Targeting a country's economic operations will likely be one of the most significant aspects of coercion in the 1990s and beyond. Again, the expansion of multinational business into new market areas and the introduction of new telecommunications technologies have begun to dramatically affect the abilities of even developing countries to take part in the international marketplace. Consequently, disrupting a country's ability to compete will have a major and immediate impact on that nation's prosperity and influence. Therefore the goal of this avenue of coercion would be to engage the voice of a targeted country's business to confront its government.

For example, the ability to access a company's computer network and manipulate design, production, and marketing data momentarily, or to go into accounting records and "zero-out" entries, would have a devastating effect on operations. Such access, once explained to the company as a precursor of things to come, could be leverage to gain government concessions. In a more simplistic approach, manipulating a company's ability to utilize its equipment by interfering with transmissions or access can also have a dramatic effect on operations and, consequently, on successful business practices.

Momentary disruption of a nation's financial markets and institutions can have a lasting effect on the attitudes of people toward the stability of their government and economy. As with an attack on industry, accessing a bank's financial records, or blocking employee access to the bank's data bases, could substantially cripple the individual bank's operations, the credibility of the country's banking system, and, by extension, the regime supporting it.

New technology can also permit coercion techniques using a country's broadcast media. We have already witnessed the effects of international media broadcasts and the dramatic impacts that they can have. From the days of the Vietnam War, when the media brought the war into the living room, to the images of thousands of starving children in Somalia, which caused an intense international humanitarian effort, real-time media reporting has had the ability to influence, intervene, and coerce governments and the public. Dramatic media stories will often result in strong public reaction, regardless of whether all the facts are in.

As multinational business continues to expand, "bad press" becomes more important and can be devastating to a company, causing it to lose its competitive edge. For example, in the 1980s the media exposed many companies that were dealing with the South African government. Public outrage, including boycotts of those companies' products, forced them to divest of their assets in that country. With the onset of the information age, the influence of the media on international business activities will continue to grow, as more people will be reached worldwide and the messages can be quite specifically targeted.

A more direct, technological approach for coercion would be to intercept and infiltrate a country's broadcast capabilities. Because much of any country's signals are now based on satellite transmission, there are few technological hurdles. In fact, in areas of Europe, given the right commercial signal receivers, it is possible to receive rough, unedited CNN news footage as it is being transmitted to the United States to be edited and turned into a story. While this is an example of intercepting a transmission traveling across several countries and using several different satellites, the technology needed to intercept a signal that stays within a country is the same. Obviously, the same concept also can be used for radio broadcasts.

The ability to take the message out of the hands of the government, especially in countries that totally control the media, and send a message directly to the people, or to an important subset of the population, effectively takes the influence out of the hands of the leadership and can specifically support intervention and coercion. There are three aspects of this technique to consider:

- Broadcasting on an unused channel that allows the population to tune in to our message at their discretion. Such an attempt at influence would, in essence, create a televised Voice of America.
- Overriding existing signals so that our message is viewed no matter which channel is selected. This type of intervention technique would both disrupt the government's operations and supply our alternative message.
- Manipulating the government's signal in order to adjust the government's message in a negative way. Such an example of this coercion technique could be accomplished with the use of the computer graphics capabilities referred to earlier. Inserting a damaging picture into the broadcast (such as the fabricated Ukrainian-Iraqi meeting postulated earlier) or manipulating the broadcast in a way that has prominent figures saying our message has the potential for significant results in our favor. A potentially more dramatic internal effect would be created if a

prominent leader appeared to be significantly changing his policy in an address to his fellow citizens. For example, a televised
speech by South African President DeKlerk, in which he re-
scinds all previous agreements concerning representation and
eventual control by South Africa's black population, could well
bring about the violent downfall of all government in that country.

While each of these options takes varying degrees of equipment
and effort, the technology to implement any of them is available
today.

Other Techniques

Other techniques and ideas are available, either now or in the
near future. Using such techniques, the United States can pursue
efforts of a more long-term nature. One case would be the use of
computer "bulletin boards" and information services that will proliferate with the introduction of the types of technology systems
that have been described. One of the more effective, albeit long-
term and slow acting, forms of political and economic influence
during the cold war period was the continuous broadcasting of our
fundamental rights, freedoms, and values into Europe via the
Voice of America (VOA), Radio Free Europe, and comparable
services. Besides providing hope for countless individuals living
under Communist oppression, the VOA provided information for
those who were seeking knowledge. While it is difficult to quantify
the effectiveness of the VOA, it is certain that such an effort
touched enough people so that their hopes were kept high and
their desires for democracy were kept fueled.

Computer bulletin boards could become the information age
equivalent of the VOA. With the advent of a global telecommunications infrastructure and the growing, worldwide access to the
resulting infosphere, the United States can use a "VOA philoso-
phy" in various parts of the world, targeting countries that are
preparing to actively participate in the international economic
arena and that have the basic technologies to get them in the door.
In these cases, while many individuals may not have personal

access to computers, access through business or academic resources is likely. Thus the information would end up in the hands
of educated individuals who would be more likely to contemplate
change. This technique would be especially valuable for dictatorships, which depend for their control on maintaining a monopoly
over information. The United States could break that monopoly.

There are various ways in which to transfer/target the data. For
example, the government could construct a standing data base
with copies of relevant documents or information relating to democratic processes or structures, to current international issues, or to
ongoing domestic issues in the target country. This could be available on-line in a data base–type configuration for anyone wishing
to query that information. Another option could be a bulletin
board format where an individual could ask questions and quickly
receive personalized answers on the bulletin board. Just as a television or radio broadcast can be manipulated, the technology is
available to infiltrate a business or government's computer system
and force entry of a textual message.

Another technique made possible by new technologies is disrupting a nation's security forces by disruption or infiltration of
their warning capability. The ability to decrease the readiness of a
military force would be an important advantage, especially if
armed intervention is inevitable. As a specific example, most military forces throughout history have kept weather predictions high
on the list of priorities of required information. The prospect of a
major storm, for example, often has an effect on planning that can
include changing (and often reducing) flight activity, postponing
troop or equipment movements, or, if the storm prediction is bad
enough, "battening down the hatches" to ride out the severe
weather. Primarily, weather prediction is based on two sources of
input—satellite data and computer programs. Intercepting and
modifying this data via infiltration of what are most often unclassified and unprotected transmissions could result in false prepara-
tions for a storm (or, conversely, no preparation for an actual
storm) and a reduced capability or readiness.

Yet another post–cold war intervention technique, this time not
dependent on technology, is the promise of financial incentives in
return for specific actions. After the break-up of the Soviet Union,

the new states were in such serious financial straits that, after extensive negotiations regarding the elimination of the nuclear weapons on their territories, the United States' promise to reward the dismantlement of nuclear weapons with significant financial contributions was at least somewhat effective in Ukraine and Kazakhstan. While this form of bloodless success is attractive, its use may be limited. The circumstances surrounding these episodes were unusual. Never before has a nuclear-capable nation broken up, and it is unclear whether such an incentive would work in every similar case. Nor is it clear whether such a technique would carry over to a situation that did not involve nuclear weapons or whether the United States would tolerate such payments if weapons of mass destruction that directly threatened our territory were not involved. Finally, the line between offering such incentives and encouraging other countries to gain these weapons in order to extract (or extort) such incentives from the United States can be thin, especially as the weapons proliferation problem grows.

Not all aspects of intervention need to be as dark as many of those included above. Providing basic necessities to the population can often result in explicit cooperation by a government. These necessities would include making food available, or improving on the quality of food that is available, and assuring that adequate shelter is provided. Likewise, supplying medicines to a population to prevent the spread of disease is the type of positive, humanitarian measure that can gain support not only from the receiving country, but also from the international community. The degree to which these actions are coercive is dependent upon the situation. For many countries the results will be indebtedness that will allow a country like the United States to have influence.

Assessing the Effectiveness of These Techniques

Having taken a quick look at the environment in which the United States is operating and the tools that are, or could become, available to conduct various forms of influence and intervention, an assessment of the relative effectiveness of such action in the post–cold war period is in order. The effectiveness of any or all of these actions will vary from country to country. Consequently, their utility in U.S. intervention policy is highly dependent on each situation. A wonderful aspect of a multipolar world is each country's individualism—unfortunately, this individualism adds complexity to planning intervention strategies and options.

One of the primary new factors is the need for flexibility. After more than forty years of the fairly predictable and stagnant foreign policy activities of the Soviet Union, it is easy for Americans to fall into the trap of making a decision on a strategy but then not revisiting that decision to see whether the situation has changed. A successful strategy using new coercion and intervention techniques requires an ever-changing mixture of these techniques and the skill to leverage one off of the other.

A principal theme in this chapter has been the emergence of technology. The technology addressed here is available, inexpensive, in demand worldwide, and, perhaps most importantly, allows access to information and information systems. As was said in the 1992 movie *Sneakers:*

> The world isn't run by weapons anymore, or energy, or money. It's run by little ones and zeros, little bits of data. It's all just electrons. . . . There's a war out there, old friend. A world war. And it's not about who's got the most bullets. It's about who controls the information. What we see and hear, how we work, what we think—It's all about the information.[1]

Understanding this technology and how to use it is one of the two keys to the success of future interventions.

Understanding the economic, social, and technical evolution of the target is the other key. Each country's national goals and priorities vary. The effectiveness of any technique will obviously depend on the state of a particular target nation's economic development. A country's sociological development also affects the type of coercion that can be used and its expected results. An obvious example is the targeting of a television broadcast, a technique only effective if there are individuals watching television. Even in countries where television has now been introduced, sociological and religious beliefs may result in a loss of the message because no one is watching. Finally, while the information age will touch all parts of the world, the pace of evolution will take its own course, so one solution will not work in every case.

It is important to keep in mind that in some instances, many of these techniques will be ineffective because of a country's specific situation. Somalia serves as a good, extreme example. Given the state of economic and social development, and the state of the government (or in this case, the lack of a government), it is likely that few, if any, of the techniques described in this chapter would be effective today.

Impacts of Coercion Policy

National resolve is the most important factor in determining the success of coercion policy and intervention strategy. The fact that we now have the opportunity to target different aspects of a nation's livelihood—especially private business—makes the stakes for intervention higher in certain situations than one might believe. If international business is vital to a nation's survival, then targeting someone's industry could be the touchstone for violent confrontation as well as for forced compliance with our demands.

Because of the emphasis on the development of multinational business, it is possible that the United States will need to find a new approach in cooperating with business. Walter Isaacson and Evan Thomas, in the book *The Wise Men,* examined the influence of prominent businesspeople on United States foreign policy after World War II. One of the key aspects of the success of Averell Harriman, Dean Acheson, John McCloy, and Robert Lovett, and those like them in this period, was that they saw the utility of bolstering the government and its influence in the world by utilizing their backgrounds and businesses for the country's development. Consequently, business interests were often synonymous with the interests of the nation. Thus while business saw cooperation with government as positive and in their mutual interests, government saw that promotion of United States business abroad was better than regulation.

Today's multinational, free market businesspeople are becoming less dependent on government and less concerned about a government's influence, unless it directly affects their business. The expansion of these businesses has far outpaced the activities, and in some cases, the influence of government. As a result, the ability of the United States to carry out an effective coercion policy may well rely upon reestablishing a relationship between government and industry that is mutually beneficial.

The values of reestablishing such a relationship between government and multinational businesspeople are many. As stated earlier, a CEO's influence in many developing countries can be more extensive than that of a government. As a result, business's access to and intelligence on foreign businesses, as well as their host governments, could supply additional tools for coercion providing there is a solid, mutually cooperative relationship between business and government. The cost for government is probably allowing business to have a stronger voice in foreign policy (and perhaps domestic policy) and giving business access to government intelligence holdings on foreign competitors. The latter issue has been debated by the Clinton administration.

As the United States considers new techniques for political and economic coercion, it is important to consider our own vulnerability to these types of techniques. If the United States is vulnerable, then an important consideration in deciding whether or not to use these techniques is whether they will provoke similar responses from a targeted country. Such a possibility should not preclude exploration and development of new capabilities, but does suggest that the United States should give attention to its own vulnerabilities as well.

The United States leads the world in telecommunications and computer development, but we are definitely not alone in the race. European and Asian telecommunications firms are fast approaching the United States in deploying this new technology. This advance in telecommunications is beneficial for the United States in that it furthers the overall development of the worldwide telecommunications grid. However it also means that there is the potential for some of the coercion techniques to be used on us. Consequently, the most prudent developers and planners of coercion techniques and policies will also give priority to developing specific countermeasures as well.

Finally, in addition to technical defenses, much of the United States' success in development and implementation of intervention policies also will depend on alliances formed for each situation and on our ability to pick and choose our "battles." We need a concerted effort to develop a mechanism to understand the possible options for coercion, the various techniques available, the specific situation presented, and the possible impacts. Without such a mechanism, it will be difficult—perhaps impossible—to take account of these new approaches in the foreign policy decision-making process.

The information age is upon us. Most of the techniques described in this chapter are here today; those that are not can be developed in the near term. While there is no way to predict all of the challenges that are on the horizon, studying the availability and effectiveness of new techniques for coercion is not only necessary but will be a continuing, evolving process. The success of a United States intervention program for the future relies on all agencies within the government, and also with the multinational business community. One cannot effectively operate without the other. Because the technological advances are from the commercial sector, government must depend on business to research and develop mutually beneficial techniques and technologies. Given the technological lead that the United States is enjoying in the early 1990s, pursuit of these ideas is timely. Because of the nature and the pace of these technological developments, the window of advantage may not stay open for long.

Notes

[1] Copyright by Universal City Studios, Inc. Courtesy of MCA Publishing Rights, a division of MCA Inc.

7

A Framework for Interventionism in the Post–Cold War Era

FAREED ZAKARIA

O n November 6, 1881, in a small town in West Africa, two local chieftains wrote a letter to the prime minister of Great Britain. It read as follows:

Dear W. Gladstone,

We both your servants have met this afternoon to write you these few lines of writing trusting it may find you in a good state of life as it leaves us at the present. As we heard here that you are the chief man in the House of Commons, so we write to tell you that we want to be under Her Majesty's control. We want our country to be governed by British Government. We are tired of governing the country ourselves, every dispute

---

FAREED ZAKARIA is managing editor of *Foreign Affairs*. Formerly, he directed Harvard University's John M. Olin Institute for Strategic Studies' research project on "The Changing Security Environment and American National Interests." Dr. Zakaria is the author of numerous articles on international affairs in the *New York Times, The New Republic, Foreign Affairs, International Security,* and other journals and newspapers. A different and earlier version of this chapter appeared in *Commentary* in December 1993. Dr. Zakaria would like to thank Jacob Kramer for his research assistance.

leads to war, and often to great loss of life, so we think it is the best thing to give up the country to you British men who no doubt will bring peace, civilization, and Christianity in the country. Do for mercy's sake please lay our request before the Queen and to the rulers of the British Government. Do, Sir, for mercy's sake, please to assist us in this important undertaking. We heard that you are a good Christian man, so we hope that you will do all in your power to see that our request is granted. We are quite willing to abolish all our heathen customs. . . . No doubt God will bless you for putting a light in our country. Please to send us an answer as quick as you can.

> King Bell and King Acqua
> of the Cameroons River, West Africa
> 6 November 1881[1]

William Gladstone received this letter at an extraordinary moment in British history. The country made up roughly 25 percent of world gross national product (GNP)—the same as America's share today—and 50 percent of European GNP. London was the unrivaled financial center of the globe. In political-military affairs Britain had defeated Napoleonic France's bid for continental hegemony and helped establish a stable balance of power on the European continent. More recently, in the Crimean War, it had thwarted Russian expansion in southeastern Europe. Outside Europe, at very low cost and to great economic benefit, it had conquered large tracts of India and West Asia. In 1881 Britain could reasonably have been called the only superpower in the world.[2]

Britain declined King Bell and King Acqua's kind invitation. But it accepted many others, so many that over the next twenty years it added 5 million square miles to its empire. Some of these extensions were motivated by greed or glory or great power competition, but many were prompted by humanitarian concerns (ending slave trading, infanticide, bride burning, and so on), and in all cases the dominant cause was a fear of instability and a desire for order. Most of Britain's interventions were, as the great historians of imperialism Ronald Robinson and John Gallagher explained, "involuntary responses to emergencies arising from the decline of Turkish authority."[3] (In the case of Somalia, over a part of which Britain established a protectorate in 1884, it was the retreat of Egypt that drew in a reluctant Britain.) With its tentacles all over the world Great Britain witnessed every outbreak of chaos no matter how distant and felt that it had to do something about each one, fearing in some cases that local conflicts might spill over, in others that inaction might damage London's credibility across the globe. Robinson and Gallagher wrote that because of these fears, "These once remote and petty interests in the Sudan, Uganda, and the northern hinterlands of the Zanzibar were changing into safeguards of Britain's world power." Not only were these areas elevated to an importance they did not deserve, the concerns about credibility, falling dominoes, and spillover turned out to have been vastly exaggerated.[4]

Meanwhile back in Europe the rise of Germany had massively altered the continental balance of power. Yet Britain and France—which during the same period added 3 million square miles of new colonies—were utterly distracted and exhausted by an unending series of crises in Africa and Asia, leaving them neither the time, energy, nor resources to address their central security problem. Ironically, Britain and France's exploits in these hinterlands made them inattentive to the very conditions that had created an era of peace and prosperity in Europe and allowed them to engage in imperialism in the first place. Finally, both powers reasserted their gaze on the central balance of power, but by then it was too late, and what they could do—and did—was ruinously expensive. Britain and France—and the world—paid dearly for these distractions.

In the post–cold war world the United States is as dominant, if not more so, as Britain was in the 1880s, and thus faces some of the same challenges that Britain did. It must, however, respond to these challenges better than Britain did. It must intervene in a substantial manner abroad in support of its central security interests. It must, of course, remain actively involved in the world and act abroad for all manner of other reasons—purely humanitarian ones, for example. But to all its foreign policy it must constantly apply the "Lippmann Test." In the early 1940s Walter Lippmann set out a fundamental rule for a nation's foreign policy. He asked that a nation ensure that it not take on commitments that exceeded its power; indeed that it always balance commitments and power so as to leave itself "a comfortable surplus of power in reserve." Otherwise, he warned, a nation's foreign policy would be bankrupt.[5] In order that it retain the resources, influence, energy, and domestic support to engage itself, *on a sustained basis,* on the most crucial issues the United States must constantly apply the Lippmann Test to itself. This is not only the wisest course for the United States but for the wider world as well. The stability and prosperity of the world depend in some large measure on America's "solvency."

This is not an argument for doing nothing in crises that are not central to U.S. security. Given America's preponderance, all crises around the world will require some level of American intervention. These may take the form of diplomacy, humanitarian aid, food delivery, logistical support for other nations' military efforts, and so on. This is, however, an argument against major and sustained U.S. interventions in certain areas of the world. The case is not based on any concern that the peoples of these countries do not want American involvement—many do—or that the United States will always fail in its missions—it will not—or on any doubts that American intervention would do good—it would. The case against substantial intervention in areas, conflicts, and crises that are peripheral to America's long-term strategic interests is that, like Britain, by focusing on the periphery America will lose the core.

The United States must devote itself almost single-mindedly to its central political and economic problems abroad. This is particularly necessary in the post–cold war world because the stable order of 1945 is unraveling and it will take every effort of the United States to arrest this descent and secure the central achievements of the last forty-five years: peace and prosperity in East Asia and Europe and an absence of serious rivalry between the great powers of the world. Great power peace is America's most vital concern, for it undergirds all else. Thus America's core strategic interests lie in the preservation of peace and prosperity between the great powers, most of which are clustered around Western Europe and East Asia (with Russia astride both). Naturally there are some areas that are connected to this central goal, but with one exception—stability in the Middle East is vital to the peace and prosperity of the great powers—these connections often tend to be greatly exaggerated. In the post–cold war world, one is struck—with apologies to Alfred North Whitehead—by the "unconnectedness of things."

The Importance of the Core

Great power peace and the resulting global prosperity are rare. They existed for the first time in modern history during Britain's economic hegemony and the stable balance created by the Concert of Europe during the mid- and late nineteenth century. During this period—which A.L. Rowse has called the *belle epoque* of interdependence—world trade grew, regimes across the world liberalized and democratized, capitalism surged, and global standards of living rose. The underpinnings of this world crumbled in the wake of World War I with the collapse of British power and the unwillingness of the United States to take its place. Then came mercantilist rivalries, depression, xenophobia, fascism, and war.

The second flowering of peace and prosperity, which took place over the last forty-five years, was a direct consequence of the cold war.[6] The Soviet threat and America's security umbrella over East Asia and Europe created a climate of stable fear in which long-standing enemies foreswore national rivalries and concentrated on the creation of wealth at home. America's political-military role, the dollar's pivotal place in the world monetary system, the free trading system (also sponsored by Washington), and American foreign investment all created an open world economy that more than any other single factor explains the extraordinary progress toward peace, democracy, and civilized conduct that has taken place in the industrial world over the last half-century.

We take this world for granted, but in fact it is fragile. Henry Kissinger argued in *A World Restored* that the nineteenth century's era of stability might have been "so pervasive that it contributed to disaster. For in the long interval of peace the sense of the tragic was lost; it was forgotten that states could die, that upheavals could be irretrievable. . . ."[7] Today we seem similarly to take the conditions of peace and stability among the great powers for granted and are anxious to move beyond "mere stability" to promote other values abroad. But the "long peace" of the cold war rested on both the Soviet threat and American power, and we must first ensure that the collapse of the world's last multinational empire does not un-hinge the balance of the world—which has been the consequence of almost every previous imperial breakdown. Strains in the bal-ance are already apparent: increasing protectionism and trade ri-valries at home and abroad; the disarray of European unity; ram-pant populism, xenophobia, and radicalism in the heart of Western Europe; and the rise of tensions among East Asia's new great powers. If the Soviet threat constituted one ingredient of the long peace, American power and purpose was the second and more important one. This is why it is important, not just for selfish and parochial reasons, that the United States husband its power and use it with wisdom and caution. If Washington gets so dis-tracted by its exploits in Africa, the Caribbean, and the Balkans that it lacks the ability to focus the bulk of its energies on Europe and East Asia, the resulting strains in global politics and economics could dwarf the crises in Haiti or Somalia.

The Cold War and Now

For the last forty-five years debates about American interven-tion abroad have been concerned with specific concerns that are now dead, as dead as the Soviet Union. It was only ten years ago that the fate of American foreign policy seemed—for both sup-porters and opponents—to hinge on aid to the Nicaraguan con-tras. Today even discussing that issue, and others like it, sounds quaint. Having passed a great historical divide, it appears pointless to study events from the *other* side of the divide to illuminate the utterly different world in which America must now make foreign policy. Yet it is worth asking what the great debates over American intervention in the cold war were about. Why were they so differ-ent from those today? Why do they seem so irrelevant? It is in explaining the old dynamic, and how it differs from the new, that we may sense where the challenges and dangers lie in the years ahead.

During the cold war, U.S. interventionism abroad resulted from a "push" from Washington for strategic reasons (the Soviet threat) and ideological reasons (anticommunism, and to a lesser extent, democratic internationalism). The number and extent of these interventions were qualified by international constraints. The constraints were clearly perceived in Washington—a fear of eroding American legitimacy abroad, of undermining sovereignty, of destabilizing popular regimes, and, most importantly, the fear of a Soviet response, though each administration ranked these various concerns very differently. Today the relationship between Washington and the world has been reversed. In the *near* future—five to ten years—American intervention abroad will result from "pulls" from the external world—power vacuums, civil wars, atrocities, famine—and will be qualified in number and extent by Washington's parochial concerns—principally a concern with domestic priorities and a fear of high costs, strategic overextension, and the loss of American lives.

The strategic impetus during the cold war urged intervention; the humanitarian one urged caution and noninvolvement. Today the roles are reversed; it is the strategists who have become cautious about far-flung ventures, and those who used to be anti-interventionists, such as the columnist Anthony Lewis, now urge "humanitarian interventions." Indeed the new interventionists urge involvement precisely in those areas where the United States has no interests—for only if America has no interests in the area can its motives be pure.

To elaborate this discussion about interventionism, then and now, let us ask three questions: why, how, and when?

Why? What is the purpose of America's intervention? What are the ends of U.S. policies in the region where the intervention might take place? This was a matter of great contention throughout the cold war. Furious debates raged over the question of whether, for instance, America's goals in Central America during the 1980s were good for Central America. The principal source of contention over U.S. interventionism for much of the cold war was the effects of those interventions in the region. Critics of Washington's involvements in Asia, Africa, and Latin America often argued that America was choosing the "wrong" side in local struggles and was worsening the political, economic, and social conditions of the people of the region. Thus Senator Christopher Dodd could argue against the Reagan administration's Central American policy by warning that the administration was "standing against the tide of history." It is remarkable to consider how the discussion on this front has changed dramatically in recent years. Today Americans seem to have fewer disputes over the direction of history, less trouble picking the good guys from the bad guys. Indeed Americans on either side of those old debates would probably agree on what they would like to see happen in most countries and regions of the world today. There is little dispute over what ends we would prefer. The questions that are asked now are when and how we should attempt to achieve those ends.

How? With regard to the means of intervention the pendulum has also swung. During the cold war people asked questions centered on the *means* of U.S. interventionism. Was military aid—say to the Shah of Iran—wise? Was aid to a guerrilla force—the Afghan rebels—a legitimate tool of foreign policy? The central dilemma of Washington since the early 1950s was that while it perceived an urgent need to counter Soviet internationalism, it could not do so with forceful and direct measures for fear of triggering an all-out war with Moscow, which could then become a nuclear war. Thus most American moves were indirect and moderate, particularly if they were in distant regions. The two cases where the moves were not moderate—Korea and Vietnam—became lessons to be avoided. Even in the Reagan administration it was clear that U.S. foreign policy had to use a creative bag of nonmilitary methods—aid, arms sales, training—in order to achieve its ends. When military force was used, it was used in a place like Grenada where the possibilities of escalation were virtually nil. Even then, most of the questions surrounding the means used by the Reagan and Bush administrations asked whether they had used too much. Indeed, at the height of the Reagan administration, Secretary of Defense Caspar Weinberger, in an address to the National Press Club in Washington, D.C. on November 28, 1984, asked whether his administration was being too trigger-happy and outlined a series of quite restrictive conditions that would have to be satisfied before American military intervention proceeded. His conditions were quite straightforward: (1) U.S. national interests should be at

stake; (2) if the United States goes in, it should go in wholeheart-
edly; (3) military force should be used in the service of clearly
defined political objectives; (4) flexibility and adaptation are important; (5) prior to military intervention there must be "some
reasonable assurance" of public support; and (6) force should always be a last resort.

These criteria are well articulated and accurately represent the
U.S. military's post-Vietnam caution. In the post–cold war world,
with American power—particularly military power—dominating
the globe, such caution could serve a useful self-restraining purpose. (While the debates during the Reagan years were over
whether the administration was using *too much* military force, early
in the Clinton administration most of the discussion surrounding
American interventions in Haiti, Somalia, and Bosnia focused on
whether America's means have been *too limited.*) All that said,
Weinberger's criteria are too restrictive, a recipe for paralysis and
inaction. They could, however, become a sound framework for
U.S. policy with two amendments: the Powell amendment and the
Shultz amendment. The first amendment concerns Weinberger's
advocacy of what some call "the all-or-nothing approach." General Colin Powell has pointed out that the distinction between
"limited" and "all-out" interventions is too abstract to be decided
in all cases in favor of all-out interventions.[8] The nature of the
intervention must depend on the political objectives that are
sought. If the objectives are broad, large-scale force will probably
be required. If the objectives are narrow—for example, the ouster
of the president of Panama—less force can be used. It is important
only that the objectives are clear, and the force allocated is sufficient to achieve them. In fact, as Samuel P. Huntington argues,
because of America's military tradition it is important that the
forces be ample, even excessive, for the mission.[9]

The second amendment, the Shultz amendment, would eliminate Weinberger's penultimate point regarding public opinion.
George Shultz, in an address at Yeshiva University in New York
on December 9, 1984, properly argued that to require public support before an intervention was to hide behind the skirts of public
opinion. Public support results from the ability of the president to
articulate the purpose behind and the reasons for the intervention.

If all Weinberger's other conditions were satisfied, an administration would have a duty to attempt to create public support for its policy.

During the cold war debates also raged about the *effect* of U.S. intervention on international norms, principally those of sovereignty, international law, and nonintervention. More surprising perhaps is that the concern over the effects of U.S. intervention on international norms has also partially evaporated. When Charles Krauthammer wrote in 1986 that respect for sovereignty was not a moral imperative, and that there were goods worth pursuing even if their pursuit undermined sovereignty, he was considered a provocateur.[10] This was, of course, in part because he was defending the Reagan Doctrine, but also because of the high standing that the idea of sovereignty enjoyed at that time. The Nicaraguan government's victory over the United States in the International Court of Justice rested in large part on U.S. violations of Nicaragua's sovereignty. Today Krauthammer's statement would be regarded as self-evident, almost banal. In most of the crises that attracted Washington's attention in 1993, state sovereignty was considered mainly as an obstacle over which lawyers and diplomats had to vault in order to promote more important goods.

This change in attitudes is caused by a broader shift in international relations. In ages of ideological discord great powers cannot agree on the purpose of intervention. During the cold war, for example, the United States and the Soviet Union wanted to intervene in the domestic affairs of other countries to produce profoundly different outcomes. In times like those, sovereignty and nonintervention become highly prized.[11] Since discord prevails over the ends of foreign policy, rules of the game become important to ensure that things do not get out of hand. In contrast, we live today in what is perhaps an age of unprecedented ideological accord. Almost all the great powers agree on what direction they would push a country's regime were they to intervene (though, of course, some would argue against doing so on prudential grounds). In such an age, sovereignty and nonintervention become less sacrosanct. (This pattern played itself out in Europe in the early nineteenth century. The normal practice of intervening in the affairs of small states on the continent of Europe became less and less common as the Holy Alliance's purpose in intervening—to stabilize conservative autocrats—began to diverge from that of Britain and France.) The "Why" and "How" of interventionism become less contentious in such a climate. That is not true, however, about the "When."

When? This question involves the broader aims of U.S. foreign policy. What events, crises, interests, or threats in the world require American intervention? Does any particular intervention enhance or diminish America's broader strategic and ideological objectives? Does the intervention help America's promotion of its interests and ideals abroad? This question was asked during the cold war—often not hard enough and not by the right people— and before. In fact, it is the central strategic question that American foreign policy makers have asked themselves from the birth of the republic onward. It is a complex question because almost all crises in the world merit *some* U.S. intervention. How one ranks the event or the interest or the crisis, however, will determine how sustained and significant this intervention should be (thus linking it to the question of *how* America should intervene). It is this question of weightage that will prove the hardest to answer in the years to come.

1993: The Year of Promises and Threats

To think about this last problem, when to intervene and to what extent, let us reflect on the three crises that captured the Clinton administration's attention in 1993. The president and his advisers began by defining America's objectives in a strikingly extravagant manner—the preservation of Bosnia as a multiethnic state within its original borders, the restoration of democracy to Haiti, and nation building in Somalia. All three goals are praiseworthy, but all three would require a significant expenditure of energy, resources, and political capital over a long period of time. Given the stakes involved, were they worth that kind of effort? Evidently the administration thought not on closer examination. As each crisis unfolded, when confronted with the reality that its goals would require a more vigorous assertion of U.S. military power, the administration backed off, sometimes scaling down its objectives, sometimes making a novel distinction between its preferences and its goals (the latter being what it thought it could achieve through consensual talks with its allies). While casual about willing the ends, the Clinton administration would not will the means to these ends. This single flaw explains the debacle of U.S. policy in all three areas.

It could be argued that the goals articulated by the Clinton administration were correct, but then it should have employed the means to achieve them. More realistically, however, the administration should have scaled back its goals so that the means it was prepared to use would have been adequate to attain those goals. In any event, to do neither was the worst of all possible worlds because it exposed the nation internationally to the image of hypocrisy and the reality of a "Lippmann Gap"—with its commitments exceeding its power. Many of the new interventionists argue that the United States loses credibility when it chooses not to intervene in foreign crises. In fact, credibility does not require that the United States respond to every act of aggression anywhere in the world at any price. It does require that the United States choose carefully its interests, that it protect those interests vigilantly, and most importantly that in all matters it make only threats and promises that it intends to fulfill. Thomas Schelling has remarked that in international relations, it is always important to remember how expensive are threats when they fail and promises when they succeed.[12] It is the casual use of threats and promises that has damaged American credibility.

In Haiti, after the first policy reversal over refugees, the administration seemed stung by the charge—entirely accurate—that it was following President Bush's policy after Clinton had attacked this very policy during the presidential campaign as immoral. The administration moved to more active attempts to restore former President Bertrand Aristide to power. The band of thugs who run Haiti, however, could not be negotiated with. Restoring Aristide would have taken the use of the U.S. armed forces—by which I mean soldiers and sailors, not technicians. The United States does have interests in Haiti. It is a country of the Western Hemisphere, with whom the United States has a checkered history. Instability in the area could destabilize the neighboring democracies. There is also the danger of an influx of refugees (though ironically this problem is in large part caused by an American action—the economic embargo). These are not, however, possibilities so fraught with danger as to justify an armed intervention. The United States should have made clear that it did not condone what the government of Haiti was doing. It should, perhaps, have broken diplomatic relations with this regime. If targeted economic sanctions could have been devised that did not simply cause general misery, they should have been put to work. U.S. policy should thus have been essentially punitive, punishing the government of Haiti for its actions rather than attempting to engineer a domestic revolution. Such a policy might well have resulted in a change of regimes; if it did, all the better. But that would not be the focus—nor the yardstick of success—of U.S. policy.

In Somalia it does appear that the Clinton administration expanded the goals of the mission in March from a food aid mission to what the *New York Times* described on March 26, 1993, as "the largest, most expensive and most ambitious operation [the United Nations] has ever undertaken."[13] It could be argued that George Bush bit off more than he could chew when he sent troops to Somalia, that nation building is implicit in famine relief. But the United States was at a decision point in March 1993, and again in August, when U.S. troops were being fired on. Given everything that we know about George Bush's instinctive caution and prudence, it is difficult to imagine his ambassador to the United Nations saying, as Madeleine K. Albright did in March 1993 about the expanded mission in Somalia, "[This is] an unprecedented enterprise, aimed at nothing less than the restoration of an entire country as a proud, functioning and viable member of the community of nations."

The famine had indeed been caused by a political breakdown. Thus it is argued that if that breakdown were not addressed, the United States would have withdrawn only to see the onset of the very same conditions that it intervened to end. In foreign policy as in domestic policy, however, an obsession with "root" causes is futile and self-defeating. For example, one can never "solve" the problem of crime, but one can alleviate its consequences. The United States should not have attempted to address the underlying causes of the famine in Somalia, if by that one means creating order out of chaos. It should have sought to alleviate its symptoms. Creating a polity in Somalia may be beyond America's capacity; it is certainly beyond its capacity at a reasonable cost. But food and medical aid are effective and important cures for a famine; they save countless lives and rescue hundreds of thousands of people from terrible suffering. Since part of the problem was that the aid could not get through, military efforts to open up channels of distribution were worthwhile. But the model should have been America's massive aid efforts during the Ethiopian famine, rather than an attempt at nation building.

Haiti and Somalia are easier cases to discuss than Bosnia because in the former, most observers agree that U.S. interests (however broadly defined) are minimal, and that while U.S. policy should be responsive and helpful, Washington cannot be asked to solve the problems of Haiti and Somalia. Bosnia is the most vexing of all three, and one of the most painful dilemmas America has had to confront in recent years. This is because in the case of Bosnia one could make a case that the United States has some strategic interests in the region, that the response to this crisis has larger implications for U.S. credibility, and that U.S. policy making under both the Bush and the Clinton administrations has failed in this area. There is truth in all these arguments, and American diplomacy—particularly the politically and morally obtuse arms embargo that should never have been imposed—has been a failure, but on final analysis I still come to the painful conclusion that while the United States should have done more than it did, it was wise to resist any significant and sustained military intervention.

Few would argue that America has vital interests in the Balkans per se (the West Europeans, by contrast, clearly have important interests in the area). The argument about U.S. national interests in the Bosnian crisis is an argument about European stability in general, and particularly about Western Europe—the most important part of the continent. For this argument to be meaningful, however, there has to be some indication that the Balkan war is likely to spread and become a more general European war. This argument has been made by many advocates of U.S. intervention, most famously by George Kenney, the former State Department desk officer, who wrote in the *New York Times* on September 30, 1992 that within three to six months the war in Bosnia would spread through the Balkans, drawing in Iran, Libya, and other Islamic nations, then Greece and Turkey, then against their will the Western powers. He predicted that by the spring of 1993 Milosevic would have conquered Bosnia, including Sarajevo. He would then turn on Kosovo, which would make Albania go to war, after which Macedonia would join in, after which Greece would enter to conquer Macedonia, after which Turkey would enter to fight Greece. The major Western powers would enter what would by then be a general European war.

As of this writing, one and a half years after the prediction, this chain of events has not occurred and does not seem likely to occur. It is important to understand that conflict in the Balkans led to a general European war in 1914 because the great powers cared *too much* about instability in the Balkans; today they care *too little*. This may cause many problems, but it cannot cause a general war. When Bismarck was asked to intervene in a similar Balkan crisis over 100 years ago, he is reported to have said that the Balkans were not worth the bones of a single Pomeranian Grenadier. His successors in 1914 believed that instability in the Balkans was dangerous, so they intervened, which drew in the other great powers. Bismarck's indifference led to peace; his successors' paranoia, to a general European war. The surest path to a wider war, ironically, would be a substantial intervention in the conflict by the great powers.[14]

The less specific argument for intervention in the Balkans is that inaction will hurt America's credibility and encourage dictators and would-be ethnic cleansers all over the world to act with impunity. Credibility and deterrence are important aspects of foreign policy, but they are complex matters. Why did America's breathtaking victory in the Gulf War—televised live all over the world—not deter the Serbs, or for that matter the Azeris, the Georgians, or the Sudanese? Most local dictators come to power because they have a very acute understanding of threats and force. They know that the United States would not send a force of 500,000 troops to liberate Nagorno-Karabakh, but that it would for Kuwait. Deterrence works when the other side will not risk finding out whether your threat is real or a bluff. The Red Army declined to cross the Fulda Pass because it believed, probably accurately, that if it did, NATO would respond with massive force. Even in deterring Soviet client states on the margins, however, the United States had mixed success during the cold war (hence the Korean and Vietnam Wars). Generalized deterrence is impossible. It is an attempt to stop the clock of international conflict—a worthy but unattainable goal.

It is impossible to discuss Bosnia without a reference to the moral issues it raises. For many, the brutal Serb aggression on the Bosnian Muslims and the even more brutal atrocities have made this a supreme moral matter in which the United States must intervene, even if it has few strategic interests in the area. To address the moral issue seriously, however, we must first ask the question, "why Bosnia?" What makes this outbreak of violence and this series of atrocities so different from others—with as many casualties—that are taking place across the globe? For some the answer is simple, "why not Bosnia?" The fact that we cannot help every nation in bloody civil war should not paralyze us so that we never act out of moral sympathy and outrage. But this argument does not stand scrutiny. It is disingenuous to claim that the United States has simply stumbled upon Bosnia in the way that a rich man notices a beggar at his door and feeds him without worrying about all the other, equally deserving beggars he is not helping. The reason that every Western news organization has cameras in Bosnia, the reason that Susan Sontag and Annie Leibovitz have traveled there—and not to Azerbaijan and Sudan—the reason that it is discussed day after day in newspapers, magazines, and chancelleries is surely not utter idiosyncrasy.

The uncharitable explanation for this extraordinary interest in Bosnia is that the people in the region look a lot like most Americans and Europeans. In my opinion, however, this does not explain the real impetus behind the zeal for intervention in the Balkans. The more serious reason for the interest in the Balkans is that for many it is unthinkable that such a thing should happen in Europe. Europe was supposed to have transcended these kinds of barbarisms. It is one thing for ethnic cleansing to take place in

Central Asia, but in Europe? This is, of course, a profound mis-reading of European history. The paradox of European civiliza-tion has always been its capacity for supreme achievements of culture and politics and at the same time for supreme acts of violence. The history of Europe is a history of fratricidal wars and ethnic cleansing. Compared to Latin America, Asia, and Africa, European civilization has been marked by almost continuous in-terstate and intrastate violence. Where else would ethnic cleansing occur but in Europe?[15]

For the last forty-five years Europe has experienced an era of peace and believed that it had transcended this history. It will now have to accustom itself to the kinds of crises and instability that other continents have always lived with. The solution does not lie, at this point, in an ambitious, futile, and probably counterproduc-tive attempt to resurrect the original Bosnian state—noble as that cause is—but to help broker an equitable, or minimally equitable, peace settlement, and to make sure that this conflict does not spread, but instead serves to immunize the rest of the continent from violent nationalism and ethnicity. War in Bosnia is tragic; a general European war would be worse.

The Morality of Focusing on the Core

President Clinton and his advisers seemed to recognize the po-litical importance of the core by 1994. They moved from spending almost all their time, energy, resources, and political capital on the three televised hot spots—Haiti, Somalia, and Bosnia—to deal with other, more consequential matters like Russia, relations with Japan, the rise of China, the General Agreement on Tariffs and Trade, and the North American Free Trade Agreement. But this is not purely a matter of politics and expediency. America's core interests involve both American interests and ideals—for example the preservation and strengthening of an open world trading sys-tem or the democratic future of Russia. These goals will not auto-matically come to fruition, but require constant and vigilant atten-tion and effort. It is these larger issues that are worth the risks of U.S. involvement and intervention. In the long run what happens in the hot spot of the moment will not matter, but these vital issues, trends, and relationships will determine the fate of the post–cold war world. If the United States wishes to see a world in which democracy and free markets flourish, in which human rights are respected, and in which countries resolve their differences nonviolently, it has a duty to its citizens and to its historic role to conduct a foreign policy that helps create and sustain the underpinnings of peace and prosperity in which such a world is conceivable.

Notes

[1] Quoted in Doyle (1986), p. 162.

[2] For an elaboration of this point see Zakaria (1992); for statistics on Britain see Kennedy (1987), pp. 149, 330, 436.

[3] Robinson and Gallagher (1978), p. 466.

[4] One scholar calls these mistaken beliefs "myths of empire"; see Snyder (1991).

[5] Lippmann (1943), p. 9.

[6] Gaddis (1987).

[7] Kissinger (1973), p. 6.

[8] Powell has been characterized as an "all-out" advocate himself, and certainly his desire for decisive force was plain during his tenure as chair of the Joint Chiefs of Staff. However, as his writings make clear, he argues for force sufficient for the purpose of the mission—no more, no less. For the best statement of this see Powell (1992/93).

[9] For a brilliant advocacy of excessive force see Huntington (1986).

[10] Krauthammer (1986). For a discussion of whether the Reagan Doctrine was "revolutionary" or not, see Zakaria (1990).

[11] For a surprising defense of sovereignty, see Walzer (1977).

[12] Schelling (1980), p. 177.

[13] See Bolton (1994).

[14] For an elaboration of this point, see Misha Glenny, "Bomb the Serbs?; A Wider War Would Follow," *New York Times*, April 29, 1993.

[15] See the well-documented article by Andrew Bell-Fialkoff (1993).

8

Organizing the Government to Provide the Tools for Intervention

JAMES G. ROCHE AND
GEORGE E. PICKETT JR.

T he objectives of this chapter are to recommend actions that would improve the government's acquisition of capabilities to support intervention and to suggest steps that would increase the effectiveness of U.S. responses in intervention situations. Different categories of intervention are analyzed, and the broader management requirements that emerge are enumerated. Drawing from experiences in industry and government, management concepts are recommended that would be useful in this post–cold war environment, and these concepts are linked to examples of specific changes that need to be considered. Particular attention is given to the increasing role of technology in developing new, or enhancing existing, capabilities to intervene.

JAMES G. ROCHE is corporate vice president and chief advanced development, planning, and public affairs officer at the Northrop Corporation. Formerly, he was the assistant to the chairman, president, and chief executive officer. From 1984–89 Dr. Roche was the vice president and director of the Northrop Analysis Center in Washington, D.C. Before joining Northrop, he was the Democratic staff director, Senate Armed Services Committee, and served as the principal deputy director of the

Whether interventions are per se appropriate, or whether certain interventions are acceptable and others are not, is a political question (and often an ideological and philosophical one). This chapter attempts to avoid addressing such issues. It probes the question of "how should one manage the intervention environment" not "should intervention occur." How to manage such situations needs to be addressed, regardless of whether the United States finds itself in intervention situations once a year or once a decade. The management issues are somewhat independent of the frequency of involvement; anyone who believes no interventionist situations will arise can bypass this chapter.

Categories of Intervention

Intervention can be defined as the deliberate intrusion of U.S. military, economic, and/or diplomatic activities into a sovereign nation, group of nations, or transnational group. Interventions are for the most part episodic actions, often in the nature of a crisis. Combat is the most destructive form, but other examples include trade sanctions, foreign aid, military assistance, and political pressure from alliances. To avoid the term being applied to all forms of interchange between the United States and other nations, intervention is considered to be an involvement that has not been requested or sanctioned by all the parties in a particular interna-

---

State Department's Policy Planning Staff during 1981 and 1982. He was a senior professional staff member of the Senate Select Committee on Intelligence (1979–81); and he was an assistant director of the Office of Net Assessment in the Office of the Secretary of Defense (1975–79). Dr. Roch is a retired captain in the U.S. Navy, having commanded the USS Buchanan DDG-14.

GEORGE E. PICKETT JR. is senior analyst/director at the Northrop Corporation. He served in the U.S. Army in Korea and Vietnam from 1964–70 and served on the staffs of the National Security Council and the Senate Intelligence Committee before joining Booz Allen & Hamilton in 1980. He joined Northrop in 1986, where he has conducted studies of new weapon acquisition policies, the defense industrial base, and defense conversion.

tional situation; one or more may have requested that the United States intervene, but at least some participants oppose such a move.

In the coming decades, the interventionist challenges that may confront the United States can be grouped into four categories. First is the potential emergence of one or more nations with major global aspirations and probably some capabilities in nuclear or other weapons of mass destruction. This would be a power, perhaps even transnational, with worldwide interests or regional interests so great as to be worldwide in their effect, whose objectives conflict with those of the United States and its allies, and whose actions could lead to ever-expanding conflicts that might eventually provoke a major war. In addition to a possible Russian resurgence, this includes the emergence of a nation like China, which could progress from regional to world power status in the first quarter of the next century, or a coalition of nations (e.g., China-Japan? several nations in the Pacific Rim? Turkey and neighboring states?) The United States also needs to be alert to the rise of a fanatical leader, regime, or movement (à la Nazi Germany) that would risk plunging the world into crisis.

The emergence of a global power would be an event with which the United States has almost a half century of international experience in dealing with and counterbalancing. As threatening as it might be for international stability, this is a class of problems for which the United States has built a vast repertoire of responses in economics, politics, military force design, etc. The United States could not halt the rise of such a nation, but it could create an international environment that would help shape the manner in which the new entrant might behave. One risk would be that, as with the U.S. response to Germany in the 1930s, the United States might be too muted in its political and economic actions and too timid militarily at the outset to affect the behavior of an emerging global power. A second risk would be that, being involved so deeply in other international and domestic issues and focused on budget reductions, the government might allow fundamental competencies to disappear that would be important in dealing with the rise of such a power.

The second class of interventionist situations is regional powers.

In some cases, the United States will be only modestly concerned about local powers (e.g., in sub-Saharan Africa and Latin America). Diplomatic ties, trade relations, humanitarian aid, and so on, could be used to influence the resolution of local problems, and new technologies (e.g., sensors for border control or nonlethal means) could provide new instruments to support diplomatic actions. As in the Falkland Islands, the United States may have to choose sides, but most crises in Latin America or sub-Saharan Africa are unlikely to endanger U.S. national security, and in the final analysis the United States could defeat such nations in this part of the world militarily if necessary.

Other regional powers and intraregional confrontations will have a more substantial impact on U.S. interests, and require U.S. involvement (e.g., conflicts in the Middle East, Europe, and along the Pacific Rim). Dexterity at managing political and economic relationships, at forming and employing alliances and coalitions, and at military action will be important in moderating the effects of such crises, and in controlling the extent of long-term U.S. involvement. The astute use of various interventionist techniques (like the application of new technology and economic sanctions) is probably going to grow in importance as more and more protagonists have modern industrial and military capabilities. Indeed, the handling of major regional crises could be the litmus test for judging U.S. competence at intervention in the coming decade.

In the military arena, the capacity to deal with such crises is declining rapidly. Desert Storm demonstrated the value of high-technology weapons, well-trained troops, overwhelming force, and the use of alliances and coalitions. But Desert Shield/Desert Storm should not be taken too literally as the example of the successes that will be possible in future regional confrontations, and its lessons need to be weighed carefully. First, Iraqi aggression clearly unified neighboring states whose differences were not so severe as to make an alliance impossible. By contrast consider the failure of the Europeans (and their American ally) to unify over the crises in the former Yugoslavia, where the interests of various states were too disparate and consequently undermined a key requirement for containing a crisis (the ability to respond rapidly). Second, Desert Storm fit with U.S. military capabilities. For example, the United States has virtually no capability to project sustainable and conventional military power into the Eurasian heartland that was fragmented with the collapse of the Soviet Union. Third, U.S. forces will be smaller and in many ways less capable in 2000 than they were in 1991.

The third class of interventionist situations is the occurrence of small but locally devastating conflicts. These have their basis in profound antagonisms and pose little threat to the world, but are nonetheless disturbing because of their brutality. They often involve complex issues of which nations outside the immediate area are only vaguely informed, and for which political-military expertise for successful intervention is relatively weak. For example, alliances may be seen as the useful tool in such crises (e.g., the NATO response to Bosnia). However, alliances may be even less skilled than the United States in understanding, controlling, and limiting commitments. They may have unwarranted optimism for the effectiveness of forces (e.g., air power), may lack the skills for providing civil affairs support in delicate situations, or may not realize that a peacekeeping enterprise for them may be seen by one or more of the protagonists as inserting an additional aggressor to be fought and resisted.

For the United States, involvement in local conflicts poses a number of risks, including subtle changes in commitments and objectives that embroil the U.S. beyond its original intent and create threats to U.S. personnel more severe than anticipated. While it is unclear that this category can be effectively managed by any interventionist tool (political, economic, military, or a mix thereof), it is abundantly clear that heavy reliance on military means is a precarious approach and requires careful thought beforehand as to military objectives, rules of engagement, criteria for determining success, and so on. The deaths of Marines in Beirut and Army soldiers in Somalia exemplify the risks. These types of conflict do not stress the United States in economic, military, or technical capabilities; they stress its capacity for crisis management and innovative application of interventionist tools as well as its willingness to inflict and absorb casualties.

The fourth category of interventionist situations is the "rogue state" problem. This includes states that could be considered re-

gional powers and in addition act in a manner that shows they
have no interest in following the rules of international behavior
(e.g., North Korea and Iraq). It also includes nations that aspire to
the status of a regional power but whose principal advantage is an
ability to impose damage far out of proportion to their underlying
economic, international political, or real military capability (e.g.,
Libya). Such states use terrorism, develop nuclear weapons or
other weapons of mass destruction, and build or buy missiles,
space vehicles, and aircraft able to deliver conventional or other
munitions to great distances.

Today the United States has various capabilities to intervene
and influence "rogue states." For example, diplomatic and economic pressures have been used to suppress or slow down the sale
of missile technology; air and naval forces have reinforced diplomatic initiatives to control the behavior of these countries; and
missile defenses have been deployed (even though their effect may
be debatable).

However, "rogue states" pose complex challenges. The capacity to control international terrorism is mixed. Future "rogue
states" may be in the central Eurasian continent and difficult for
the United States to reach militarily. Desert Storm's very limited
success with Scuds shows that highly selective targeting remains
difficult. Such capability against "strategic relocatable targets"
may improve if continued advances are made in sensors, sensor-
processing technologies, precision-guided weapons, and munitions
design, all using long-range delivery systems. Finally, "rogue
states" can pose a challenge to fundamental principles of U.S.
foreign policy. For example, no matter how urgent it may be,
preemptive attack (e.g., the Israeli 1981 air attack on Iraqi nuclear
capabilities) is a politically difficult action for the United States;
also challenging is whether, ideologically, the United States can
allow itself to target specific individuals for attack (e.g., a rogue
leader), a capability that modern technology makes a real possibility.

The Techniques of Intervention

For the United States to respond to the varied types of interventionist situations outlined above will be a major challenge in for-

eign policy. The menu of potential opponents, their military and economic capabilities, their objectives, and the confrontational situations that may arise are rich, varied, and unpredictable. The numbers of interventionist situations may increase, stressing the capability of government to handle simultaneous crises. The strain of competing demands on the government's budget is limiting U.S. flexibility overseas and reducing the margin of error that can be tolerated in making decisions. The U.S. initiatives toward Russia suggest a form of American intervention not often seen: long-term and deep involvement in another nation. That too spells a management challenge: how to focus agencies for long-term operations without losing sight of the broader foreign policy objectives.

The break-up of the bipolar world has created a more fluid environment in which the United States can employ a variety of political techniques (aid, coalitions, moral suasion, promises, military assistance, etc.) to exert influence. Indeed, the choice among political tools available to respond to problems presents a major challenge to government management. Are there sufficient country and area experts to provide advice and assistance? How does the government tap knowledge in the private sector and academia for parts of the world that it has largely been able to ignore by subsuming them under the rubric of being part of the Communist bloc? How does the government establish policies to guide its relations with nations and regions whose long-term health, value, or threat remains unclear? How does the government avoid being caught up in the management of multiple situations that lead to losing sight of longer-term problems in the international arena (e.g., focusing on crises and not on controlling the rise of a new global power)?

The role of economic tactics in intervention will continue to change in the next several decades as the world reaches higher levels of market integration, and more nations begin to have a stake in those markets. By the early part of the next century, economic power will be even more broadly shared among the countries of North America, Europe, Asia, and the Pacific Basin, and this will provide complex linkages among national and subnational actors that may be used to influence situations. For example, technology will provide the basis for much of that integration, from the communication and automation advances that support complex corporate and government enterprises to the flow of technologies that shift and redefine market power among states in products and industries.

The exploitation of such technological linkages for political effect (beyond trade sanctions and other devices now used) may provide new leverage for the United States in intervention situations. It will also raise difficult questions for U.S. trade, economic and industrial policy, and politics. For example, should the U.S. government spy on foreign corporations? Should American corporations be used to implement sanctions? Should the U.S. government intrude into a nation's financial transactions by monitoring and possibly even covertly altering information flows? Legal, political, and cultural obstacles may be far too strong to permit the use of some effective and innovative techniques that are becoming available.

At this time, and for the foreseeable future, at the broadest strategic level the critical underpinnings of interventionist capabilities remain military in nature. In diplomacy the effectiveness of political persuasion often depends on perceptions of the capability of the United States to act militarily, even if military power is not routinely exercised. Similarly, economic tactics, for all their merits, have limited use in the long term without the perception that a nation has the military capability to be viewed as a world power (witness the Japanese, who for all their economic strengths are limited in their international effectiveness because they are not viewed as a great power). Nations without a serious military capability can be viewed as helpful, but limited in their influence.

The continuing spread of technology throughout the world provides a richer range of political, economic, and military options than in the past. For example, new tools (e.g., nonlethal systems, intelligence sensors, etc.) can provide means to assist one or more sides in confrontations (e.g., closing borders, intimidating one side by providing intelligence to the other, or intimidating both sides by publishing data on each). Geolocation and electronics are approaching points at which weapons can be programed not to operate in certain regions of the world, or to shut down after a certain time period. Such innovations would make seemingly offensive weapons only useful defensively, and could force countries to behave responsibly or face the refusal of supplier nations to restart their systems. More broadly, the United States could provide highly classified intelligence to friendly regional powers to establish a "knowledge gap" in favor of an alliance. This could also impress allies with the extent of U.S. capabilities, discouraging them from attempting to develop independent capabilities and encouraging them to follow the United States in future crises.

The growing potential of technology creates one of the newer difficulties for intervention management: how to coordinate its use across various political, economic, and military applications, and across agencies with widely differing perceptions and understandings about technology. The complexity of integrating government subcultures can be imagined by thinking of a meeting on the use of information technology against a nation and how it would proceed in a room with an engineer from the Department of Energy (DOE), a political analyst from the State Department, a foreign sales analyst from Commerce, a Department of Defense (DOD) military planner, and lawyers from Justice and the Securities and Exchange Commission (SEC). How, for example, would these parties work together to use U.S. capabilities in information technology to influence Japan and China to resolve a confrontation over the pollution of Japan's air by coal plants that China is building to provide power for China's further growth?

Considering the demands of the four types of intervention situations and the diversity of political, economic, military, and technology tools, the future organization of government should be driven by seven factors.

Uncertainty—The difficulty of predicting the appearance and content of future crises makes it hard to prepare standard response plans beforehand, and requires flexibility, responsiveness, and adaptiveness.

Diversity—Crises may be both geographically dispersed and of very different types, making institutional learning by experience more difficult and requiring more extensive coordination among agencies.

Number—Interventionist situations may be more numerous and even occasionally simultaneous (e.g., Somalia and Bosnia), requiring management approaches that effectively use the limited time and attention of key decision makers, and decision-making groups.

Constraints—The options available to the United States will be bound by external limits (e.g., alliances) and internal hurdles (e.g., legal questions and trade interdependencies), requiring an ability to fashion solutions within a maze of complex limitations.

Tools—The techniques of intervention will be more varied, and technology will provide options unlikely to be considered by uninformed participants. This requires government management to coordinate a greater variety of participants and provide training and education in the application of these techniques.

Vision—Compelling pressures will arise for short-term decisions that can have long-term effects (e.g., ending a crisis in a manner that sends the wrong signals to the next potential opponent), necessitating a decision-making framework that ensures congruence with long-term objectives and strategies.

Timeliness—Crises will require (as in the past) rapid response, particularly challenging when deciding on difficult policy actions (e.g., preemption), and the demand for timeliness will tax the government's ability to provide top-level decision makers (e.g., the president) the information they need.

Management concepts to address these characteristics exist in both the government and commercial environments, although in many cases private industry and academics are far ahead of the public sector. In the middle part of this century, corporate America often drew from the government in such areas as long-range planning and logistics management, but for the past several decades, commercial concepts of strategy and management have progressed faster and in new directions that have often left the government far behind. The concepts that have emerged are relevant to the government today because they are based on solving the same type of problem—how to change and direct large organizations in fast changing environments with uncertain futures.

Concepts and examples are presented in the following pages in three categories: strategy and planning, organization structure and functions, and organization processes and operations.

Strategy and Planning

Determining basic U.S. objectives and strategies in intervention is an important step because these not only provide policy guidelines, but also influence how government is organized. However, the search for objectives and strategies will probably be a long-term affair for the government, because it will find that complex issues are resolved not in the immaculate and sudden conception of a strategy, but in the development of strategy through the crucible of experience and deep involvement in solving real problems. In the majority of cases, good strategies evolve, they do not suddenly appear.

In developing new strategy there should be a probing examination of many concepts that have their roots in the cold war. Terms such as "deterrence," "intervention," "preemption," "proliferation," and "arms control" carry a number of underlying assumptions about the behavior of nations in general and what constitutes acceptable behavior by the United States. For example, deterrence in the past often meant the threat of nuclear attack to discourage another nation from using nuclear weapons, but with advances in precision weapons the United States could use conventional weapons to impose as severe or crippling a blow against a rogue nation. Should the United States develop the capability to impose nonnuclear strategic attack rather than be more tightly constrained to have to use nuclear weapons in response to another nation's first use?

Strategies or policies are needed for a number of areas related to intervention. To maintain U.S. competitive advantage over potential adversaries requires a set of goals and actions to develop and exploit opportunities in commercial and military technology, to make systems available to the government when they are needed, and to balance cost, schedule, and risk. Arms control approaches need to be redefined to transition from agreements with a nation no longer the key adversary, to agreements that are relevant to dealing with the activities of new participants (e.g., should the United States be bound by limits set with the Soviet Union but not followed by new potential opponents?) The behavior of U.S. government agencies needs to be guided to ensure that individual crises or interventionist situations are not viewed only through the narrow lens of the situation; how a crisis is handled affects how other nations behave in the future.

The private sector, confronted in the past several decades by the explosive growth of overseas markets, competitors, and technology, has evolved several techniques for determining and managing strategy. Just as in the government today, these were developed to guide long-term behavior in highly uncertain environments, where risks could be high and rates of change rapid.

Core Competencies

Core competencies appeared in the late 1980s in industry as a way to think about strategy. Core competencies are talents or capabilities that have an enduring quality, that are applicable in a variety of settings, that are seen as significant by potential opponents, and that are not easily duplicated by adversaries. For example, Honda has used its core competencies in engine and drivetrain design to successfully penetrate such dissimilar markets as automobiles, motorcycles, and lawnmowers. In industry individual companies have used the concept to guide long-term investments in basic technologies and in people skills, facilities, processes, etc. that are unique to a company and give it the potential for long-term advantage (e.g., in distribution, product design, market creation, etc.).

U.S. strategy and planning have for decades been closely tied to a specific opponent and the means to counter it. The analysis and then presentation of a threat was an essential first step in any effort to develop a new weapon or a new way to operate forces. With the seeming departure of the Soviet Union, the quandary for conceptualizing the organization, doctrine, and weapons of the U.S. military is that force investments are difficult to select and defend when no definitive threat can be identified. Consequently, valuable capabilities may be lost, and less important (but bureaucratically strong) ones may be retained.

Core competencies reshape such decisions away from finding specific threats and toward the questions of which enduring skills of the United States should be retained because they can support a variety of applications and situations. For example, the United States leads the world in such capabilities as distant naval operations, long-range air combat, intelligence, and long-distance logistics. It also appears to be among the best at integrating advanced weapons with combat units and operations, because these exploit the high skill levels of its soldiers and the quality of their training. National security planning based on core competencies would focus on preserving and enhancing such capabilities in order to provide a basic ability that can be tailored to the needs of a particular crisis or to the (now unpredictable) emergence of new or stronger political-military actors in the future.

Scenario Based Planning

Scenarios provide a planning technique that can avoid extensive debates over who has the most accurate prediction of the future against which to plan. Rather than try to precisely guess the future, strategists develop a number of possible futures and evaluate their impact on the organization. Planning and policy decisions are then made based on future outcomes that would (if they occur) pose some of the greater challenges to U.S. economic, political, and military capacities. In the corporate world, this approach has been successful in focusing managers not on debating which future is right, but on identifying what changes have to be made to exploit the futures that might emerge.

Scenario planning is already being explored in the government, for example, in exercises and forecasting efforts involving how nations and crises may emerge ten to twenty years in the future. Their power lies in decoupling policy from intelligence, which is inherently weak in estimating a few years (much less decades) in the future, and in focusing policy debates on what the differences are in how the government should operate. For example, a resurgence of a hostile Russia as a superpower would be an international tragedy, but the United States developed a national security system in the last half century focused on countering just such an adversary. The impact on the overall style of government would be modest. On the other hand, the rise of a "rogue state" in the Eurasian heartland would be a much more significant challenge because U.S. political thinking and military capabilities have not been focused on how to negotiate, pressure, or apply force against such a nation. For example, how would military power be projected to a place too remote to be able to supply and sustain Army divisions?

Time Oriented Strategies

Time management, both in daily activities and as an integral part of longer-term corporate strategies, has become a central tool of some modern industrial enterprises. The introduction by some automakers of new car models at more frequent rates than competitors has been used to undercut competitors' reputations for design and innovativeness. In retailing, the rapid movement of products from manufacturers to retail shelves (reducing stockage costs and store size) has opened new markets in smaller towns for discounters. Just-in-time inventory practices on production lines have led to reduced costs and improved quality.

In government, reducing the time to develop new technologies and new ways to operate would provide strategic robustness to deal with international competitors. It could enable the United States to introduce new capabilities that would sustain its leadership and deter opponents. It could provide a capacity to respond more rapidly to unanticipated actions by potential opponents. The use of time should not be viewed as a mundane efficiency issue because it has a much broader strategic dimension.

For example, increasing the frequency of innovation in military systems and doctrine, and timing introductions for political impact, can communicate to adversaries the uselessness of attempting to keep up. Ironically, the U.S. government has proposed on occasion to increase the development times for new capabilities while industry worldwide has been attempting to reduce those times. With the wider dissemination of technology and modern manufacturing techniques in the world, the United States should also expect to find nations, as a logical consequence of their industrial development, reducing the lead-time advantage the United

States has had in areas important to military effectiveness (e.g., sophisticated communications, encryption, geolocation, microelectronics, and material science). Will nations that are closing on U.S. leadership perceive (however ill-advised) that they are approaching parity with the United States and thus be able to act more aggressively (e.g., Iraq's invasion of Kuwait)?

Time oriented management also has second-order, beneficial effects, such as reducing the cost of government activities and the risk of new technology. In technology development, a high percentage of costs are "period" costs. They are incurred during a year regardless of the volume of work (e.g., the cost of heating a manufacturing plant is substantially independent of the number of units produced). Reducing the time during which a project is executed reduces these costs. Attempts to achieve major advances in technology (with the attendant increases in risk) result in part because of long gaps between the generations of new systems. Collapsing the time between generations reduces the need to undertake high-risk technologies. (Accelerating innovation rates also narrows the gap between the defense industrial base and commercial companies and eases the challenge of employing commercially available systems.) Finally, reducing time by accelerating change forces greater reliance on the skills of U.S. personnel to adapt to change. In the military, at least, this exercises a unique talent of U.S. forces (the quality of the individual soldier, and the adeptness of the military in employing new systems in multiunit operations).

Organization Structure and Functions

Since the emergence of the modern corporate structure in the early part of this century (in General Motors, for example), the concepts of how to divide work and assign responsibilities have continued to evolve. Concepts such as centralization, divisionalization, vertical and horizontal integration, and matrix management reflect the seeking of fundamental ways in which to organize work to provide strategic direction to an organization and efficiency in its operations. These ideas of structure have been equally valuable in private and public institutions.

One insight over the past several decades is that in organizations, anatomy can be destiny. While institutions may be organized originally on some overriding objectives and strategies ("structure follows strategy"), eventually the institution itself becomes a constraint on adapting to new environments. How tasks are prioritized and executed becomes determined by structure, functions, and procedures. The quality of insight is constrained by the type of skills of the people who have been acquired to fill that structure. The range of feasible solutions to problems is bound by how previous tasks have been successfully or unsuccessfully accomplished. Strategy, then, follows structure.

Today the U.S. government is not well structured to operate as effectively in the interventionist environment of the future as necessary. It lacks broad expertise in many foreign countries, regions, and their languages. Its overall focus may be driven by cold war management cultures (e.g., the shift of bureaucratic power within major agencies and departments may be moving too slowly from Soviet/European expertise to Asian/Pacific talent). Restructuring of military development and acquisition activities is occurring only superficially; changes are not being made in the fundamental manner in which requirements are developed, options considered, and solutions implemented. New technologies may not be developed rapidly to support political leaders, and very innovative technologies and operational practices may not emerge except over decades. Finally, declines in the resources available to national security are not being paralleled by sufficient decreases and restructuring of the bureaucracy of national security.

The current contraction of the Defense Department provides the most publicized view of this tension between strategy and structure. The end of the cold war has prompted the obvious examination of the defense establishment (e.g., new joint commands, canceling of weapon systems, debates over depots) in parallel with major reductions (e.g., our military personnel level may be 1 million people in the next century). The resulting struggles over roles and missions, as well as military strategies, in part reflect constituencies trying to protect their positions. It also demonstrates that both organizations and people have great difficulty doing things differently from the past. But the problem is much broader than defense. Across all agencies one determining factor in shaping the government's overall responses to the end of the cold war may be what people in its agencies traditionally think about and pay attention to for most of every working hour. Unless vigorously led and reorganized, past cultures will set the limits of defense and other capabilities in the future, and will dramatically affect strategy.

Differentiation and Integration

This concept recognizes that like activities need to be grouped together in order to obtain both efficiency and learning, and to respond to the unique characteristics of the work and people involved (e.g., in business this usually means having accounting functions, R&D efforts, manufacturing, etc. in separate organizations). These separate activities then need to be linked together to provide products and services through various coordination devices (e.g., committees, teams, bureaucratic procedures). For example, in government, the work environment and type of people essential to research in advanced technology are different from the work environment and people essential to conducting military operations. Successful organizations figure out how to organize to obtain the best in research and in operations, and how to link these together to develop affordable systems that perform when needed.

While the concept is easy, the power of this division and recombining lies in understanding the subtle characteristics of different types of work and in finding the appropriate integrating mechanisms. At the broadest level, for example, the division of tasks between the State Department and Defense Department reflects not just bureaucratic history, but the fact that people who must be highly competent in combat operations are different in their skills from those who are diplomats. The type of training and the sense for what is important at a fundamental level are different. Homogenizing them in one agency would risk marginalizing their skills in a way that makes each less effective. It is in part for this reason that the National Security Council (NSC) system, which integrates across departments, is potentially so useful. It permits differentiation, while providing the means for integration.

At least three challenges in differentiating and integrating people and organizational talents face the government. First, the development of new tools in intervention (i.e., new economic/trade opportunities and new technologies) invariably will require new skills (new needs for specialization). Is the State Department adequately skilled in the technologies of intervention to link them to its traditional diplomatic roles? Will the DOD adequately support the evolution of new technologies and new capabilities such as rapid, long-reach warfare and information warfare to make them more applicable to interventionist situations? Can the Commerce Department develop aggressive trade and other economic tactics into a portfolio of potential actions?

Second, the presence of new tools of intervention and the variety of interventionist situations will demand more integration across agencies and departments at the national level. Agencies such as Energy, Commerce, Justice, and the SEC may at various times be part of the response mechanisms organized at the Washington level to assist the president in shaping the U.S. role in a crisis. The current NSC mechanism provides the flexibility in a broad institutional sense to capture and coordinate the talents of these organizations, and the NSC system is fluid enough to respond to the operating styles of individual presidents. On the other hand, the complexity and subtlety of coordinating organizations is often underestimated, and more attention is required by the government to developing such integrating skills. (Past crises have shown, for example, that the NSC system operates better with practice, a phenomenon occasionally overlooked by senior administration officials until they observe rusty performance in a crisis.)

Third, integrating across agencies may already be a weak point in intervention management outside of Washington. For example, military deployments to regions (e.g., Desert Storm) are accompanied by command structures that, despite some criticisms as to their effectiveness, do coordinate across military services, operational missions, and geographic areas. No such similar structure coordinates U.S. political or economic relationships on a region-wide basis. Consequently, senior military commanders may be thrust into political and economic issues that divert their time, and for which they may not be adequately prepared. Embassy structures and "country teams" of agencies are not an appropriate response, because they are country and not regionally focused. Day-to-day political and economic management of in-theater issues in a regional crisis cannot be accomplished from Washington, and this absence of an integrative mechanism creates the risk that important political issues may not receive the attention and timely action they require.

Shallow Hierarchies

For a number of reasons, corporations have been removing the middle and senior layers of their management structures. While this certainly relates to cutting costs, the decrease in hierarchy also recognizes more profound strategic issues. Hierarchies consume time, and in a rapidly changing environment organizations must be able to move fast to respond to competitors. Hierarchies shape and control information, and senior decision makers increasingly recognize that accurate information is essential to decisions. Hierarchies lead to power centers within organizations, which then control the type of people who populate important positions. The effect of these constraints is to impair the flexibility of companies to respond to changing environments. Removing hierarchy can increase agility.

While it is an extremely difficult challenge to the government, the removal of management levels and a focus on agility would be major improvements. The relevance to intervention can be seen on several levels. First, experts in the unusual countries that may be the focus of future crises may be too far removed from the president and senior decision makers. When the Soviet Union was the focus of attention, the government was populated by large numbers of knowledgeable individuals, often organizationally close to top-level people. Except for the Middle East, in the case of the lesser states that will rise to attention in the future, the experts may be very difficult to identify and far removed in the hierarchy.

Second, the unpredictability of the future crisis environment requires responsive organizations, and hierarchies create obstacles to responsiveness. This effect is not malicious, but it is inherent in hierarchies. For example, years of experience have led to certain staffs in agencies and departments becoming centers of bureaucratic power (often those with expertise in Russian and European affairs). This power may have to shift to staffs focused on Asia and the Pacific. As a second example, the efforts to modernize the government's approach to system acquisition are constrained by the presence of over 300,000 government workers in a highly layered structure of agencies and procedures (one reason why most attempts at reform since World War II have stalled after changing a few top-level positions in the Pentagon). For introducing technologies that may be useful to creative intervention, this layered structure with rules that lead to decades-long development times will be a major obstacle. In a world where opponents may use current technology against the United States, a cumbersome hierarchy can doom the United States to competing on an unequal basis.

Adaptive Organizations

In parallel with core competencies and shallow hierarchies is the increasing realization that effective institutions are those that adapt to external changes and internal opportunities. In markets that have short product life cycles and in which new competitors can appear and old ones can introduce surprising challenges, companies that succeed have mechanisms that enable them to collect and accurately assess information on the external environment, and reshape themselves to respond. For this to happen, the assigned functions of individuals and suborganizations cannot be rigidly defined (so they have latitude to change), healthy tension and competition among elements are tolerated (to maintain their competitive skills), and some redundancy is permitted (to reduce the chance that the wrong solution will be the only one pursued).

Adaptation in the broadest sense is an endemic problem for all governments, occasionally cited in the tragic failures of military organizations to adapt to new technologies and new battlefield conditions (e.g., the trench warfare of World War I and the failure to respond to the Nazis' development of blitzkrieg in the late 1930s). Implicit in the National Performance Review led by Vice President Al Gore in 1993 is a call for improving the adaptability of government. An example of such an application, although not in the National Performance Review, would be the use of controlled competition among agencies. Government, rooted in early twentieth century management cultures, works to eliminate duplication except under tightly constrained conditions (e.g., funding separate research and development approaches to solve the same problem). Yet, competition between agencies can stimulate innovation. The struggle between the military services over various ways to deliver close air support, for example, has resulted in different and, in some cases, better approaches to accomplish the mission than a single service would have pursued.

The reexamination of roles and missions among the military services that is getting underway can result in creating institutions with a long-term focus on adaptation. For example, the military may contract to a million personnel, less than half the strength of the cold war. Apart from any debates over the adequacy of this number, it will force addressal of the roles of the individual services. In general, should military missions be assigned to eliminate all forms of internal competition? Would managed competition provide useful stimuli and counterbalances to encourage creative adaptation to change? More important, the military will have to become far more compatible with operational concepts of combined arms, such as U.S. Air Force long-range bombers on alert becoming integral to U.S. Navy deployments overseas. As roles are redefined to incorporate this need, what capabilities will be lost and what steps will be taken to restart such capabilities if necessary (i.e., to adapt to an unexpected need)?

Much attention in reorganization is focused on the Defense Department, but similar actions are undoubtedly needed in the Departments of State and Commerce and the Central Intelligence Agency. Each is structured much as it was during the cold war. While the regional and functional bureaus in State may be highly adaptable for the new national security environment, it is unlikely that the entrenched bureaucracies will be able to lead in thinking about and developing new mechanisms for diplomatic intervention. Rather, when moved by a tenacious outside force, like a willing president, State will do its best to combine existing diplomatic approaches to respond to new problems. It will most likely fall further and further behind in understanding the increasing role of technology in state-to-state relations, multinational businesses, and warfare. Further, it will be held hostage in its thinking by its historic focus on Europe and Russia. In so doing, it may well miss the opportunity to shape the environment in which the powers of Asia, for instance, may emerge. To a lesser extent, Commerce is unlikely to innovate in the area of economic intervention capabilities for basically similar reasons.

Organization Processes and Operations

Organizations have three components that define their operational potential: the hierarchy or structure, the roles or functions assigned to individuals and groups in the structure, and the processes that are used to accomplish work. In the past several decades, industry has become increasingly aware of the critical importance of process management and improvement as a source of efficiency (e.g., increasing output per unit of cost) and for strategic effectiveness (e.g., for quickly responding to changes in the environment). For example, in core competencies the talents that are often seen as key are the unique processes by which a company operates. Any firm can acquire tools, factories, skilled workers, and so on. Secure advantage rests in being able to integrate those capabilities more effectively than others.

Process improvements are as difficult as they are critical. In part, processes are tailored to respond to the structure and functions of an organization; teams, for example, are a process approach used to link across defined functions in a structure. Changing the structure, therefore, implies changing the teaming process. In part, the difficulty of changing processes also rests in the intricate nature of processes. Altering them requires detailed understanding, which is why decentralized and group oriented efforts are so frequently key steps in process improvements. Three processes are discussed in the subsequent paragraphs as indications of the complexity of process improvements and their importance to altering the government's performance in interventionist capabilities.

Improvements in DOD Planning and Budgeting

The Planning-Programing-Budgeting System (PPBS) of the DOD and the authorization and appropriations processes of the Congress have been criticized for years for impeding modern management. For example, the annual appropriation process discourages long-range programing. Line-by-line changes made by all levels of the executive branch and the Congress limit the capacity to manage programs, and the practice of removing budgeted amounts that have not been obligated encourages wasteful spending practices. However, many of these weaknesses are deeply imbedded in the historical political processes of the government (e.g., the congressional practice of giving very specific instructions to the military in appropriations can be traced back at least to the nineteenth century). The probability is remote that major changes can be effected.

Moreover, even though the first "P" of PPBS is considered still to be "silent" (i.e., virtually nonexistent), the discipline of the PPBS serves a useful function. While it may be executed in a cumbersome manner that consumes excessive amounts of energy, the PPBS does force people at all levels of the government to consider long-range needs, to evaluate programs to meet these, and to allocate the limited amount of available funds among them. Top-level managers should have the capacity to intervene and elevate to higher priority those programs that the government's long-term needs require be given greater support. The challenge is to adjust the process to meet the needs of the post–cold war period.

Within the confines of the PPBS the process can be streamlined and made more relevant to the interventionist environment of the future. For example, three changes could be implemented that would improve the system: replacement of the Major Force Programs (MFPs) with new categories closely allied to the types of forces the United States will need; the use of scenarios in a serious planning phase; and the institution of capabilities based planning in place of the threat based focus. The latter two have been discussed under *Strategy and Planning*.

The DOD organizes all of its military forces, weapons, technologies, facilities, and so on into eleven categories of Major Force Programs. The key MFPs are I (Strategic Forces), II (General Purpose Forces), III (Intelligence and Communications), VI (Research and Development), and XI (Special Operations Forces). Ten of the eleven categories were established in the early 1960s, at the height of the cold war, and have endured for more than thirty years; the eleventh (Special Operations Forces) was added in the mid-1980s.

The categories constrain thinking and investing in forces for the new environment. For example, MFP II (General Purpose Forces) contains virtually all the air, naval, and ground combat forces used in conventional operations. A more useful approach to focus top-level attention would be to subdivide these into smaller increments focused on the specific applications, much as was accomplished with the creation of MFP XI (Special Operations Forces). As a second example, long-range bombers have been in MFP I (Strategic Forces) since the 1960s, despite their conventional capabilities and their repeated use in conventional conflicts. They have competed for resources against land based and submarine launched missiles, and the subtle incentives of thinking about them largely from a nuclear viewpoint have probably delayed the development of precision-guided conventional bombs for bombers (the development of precision-guided weapons traces to tactical air forces in the 1960s). Only with the introduction of the B-2 bomber has the DOD recognized the dramatic interventionist capabilities of bombers equipped with significant numbers of conventional, precise munitions.

Decisions on future forces for interventionist roles would be made more explicit if major force categories were created that grouped programs by the functions that will be important in the coming years. For example, such a new set could be:

I Strategic-Nuclear Missile Forces

II Naval Warfare/Sea Control

III Theater Combat Forces

IV Long-Range Strike/Power Projection

V Special Operations

VI Long-Range Logistics (Airlift/Sealift/Ground)

VII Intelligence

VIII Communications

IX Research and Development

X Administrative

This grouping is not organized by joint commands because the command structure should change from time to time as military strategy changes. The recommended categories have a more enduring character.

Improvements in Technology and System Acquisition

The acquisition system, like the PPBS, has come under repeated criticism over several decades of studies and reviews by panels in and out of government. The endurance of many of the most criticized aspects of the system strongly suggests that fundamental political, economic, and technical forces are at work. While this resistance to change is often blamed (rightfully) on the vested interests of various constituencies, the acquisition process also results from the inherent differences between defense systems and those produced in the commercial sector, and from the demands imposed by a single-buyer market (monopsony). Military systems (particularly systems like ships, armor vehicles, and combat aircraft) are in fact unique in their tolerance for damage, their performance capabilities, and their packaging of high-technology subsystems to give their operators an edge in combat. The government as the only buyer (the monopsonist) enforces unique requirements on companies, in part reflecting social objectives (e.g., minority contracting and profit limitations), and in part reflecting bureaucratic preferences (e.g., requiring unique accounting systems).

The acknowledgment of inherent differences is not to excuse the increases in cost, lengthy product development time, bizarre contractual forms, unbelievably cumbersome and expensive oversight, or departures from quality that could be corrected with more modern management practices. Nor does it excuse the additional costs incurred when products that do not inherently differ dramatically from commercial items are acquired with the full cost burden of a military acquisition. On the other hand, the sweeping calls for commercial items to be used for military purposes occasionally overlook the valid reasons that exist for the military character of some systems.

An overhaul of the system is needed. However, changes in top-level acquisition management that have been made in DOD over the years have had little effect because the day-to-day activities of those who implement the acquisition processes remain largely unaffected. What is required is a process approach that reaches deep into the hierarchy of several hundred thousand government workers, starting with dramatic downsizing of this bureaucracy. Of the many proposals for change, the processes that would most improve intervention capabilities are those that: (1) reduce the time for concepts to reach the field as operating systems; (2) increase the rate of innovation; and (3) protect both the manufacturing and the technology base. A new industrial model will be needed that preserves both research and manufacturing capabilities while operating at a much lower funding level. Absent an ability to produce continuously at low rates, for example, the United States could find itself in the next century with little industrial capability in militarily important areas. (It was the vision of such a risk that led the government to identify submarines as an industrial base issue.)

Moreover, the United States may face challenges in the coming decades from opponents whose approach to military systems design and whose time to acquire systems may be markedly different (i.e., several years as opposed to decades). As mentioned earlier, the growth in the international market and the dissemination of technological talent among more nations are a positive sign for global development. But it also means that the United States will not be able to monitor or control the military modernization of other nations with the dexterity of the past. For example, nations in the Pacific Rim, having achieved enormous economic success in industrial development for commercial products, may choose to emulate their commercial management approaches if they decide to develop larger armed forces. They may easily collapse the development times for new weapons (in contrast to the decades it requires in the United States). The current acquisition system requires too much time to provide reasonable responses, and by doing so it shapes strategy.

Training and Development

Future interventionist situations are going to involve encounters with a variety of states and alliances that will be very different from both the United States and the Soviet Union in their operating styles, approaches to solving problems, perceptions of their roles in the world, and their relations with the United States. For example, at the alliance level, confrontations in Europe will probably be acted out within the structure of coalitions (e.g., NATO) that have existed for decades, which provides processes (and constraints) for developing solutions. However, the states of the Pacific Rim do not have a half century of "NATO-like" alliance processes for conflict resolution. Unexpected alliances or coalition solutions might be developed in the Pacific to deal with emerging problems (e.g., suppose these nations choose to develop processes to resolve conflicts that are based on their business relationships).

The training challenge facing the government is to develop the talent pool to respond to the new dimensions of the international environment and provide insights that lead to useful policy solutions. From a substantive standpoint, this means developing regional and area experts, or providing access to them in the private sector. In functional areas, such as manufacturing, finance, and various branches of science, the government will need mechanisms to enlist outside experts. More generally, the government's work force may not be adequately trained in technical areas to integrate technology actions into interventionist policies and crises.

From a conceptual perspective, the challenge facing the government is to develop an adaptiveness of mind among its analysts and policy makers that parallels the organizational adaptiveness that is also needed. Analysts historically have had difficulty viewing other nations (e.g., the Soviet Union) other than through the lens of their own experience. Such limitations can be very significant. For example, in Desert Storm, analysts completely misunderstood the extent and intricacy of the Iraqi nuclear program. They did not realize or think through how the Iraqis might have changed their program following the 1981 Israeli attack on their reactor. Nor did analysts think the Iraqis would use technology the United States itself had long ago set aside. The result was that the number of nuclear sites discovered after the war was more than twice as great as believed at the war's outset, the closeness of the Iraqis to having a bomb was underestimated, and the fact that the Iraqis had shifted in the 1980s to developing a uranium rather than a plutonium bomb was overlooked.

Moreover, prediction—which was difficult enough against the Soviets—will be even more difficult in the complex post–cold war world. Scenario planning, core competencies, and adaptive organizations are all mechanisms to diminish the criticality of predictive accuracy. They also suggest greater investment in flexible and responsive systems and structures, and less investment in classic intelligence systems to help analysts. Acquiring more complex and expensive collection platforms, for example, is unlikely to improve the accuracy of predicting the emergence of regional powers ten years in the future. The criteria for determining whether to buy expensive collection systems should, therefore, be their short-term, immediate benefits (e.g., for negotiation support, monitoring forces, and tracking economic developments), and these systems should be forced to compete with alternative nonintelligence means. The funds saved could be committed to training analysts, opening up paths to experts in the private sector, and acquiring the systems that can respond to crises when they erupt.

Finally, training and exercises are two processes that can improve performance in interventionist situations. It can be "very expensive" for government to "learn on the job." At all levels of the government—but most particularly at the political appointee and elected official level—exercises and other training techniques need to be pursued to ensure that the president and others are well supported in a real crisis. Senior officials are the most likely to be the least well informed on the competence of various government agencies and the private sector to respond to their needs, and exercises can enable them and those in the agencies to understand key capabilities. Fortunately, technology is moving in directions to ease the challenge of such learning. Distributive, computer based communications enable leaders and followers alike to interact in a crisis exercise although they may be a continent apart. An additional innovation would be to enlist private sector individuals and organizations as participants.

Summary

The United States is moving into a period in the post–cold war environment in which intervention questions may be a more central part of U.S. foreign policy than in the past. The contrast to the cold war may be dramatic. More incidents of intervention will probably arise than in the past, and the situations will be highly varied in their participants and contexts. The United States will need to be more deeply involved or interested in the internal activities of nations. Often such actions will be on a multinational basis, confronting the United States with challenges to control the limits of its commitments in the face of subtle influences that may alter the actions of such coalitions.

The nation has the inherent skills and capabilities to participate effectively in this highly varied environment. Its position as the leading military power in the world gives it leverage, in addition to the actual pressure it can bring to bear through economic, diplomatic, and military means. The United States can, provided it commits to the effort, develop strategies and concepts to leverage its competitive advantages over adversaries, including periodically unveiling dramatic technology innovations, and over friends and allies who might someday consider confronting it in some manner. This can be done with defense budgets below those of the cold war period, but maintaining this country's position as a real, as compared to a self-deluded, superpower will not be cheap.

The achievement of this capability, however, requires major changes in the management of government. The end of the cold war not only forced an addressal of the question of how much to spend on defense and what military strategies to pursue. It also removed the support for many fundamental aspects of the style of government (cold war management has spread far beyond the Pentagon). To meet the requirements of the future, the government has to be more adaptive and responsive to increasing and unpredictable change. It has to form organizations and processes that integrate functions across government in a manner that ensures that top-level leadership is fully cognizant of policy issues. It has to develop practices that sustain underlying defense capabilities to support near-term regional interventionist situations, while hedging against the longer-term risks of a new major power. It also must learn to use its military, technological, and doctrinal strengths to deter any emerging power from thinking it can successfully challenge U.S. interests abroad.

Bibliography

Bell-Fialkoff, Andrew. 1993. "A Brief History of Ethnic Cleansing." *Foreign Affairs* 72:3, pp. 110–121.

Bolton, John R. 1994. "Wrong Turn in Somalia." *Foreign Affairs* 73:1, pp. 56–66.

Boutros-Ghali, Boutros. 1992. *An Agenda for Peace*. New York: United Nations.

Doyle, Michael W. 1986. *Empires*. Ithaca: Cornell University Press.

Gaddis, John Lewis. 1986. "The Long Peace: Elements of Stability in the Postwar International System." *International Security* 10, pp. 99–142.

———. 1987. *The Long Peace: Inquiries into the History of the Cold War*. New York: Oxford University Press.

Hufbauer, Gary Clyde, Jeffrey J. Schott, and Kimberly Ann Elliott. 1990. *Economic Sanctions Reconsidered*. Washington, D.C.: Institute for International Economics.

Huntington, Samuel P. 1986. "Playing to Win." *The National Interest*, Spring 1986, pp. 8–16.

International Institute for Strategic Studies. 1993. *The Military Balance, 1993–94*. London: Brasseys.

Kennedy, Paul. 1987. *The Rise and Fall of the Great Powers: Economic Change and Military Conflict from 1500–2000*. New York: Random House.

Kissinger, Henry A. 1973. *A World Restored: Metternich, Castelreagh and the Problems of Peace 1812–1822*. Boston: Houghton Mifflin.

Konovalov, Alexander, Sergei Oznobistchev, and Dmitri Evstafiev. 1993. "Saying *da,* saying *nyet.*" *The Bulletin of the Atomic Scientists* 49:9, pp. 28–31.

Krauthammer, Charles. 1986. "The Reagan Doctrine: The Rights and Wrongs of Guerrilla War." *The New Republic,* September 8, 1986, pp. 17–24.

————. 1991. "The Unipolar Moment." *Foreign Affairs* 70, pp. 23–33.

Lippmann, Walter. 1943. *U.S. Foreign Policy: Shield of the Republic.* Boston: Little, Brown & Company.

Mueller, John. 1989. *Retreat from Doomsday: The Obsolescence of Major War.* New York: Basic Books.

National Security Strategy of the United States. 1993. Washington, D.C.: The White House.

Powell, Colin. 1992/93. "U.S. Forces: Challenges Ahead." *Foreign Affairs* 71:5, pp. 32–45.

Robinson, Ronald, and John Gallagher, with Alice Denny. 1978. *Africa and the Victorians: The Official Mind of Imperialism.* 2nd ed. London: The Macmillan Press.

Rowland, Peter. 1975. *David Lloyd George: A Biography.* New York: Macmillan.

Schelling, Thomas C. 1980. *The Strategy of Conflict.* Cambridge: Harvard University Press.

Snyder, Jack. 1991. *Myths of Empire: Domestic Politics and International Ambition.* Ithaca: Cornell University Press.

Stuermer, Michael. 1993. "Global Tasks and Challenges: The Difficult Search for a New World Order." *AUS Politik und Zeitgeschichte,* vol. 17.

Toth, Robert C. 1994. "In Search of a Foreign Policy." *Foreign Service Journal,* January 1994, pp. 31–35.

U.S. General Accounting Office. 1992. *Economic Sanctions: Effectiveness as Tools of Foreign Policy.* Washington, D.C.: U.S. GAO.

Walzer, Michael. 1977. *Just and Unjust Wars: A Moral Argument with Historical Illustrations.* New York: Basic Books.

Zakaria, Fareed. 1990. "The Reagan Strategy of Containment." *Political Science Quarterly,* Fall 1990, pp. 373–95.

————. 1992. "Realism and Domestic Politics." *International Security,* Summer 1992.

Final Report
of the
Eighty-Fifth American Assembly

At the close of their discussions, the participants in the Eighty-fifth American Assembly, on "U.S. Intervention Policy for the Post–Cold War World: New Challenges and New Responses," at Arden House, Harriman, New York, April 7–10, 1994, reviewed as a group the following statement. This statement represents general agreement; however, no one was asked to sign it. Furthermore, it should be understood that not everyone agreed with all of it.

Since Vietnam, perhaps no national security topic has been as politically divisive as the question of U.S. intervention. This debate threatened to rekindle as the American experiences in Somalia, Bosnia, and Haiti combined to feed growing public and congressional doubts about both the wisdom of U.S. intervention and our ability to intervene successfully.

The Eighty-fifth American Assembly addressed the question of whether and when coercive intervention can be an effective and appropriate instrument of U.S. foreign policy in the post–cold war world. By "coercive intervention" we mean the deliberate involvement by the United States in the affairs of another state or transnational organization in order to change its behavior or character, using techniques that run the gamut from targeted information activities to economic sanctions to military force.

This Assembly began with two premises. First, intervention is a fact of life; a neoisolationist policy of strict nonintervention is neither realistic nor desirable. Second, in a world of eroding state sovereignty, intervention is neither intrinsically good nor intrinsically bad, but must be judged on the basis of its purposes, costs, and prospects in each case. We considered how new techniques and new technologies might affect the costs and benefits of intervention. Finally, we formulated policy guidelines for decisions on future U.S. intervention.

The Post–Cold War World

The most dramatic change since the end of the cold war is the disappearance of a single dominant security threat to the United States. This change has led to, or has been accompanied by, other developments that together constitute key features of the post–cold war landscape:

• With the collapse of the Soviet empire, our threat-driven approach to intervention disappeared as well. The removal of the single, well-defined threat uncovered a multitude of lesser immediate situations that we may or may not find threatening, and longer-term threats of a nonmilitary character—e.g., environmental degradation and population growth—that may seem less compelling because they do not have serious, short-term consequences. This change has created the need to find a new consensus on criteria for deciding when and where to intervene.

• The post–cold war world may be characterized by growing instability, but we can pursue many of our interests in a messy and unstable world. The United States should not feel driven to inter vene everywhere stability is jeopardized, but should only consider intervention where our interests and values are threatened.

• Because the international environment has become less predictable, it is more difficult to know which threats to plan for, or to calculate accurately the costs and benefits of particular courses of action. This uncertainty leads to increased political controversy and greater potential for miscalculation.

• Finally, the near elimination of the Soviet military threat has both increased the prominence of longstanding interests (such as preventing proliferation of nuclear, chemical, or biological weapons) that were submerged by the superpower competition, and allowed us to redirect national resources to additional, largely domestic, interests. In particular, economic interests now play a dominant role in our foreign policy.

U.S. leadership—in either unilateral or multilateral settings— remains crucial. This does not mean that we should adopt every problem and cause as our own. We cannot and should not. But it does mean that we must recognize that if we don't respond to threats or seize opportunities, we cannot count on anyone else to protect our interests.

U.S. intervention policy remains subject to constraints, but the nature of these constraints has changed. The *external* constraints on the United States have become fewer and weaker, except for the possibility of retaliation through terrorism as destructive power devolves into less state directed and less deterrable hands. At the same time, *internal domestic* constraints have become much more substantial.

The lack of a dominant, widely accepted external threat has reduced the political priority assigned to international problems at the same time as it has eroded the previous consensus about our foreign policy priorities. There is now *no* domestic consensus about the organizing principles of U.S. foreign policy.

The challenge of establishing new, post–cold war foreign policy priorities is further exacerbated by the expanding impact of the international media, which can play a major, if often unpredictable, role in determining what gets on the national agenda. Meanwhile, the growing priority of economic interests means that intervention policies and the capabilities needed to implement them are increasingly judged by their economic impact, both in terms of their resource requirements and their expected economic costs and benefits.

Another constraint on U.S. intervention policy arises from the strong presumption in favor of multilateral action. It is striking that the "assertive multilateralism" of the early Clinton administration has been replaced by "cautious" multilateralism, not by unilateralism. Especially for interventions involving the use of force, multilateral action (or, at least, authorization) is becoming the norm and unilateral action the exception. This is less a matter of preference than a political fact of life in the post–cold war world.

These developments increase the importance of the national leadership engaging the American people on where our interests lie and on what must be done to achieve them.

One of the most striking features of the current period is the mismatch between our rhetoric and our resources. The administration's announced strategy of enlarging the community of democratic market-economy nations implies a growing demand on resources. The end of the cold war, however, has resulted in a steady and substantial decline in defense spending and other resources for intervention. Absent a clear sense of priorities among competing foreign policy interests, as well as a clear sense of priority between domestic and foreign policy concerns, there is a real risk that shrinking resources will be spread too thinly to accomplish any of our priorities.

It would be a mistake to attribute these trends to inexorable domestic political pressures to turn inward and concentrate solely on our problems at home. Americans understand that we live in an increasingly interdependent world. There was disagreement among participants on the extent to which Americans were willing to accept any significant level of casualties in responding to the new challenges of the world. However, most agreed that if Americans are asked to take risks, they must know why they are taking them.

Perhaps the greatest need, therefore, is for a new vision to give coherence to our foreign policy. In our system, such a vision can only come from the president. Over forty years ago, another president, faced with a new world following the end of a major war, commissioned a sweeping examination of the world, America's interests, and the steps needed to promote those interests. The resulting concept—known as containment—became the blueprint for U.S. policy in the cold war. *The first, and in many ways the most important, recommendation of this American Assembly is that the president direct a similar sweeping examination of the post–cold war world.* This examination should lead to a clear articulation not just of the kind of world we would prefer, but of what changes in the world are so important to us that we are willing to commit resources and undertake various forms of intervention to bring them about, given our competing priorities.

The world will not stand still while awaiting the crafting of a new vision. Presidents and their advisers will continue to face a large and growing number of intervention decisions. The remainder of this report is intended to help them make wise choices.

Military Responses to Post–Cold War Challenges

U.S. forces are well structured and prepared for high-intensity operations, but less so for peace operations and lower-intensity intervention. Particularly given projected shortfalls in current defense budget plans, the United States must give special attention to ensuring that there are adequate forces for intervention across the spectrum of conflict.

There are many situations such as traditional United Nations peacekeeping in which U.S. allies or others can play a leading role. In such cases, any U.S. involvement will likely be in a supporting role, exploiting our comparative strength in strategic lift, communications, intelligence, and logistics.

When military forces are used, they should first be used, along with diplomatic and economic means, to deter conflict. If preventive measures fail and actual military force is necessary, committing sufficient forces, carefully tailored to the threat, increases the chances that the conflict will be resolved promptly, with minimal loss of life and collateral damage.

While U.S. forces are sufficient for large-scale intervention, they are not optimized for peacekeeping and other peace operations, or for other types of low-level conflict. These operations demand specialized training and preparation. It is not enough to have regionally oriented special operations forces; general purpose forces—the most commonly used instrument—must also be better prepared for peace operations and low-level conflict, especially since the frequency of U.S. participation in such activities is increasing.

This Assembly noted the following potential weaknesses:

- Lack of an agreed strategic concept within the U.S. government for military intervention;
- Inadequate capabilities for multilateral operations and doctrine for peace operations;
- Insufficient language capabilities for both traditional and non-traditional areas of operation, such as sub-Saharan Africa and Central Asia;
- Inadequate human intelligence capability and a maladapted national intelligence capability; and
- Slow procurement and integration of those high-technology capabilities that enhance military effectiveness and reduce casualties (especially civilian casualties) during military interventions.

This Assembly discussed nonlethal technologies that include a wide range of ideas and devices with the potential to complement our forces' lethal capabilities, especially in peace operations or small-scale interventions where current military capabilities have substantial shortcomings. These technologies may also be employed as stand-alone instruments to further some strategic objective such as diplomatic coercion. They may save lives, lower dollar costs, make our forces more effective, and their use more acceptable politically. They will not, however, obviate the need to make hard policy choices based on national interests and values.

Nonlethal technologies also may have downsides. The attractive label "nonlethal" may promise more than the device can always deliver. For example, some applications, such as rubber bullets, may kill if used at close range, even though they are clearly intended to be nonlethal. Also, some nonlethal measures, such as those that operate against widespread computer networks, could be turned against us with devastating effects. We need to consider carefully whether U.S. use of such capabilities would make it more likely that an adversary would use them on us. In any event, there are vulnerabilities to U.S. systems for which countermeasures must be developed. The potential costs and effectiveness of these systems must also be carefully assessed. Finally, a significant minority of our participants was concerned that effective nonlethal technology might increase the chance that we would intervene simply because we could, rather than because we should.

Despite the skepticism of many participants about the utility of nonlethal technology in improving our coercive capability, we all recognized the dangers of ignoring new things that don't fit into our established thought patterns. The issue calls for more analysis, more research and development, and organizational efforts that foster, rather than stifle, innovation.

Which government agency should take the lead is not clear. In general, the Department of Defense should develop technologies with the potential to enhance existing military capabilities or to create new options. Other agencies such as Justice, Treasury, Commerce, and the United States Information Agency should be included in the requirements and evaluation process.

This Assembly could not evaluate either the recommendations of the proponents of nonlethal technologies or the objections of skeptics. *The National Security Council should direct an urgent interagency examination of nonlethal and other new technologies including political, ethical, legal, and organizational factors.* This Assembly found "no free lunch, and no silver bullets."

Nonmilitary Responses to Post–Cold War Challenges

Not all of the post–cold war challenges call for coercive responses. The end of the bipolar military confrontation also created conditions for resolution of long-festering disputes through negotiation and multilateral processes of conflict resolution. The United Nations settlement in Cambodia and progress in the Middle East peace process suggest the opportunities that exist for noncoercive U.S. intervention.

From this perspective, we should encourage preventive diplomacy, support humanitarian relief operations, and use our moral and political influence to support negotiated resolution of international disputes. Our ability to carry out such efforts successfully will be significantly enhanced by multinational cooperation. One of our objectives should be to encourage the development and strengthening of multilateral organizations and coalition efforts in support of such goals as regional security, control of the proliferation of weapons of mass destruction, and disaster relief.

Still, the need for coercive intervention will remain. There are a variety of nonmilitary intervention techniques available to the United States. Despite a spotty record of success, economic sanctions are likely to remain one of the first coercive measures used in an intervention. They provide a method by which to signal the international community about U.S. intentions, to seek changes in the behavior of targeted countries, to punish governments for specific behavior, and to isolate outlaw regimes.

The decision to impose economic sanctions should be linked to a calculation of their likely success. Effectiveness is related to several factors, including the degree of domestic and international support for the actions, the duration of the sanctions, the degree to which the target country is dependent on external capital, trade, and resources, and whether the stakes are sufficient to sustain the sanctions and any subsequent decisions to impose additional coercive measures should they become necessary. The moral element should not be ignored. Regardless of the prospect of economic effectiveness of sanctions, there will be cases where we will simply not want an economic relationship with an outlaw regime.

Sustaining sanctions is difficult. They are costly to implement, slow to take effect, and frequently inflict more hardship upon the civilian population than upon the targeted political or military leadership. Their chances of success also are substantially lessened if the targeted leadership doubts our commitment to persevere.

In an increasingly interdependent economic world, unilateral sanctions are less likely to accomplish their objectives than are multilateral sanctions. The growing ability of countries to provide what they need themselves, the increasing number of nations eager to sell whatever else a given country may need, and the increased integration of the world's economy (which means that sanctions hurt innocent states as well as their targets) combine to continue to degrade the effectiveness of even multilateral sanctions. This creates a dilemma for policy makers because economic sanctions—notwithstanding their problematic effectiveness—are likely to be the most politically acceptable and available means of coercive intervention that satisfy the public desire to do something and yet remain at arm's length.

The information revolution creates potential new avenues for nonmilitary coercive intervention. Increasing international interdependence and growth in telecommunications and similar technologies present both opportunities and dangers. Subtle means to alter broadcasts, to manipulate computer data bases (such as bank records), or to silence telephone communications all could provide powerful disruptive measures, albeit with uncertain coercive effects.

These technologies, however, also present serious threats to the information and technology dependent U.S. society and economy. Overt or discovered covert use of these technologies risks delivering these means to hostile actors, legitimizing the use of these methods, and unleashing responses in kind. In addition, the consequences of many of these methods are unclear; for instance, a computer virus introduced in a targeted country may spread in unpredictable ways to friendly hosts.

Targeting these methods against the internal networks of a single hostile country does not raise the same problems that manipulating international information resources and networks would. They also may provide important techniques to enhance the effectiveness of efforts by the United States and the international community to change the behavior of, for example, genocidal governments or fomenters of state supported terrorism. Even when the effect can be confined to the target country, however, it is unclear that the benefits of manipulating local information systems of hostile countries warrant the threat to U.S. security resulting from seeming to legitimize the use of such means in the eyes of the international community. *Therefore, this American Assembly recommends:*

- *New, unconventional means of communications intrusion—because of political and ethical sensitivities, practical problems, and the danger that it could be construed as an act of aggression—should only be undertaken after most careful consideration and under the most stringent political controls.*
- *Development of countermeasures and security should be undertaken, along with consideration of international initiatives to limit, if not proscribe, some forms of communications intrusion.*

U.S. Intervention Policy for the Future

We have described a post–cold war world that denies us the possibility of a neoisolationist policy of strict nonintervention. It is a world in which the threat-driven policies of the cold war no longer are relevant, but have not yet been replaced by new organizing principles that better fit the new strategic environment. It is a world in which a growing number of U.S. interests are affected by developments beyond our borders, but for which traditional economic and military instruments of intervention are increasingly inadequate. It is a world in which the opportunities to advance American interests and promote American values are expanding, but in which Americans seem to be less willing to devote resources to foreign policy priorities.

The fluidity and unpredictability of the post–cold war world may increase the difficulty of formulating new guidelines for intervention, but they do not relieve us of the requirement to do so. As Bosnia, Somalia, and Haiti make clear, sustained intervention requires sustained domestic and international support. We likewise cannot expect to persuade the American people that the resources devoted to American leadership abroad are well spent without relating them to the concerns and priorities of the American public.

Decisions about where and when the United States should intervene abroad will not wait for formal policy development. Events will continue to force our hand, whether or not we are prepared. Accordingly, this American Assembly has formulated the following guidelines to inform the decisions our leaders are facing with growing frequency.

I. Any decision about a prospective intervention should start from the presumption of nonintervention. In other words, any decision to intervene bears the burden of demonstrating that U.S. interests and values would be better served by intervention than by inaction.

II. The magnitude of the burden that must be borne depends upon the interests at stake, such as:

- Protecting American security and values at home;
- Maintaining commitments to allies;

- Promoting open markets in regions of major importance to the United States;
- Controlling proliferation of weapons of mass destruction, and managing its consequences;
- Responding to threats to international peace and security, including threats to regional stability that could threaten U.S. interests;
- Supporting international norms, regimes, and institutions that contribute to stability, open trade, and extensions of the rule of law;
- Maintaining U.S. influence abroad to advance these interests;
- Supporting efforts to alleviate human suffering; and
- Dealing with the causes of longer-term threats to stability and prosperity, e.g., population growth, environmental degradation, and mass migrations.

A smaller burden of proof is required to justify interventions—and more coercive means of intervention—to defend those interests that are of critical importance to the American people. Conversely, a greater burden of proof is needed to make a positive intervention decision—and to expend blood and treasure—on behalf of interests that are of lesser importance to the American people.

III. A decision to intervene must satisfy the following practical considerations:

- Have a clearly understood objective with yardsticks for measuring success, and a strategy for termination;
- Build and sustain domestic political support for the duration of the intervention;
- Preserve the capability to intervene in higher priority contingencies;
- Regularly reassess the ongoing intervention in light of changing circumstances;
- Seek multilateral consensus and participation; and
- Have a high probability of success.

IV. Finally, the decision to intervene must satisfy the following ethical considerations:

- The means of intervention must be proportional to the objectives sought.
- Collateral damage and innocent casualties should be minimized.

This approach describes a role for the United States that is neither neoisolationist nor uncritically interventionist. It is intended to guide U.S. involvement in a disorderly world until a new post–cold war foreign policy achieves broad acceptance among the American people.

In the longer term, America's success in promoting its interests and its values in the world does not depend primarily on its ability to intervene coercively. Rather, it is also dependent on its ability to inspire; to lead; to respond to human needs; to promote conflict resolution, international cooperation, and widespread political and economic development; and to foster institutions and mechanisms to further these goals.

But in the world described in this report, opportunities to promote U.S. interests and values are multiplying at the same time that the appropriateness of traditional military and economic instruments is declining. Existing means, therefore, should be enhanced by every idea, procedure, and technology that demonstrates its worth. The recommendations in this report are designed to contribute to this end.

Participants
The Eighty-Fifth American Assembly

JOHN B. ALEXANDER
Program Manager for
  Nonlethal Defense
Los Alamos National
  Laboratory
Los Alamos, NM

**TERRY ATLAS
Diplomatic Correspondent
The Chicago Tribune
Washington, DC

JOHN BARRY
National Security
  Correspondent
Newsweek
Washington, DC

JOHN L. BARRY
National Security Fellow
John F. Kennedy School of
  Government
Harvard University
Cambridge, MA

THERESA BARTON
Professor of Social Sciences
United States Military
  Academy
West Point, NY

RICHARD K. BETTS
Department of Political
  Science
School of International &
  Public Affairs
Columbia University
New York, NY

L. PAUL BREMER
Managing Director
Kissinger Associates
New York, NY

LINTON F. BROOKS
Distinguished Fellow
Center for Naval Analyses
Alexandria, VA

EDWARD A. BROWN
Director for Program Support
Advanced Concepts & Plans
  Directorate
Army Research Laboratory
Adelphi, MD

‡TYRUS W. COBB
President
Business Executives for
  National Security
Washington, DC

**JOSEPH COLLINS
Director of National Security
  Studies
Department of Social Sciences
United States Military
  Academy
West Point, NY

TIMOTHY G. CONNOLLY
Principal Deputy Assistant
  Secretary for Special
  Operations/Low-Intensity
  Conflict
U.S. Department of Defense
Washington, DC

‡MARION M. DAWSON
President
Dearfield Associates, Inc.
Greenwich, CT

JAMES F. DOBBINS
Special Somalia Coordinator
U.S. Department of State
Washington, DC

RALPH EARLE II
Chairman
Lawyers Alliance for World
Security
Washington, DC

KIMBERLY A. ELLIOTT
Research Associate
Institute for International
Economics
Washington, DC

HENRY H. GAFFNEY, JR.
Director
Concepts Development Group
Center for Naval Analyses
Alexandria, VA

RICHARD L. GARWIN
IBM Fellow Emeritus
T.J. Watson Research Center
IBM Corporation
Yorktown Heights, NY

MICHAEL GLENNON
Professor of Law
School of Law
University of California,
Davis
Davis, CA

**MARGARET HARRELL
The RAND Corporation
Washington, DC

MARY ELIZABETH
HOINKES
Acting General Counsel
U.S. Arms Control &
Disarmament Agency
U.S. Department of State
Washington, DC

ARNOLD KANTER
Senior Fellow
The RAND Corporation
Washington, DC

CARL KAYSEN
Professor of Political Economy,
Emeritus
Defense & Arms Control
Studies Program
Massachusetts Institute of
Technology
Cambridge, MA

KENNETH H. KELLER
Senior Vice President & Philip
D. Reed Senior Fellow for
Science & Technology
Council on Foreign Relations
New York, NY

REAR ADMIRAL J. M.
LUECKE, USN
Director of Plans & Policy
U.S. Central Command
MacDill Air Force Base, FL

‡JOHN W. MASHEK
Political Correspondent
The Boston Globe
Washington, DC

‡DOYLE McMANUS
National Security
Correspondent
The Los Angeles Times
Washington, DC

CHRISTOPHER C.
MORRIS
Morris & Morris
West Hyannisport, MA

JANET E. MORRIS
Morris & Morris
West Hyannisport, MA

†*JOSEPH S. NYE, JR.
Chair
National Intelligence Council
Central Intelligence Agency
Washington, DC

MICHAEL F.
OPPENHEIMER
Partner
InterMatrix Group
New York, NY

GEORGE E. PICKETT, JR.
Director
Analysis Center
Northrop Corporation
Arlington, VA

‡SAMUEL POPKIN
Professor of Political Science
University of California,
San Diego
La Jolla, CA

BARRY R. POSEN
Professor of Political Science
Defense & Arms Control
Studies Program
Massachusetts Institute of
Technology
Cambridge, MA

TIMOTHY R. SAMPLE
Executive Director
The Potomac Institute for
Policy Studies
Washington, DC

ENID C.B. SCHOETTLE
National Intelligence Officer
for Global & Multilateral
Issues
National Intelligence Council
Central Intelligence Agency
Washington, DC

SARAH SEWALL
Deputy Assistant Secretary for
Peacekeeping and Peace
Enforcement Policy
U.S. Department of Defense
Washington, DC

STEVEN SIMON
Director for Policy & Plans
Political-Military Bureau
U.S. Department of State
Washington, DC

*DON M. SNIDER
Director for Political-Military
Studies
Center for Strategic &
International Studies
Washington, DC

*RICHARD H. SOLOMON
President
United States Institute of Peace
Washington, DC

BRENT TALBOT
Department of Political
    Science
United States Air Force
    Academy
Colorado Springs, CO

RICHARD THOMAS
Executive Producer
News & Public Affairs
WETA
Arlington, VA

BERNARD E. TRAINOR,
    USMC (Ret.)
Director
National Security Program
John F. Kennedy School of
    Government
Harvard University
Cambridge, MA

ASTRID S. TUMINEZ
Research Associate
Carnegie Corporation of New
    York
New York, NY

JOHN A. WARDEN, III
Commandant
Air Command & Staff College
Montgomery, AL

‡SIMON WEBB
Minister (Defense Materiel)
British Defense Staff,
    Washington
Washington, DC

‡MALCOLM WIENER
Historian; President,
Institute for Aegean Prehistory;
Chairman,
The Millburn Corporation
New York, NY

*ELIZABETH G. WYLIE
Executive Director
Naval War College
    Foundation, Inc.
Naval War College
Newport, RI

FAREED ZAKARIA
Managing Editor
Foreign Affairs
New York, NY

WARREN ZIMMERMANN
Senior Fellow
The RAND Corporation
Washington, DC

STANLEY A. ZUCKERMAN
Institute for the Study of
    Diplomacy
School of International Affairs
Georgetown University
Washington, DC

 *Discussion Leader
**Rapporteur
 †Delivered Formal Address
 ‡Panelist

About The American Assembly

The American Assembly was established by Dwight D. Eisenhower at Columbia University in 1950. It holds nonpartisan meetings and publishes authoritative books to illuminate issues of United States policy.

An affiliate of Columbia, the Assembly is a national, educational institution incorporated in the state of New York.

The Assembly seeks to provide information, stimulate discussion, and evoke independent conclusions on matters of vital public interest.

American Assembly Sessions

At least two national programs are initiated each year. Authorities are retained to write background papers presenting essential data and defining the main issues of each subject.

A group of men and women representing a broad range of experience, competence, and American leadership meet for several days to discuss the Assembly topic and consider alternatives for national policy.

All Assemblies follow the same procedure. The background papers are sent to participants in advance of the Assembly. The Assembly meets in small groups for four or five lengthy periods. All groups use the same agenda. At the close of these informal sessions participants adopt in plenary session a final report of findings and recommendations.

Regional, state, and local Assemblies are held following the national session at Arden House. Assemblies have also been held in England, Switzerland, Malaysia, Canada, the Caribbean, South America, Central America, the Philippines, and Japan. Over one hundred sixty institutions have cosponsored one or more Assemblies.

Arden House

The home of The American Assembly and the scene of the national sessions is Arden House, which was given to Columbia

University in 1950 by W. Averell Harriman. E. Roland Harriman joined his brother in contributing toward adaptation of the property for conference purposes. The buildings and surrounding land, known as the Harriman Campus of Columbia University, are fifty miles north of New York City.

Arden House is a distinguished conference center. It is self-supporting and operates throughout the year for use by organizations with educational objectives. The American Assembly is a tenant of this Columbia University facility only during Assembly sessions.

Index